Make every day count.

Neal Peter

JOURNEY OF A
HOPE MERCHANT

JOURNEY OF A HOPE MERCHANT

*From Apartheid to the
Elite World of Solo Yacht Racing*

NEAL PETERSEN

With William P. Baldwin
and Patty Fulcher

University of South Carolina Press

© 2004 Neal Petersen and William P. Baldwin

Published in Columbia, South Carolina,
by the University of South Carolina Press

Manufactured in the United States of America

08 07 06 05 04   5 4 3 2 1

Library of Congress Cataloging-in-Publication Data

Petersen, Neal, 1967–
    Journey of a hope merchant : from apartheid to the elite world of solo yacht racing / Neal
Petersen with William P. Baldwin and Patty Fulcher.
        p. cm.
    ISBN 1-57003-564-4 (cloth : alk. paper)
    1. Petersen, Neal, 1967– 2. Sailors—South Africa—Biography. 3. Sailors, Black—South
Africa—Biography. 4. Sailing, Single-handed. 5. Yacht racing. I. Baldwin, William P. II.
Fulcher, Patty. III. Title.
    GV812.5.P48A32 2004
    797.124'092—dc22

                                                                                          2004017350

To Darlene Kristi-Petersen, my wife, best friend,
business partner, and so much more

CONTENTS

ILLUSTRATIONS

PROLOGUE
Darlene Kristi-Petersen

I thought I was in love, and at age fifteen I found myself pregnant and married the father. When I entered the job market at eighteen, I had no real marketable skills. My first job, much to my astonishment, was handing out towels to male bathers in an asylum. The jobs got better and better. The marriage didn't. We divorced ten years later, and I finally took control of my life. I hadn't sailed around the world alone, but I'd had my own set of knocks and challenges. I'd grown up impoverished, with parents who did the best they could, an alcoholic father and a mother who blamed him for her misfortune, three brothers, and a home where not a book was to be found or any plan for my future. Through hard work and a bit of luck, in 1992 I established my own firm and was then dependent on no one.

So, I created a life for myself—in a way I had, through much effort, invented myself. In 1997 I was living in Philadelphia with my grown son, Rick. That's when I began to sense I should be near the ocean. I'd always listened to my inner voice—I just didn't always heed its advice. This time the voice was persistent: move near the sea! I am a corporate headhunter. My business provides a generous income and a means to live wherever there is an Internet connection, phone lines, and an airport, so I could head south. I rented a beach house on the Isle of Palms, a beach community just outside Charleston, South Carolina. At night, I'd walk down to the beach, sit on a blanket, and wait—watching for the moon to rise out of the ocean. I felt comfortable and privileged to be living in such a beautiful place, but I still wished for more. That's when I decided to try something different. I vowed from then on, whenever I had to make an important decision, I'd choose the opposite. Whatever the "old" Darlene would normally do— I'd do the "opposite." I'd step into unknown territories, swim uncharted waters. Have some fun!

I usually spent three weeks every year in Portugal. Not this year! This time I'd do missionary work in Haiti for two weeks and then on to Portugal. Clearly an opposite! I would give first and then receive. At a Haitian hospital in Limbé I cared for orphaned infants. Each morning I'd get up very early and head over to the ward. Being the first to arrive, I got "the big surprise." What a sight and what a smell! I'd throw open the shutters to let the sunshine in and the smell out, then turn to my tedious task of bathing babies. It was cold water only, with pieces of soap no bigger than sugar cubes (the supplies I brought down were nowhere to be seen). Once all the babies were dressed, I would massage them, one by one; all thirty of them were rubbed and coddled for several minutes each. One day, I offered a massage to one of the caregivers. As soon as I started, others quickly formed a line. The hall was soon filled with anxious caregivers all wanting a massage! So, I proceeded to massage them all! The head nurse, Madam, walked in, scooped seven newborns off the table, and lay down. Without speaking I understood—that was how she wanted her massage!

With no common language, I began communication with the people of Haiti. One day, when the work was done, I started dancing in the ward. I hummed my own music out loud and danced with the babies in my arms. I encouraged one particular caregiver to dance with me. Hesitantly, at first, then little by little, then we were all dancing and laughing. Originally, I had thought, what could I offer the people of Haiti except a big, open heart? Soon I understood: touch, dance, and laughter were the universal language of the heart.

Returning to South Carolina, I read a newspaper article about a sailor, Neal Petersen, whose house had just burned down. I hadn't really followed the frenzy of the Around Alone race, here in Charleston, except for the occasional story of the most-publicized entries—Giovanni Soldini and Isabelle—so I didn't recognize his name, but he looked very forlorn. My first thought was here is this poor man who has sailed alone for nine months, then lost all his possessions; aha! I could do missionary work here in my own community. An opposite! I called the Rotary Club and asked if they were going to rebuild the house, as I wanted to be a part of the group. I had some tools, time, plenty of energy, and some cash. I could help. After sending that same message to Neal via e-mail, I transferred 118 dollars into a checking account set up in his name by the Rotary Club for donations.

The 118 dollars was "miracle money." For eight years I'd had the same sunglasses, and they'd recently been stolen from my car. So in a completely frivolous and opposite act, I paid 118 dollars for a new pair. On reporting the theft to the Isle of Palms police department, I found they'd recovered the first pair. I returned the new ones, received the refund, and, as an "opposite," thought that I should give that "miracle money" to the man who had lost everything. I did, and Neal called up to thank me. That's how I met Neal Petersen on August 6, 1999.

Looking back to when I first arrived at the Isle of Palms, I remember sitting on the beach, watching the moon gloriously rise out of the ocean, joyously clapping my hands, knowing that that harvest moon rising out of that silver sea was the most beautiful sight, and thinking it was a gift, just for me. What I didn't know was that sailing toward me was my truest gift, Neal, my husband, the man from the sea.

1973

One of my earliest memories is standing on a large sand dune, looking out at the calm ocean. I was five years old. We were near Cape Town, South Africa, and the ocean was the Southern Ocean I would someday sail. In one hand was a bucket and in the other a plastic shovel. I'd been building sand castles, packing sand into the bucket to make turrets, shoveling out the moats to create walls. The tide would rise and sweep them away, and I'd build another and another and another.

This was during a school outing for the older children, a trip that their biology teacher, Mrs. Petersen, had arranged, and since she was my mother, I was brought along. Mom was tall with skin the color of light cocoa. She smiled often. She was a woman of presence.

I think I remember this outing in part because it was just before my last operation. I'd been born with a partial hip socket on the left side, and, before the age of six, I underwent three operations to correct the problem. I don't recall anything about the first two operations, but I assume that, like the last, they were traumatic experiences. Going into a hospital was linked in my mind with being left behind, with being abandoned, and as a child that was my constant fear. If a white-coated doctor was in sight and my mother wasn't, I went ballistic.

In preparation for the last operation, Mom bought a little blue car, a car she would need to transport me from place to place, a car she would keep for another twenty-seven years. Someone gave me a mouth organ. I don't know if I ever blew a single harmonious tune on that mouth organ, but I blew it a lot. Mom handed it to me and said something about us going to the hospital. She stopped on the way to get gas, and I remember the man pumping the gas calling me "a chipper chap." I didn't hear Mom whisper but found out later, as she repeated this story often, that she said, "He doesn't know it, but he's going somewhere to stay for several months." I kept blowing away on the mouth organ. We reached the hospital, but I assumed this was just another checkup. A nurse joined us, and we started down this incredibly long corridor. It went on and on. To a five-year-old boy it seemed endless. But it had to be long. The hospital was divided into so-called white and nonwhite patients. The two didn't mix. Being colored, we weren't allowed even to walk through the white section and had to follow a long corridor that circled it. There were lines painted on the floor, differently colored lines, and we were following the yellow one.

Finally we arrived at the children's wing, and Mom knelt down and tried to explain the situation. I said, "I'm going home with you." I'd already seen this was a different area of the hospital and knew something was amiss. I was put in a hospital gown, and Mom said, "I have to go. I'll come see you on Saturday." I clung to her and began to howl. The sister in charge of the ward whispered to Mom, although this time I heard, "Keep walking and don't look back." I remember her walking off down that corridor and the nurse holding on to me. Years later, Mom told me that she heard my screams all the way back to the hospital entrance.

Being left at that hospital and the sense of abandonment it engendered in me as a small boy certainly had an impact on my life. And, in an odd way, I think it enabled me to become a world-class single-handed sailor, for such a person must be able to say goodbye, to let go of loved ones and deal with the radical change of being alone. In a way this has to do with confronting your worst fears. The fear itself, the anxiety over what is to come, is far worse than the reality you're about to experience. In my case the fear was of being alone. It's like learning to swim. At first you are frightened of being in over your head, but once that step is taken and you're swimming, the sense of exhilaration is your reward. You prefer that freedom to the uncertainty of standing tiptoe in the surf. In the years to come, swimming was my path to physical fitness and to becoming an able and self-reliant adult.

I quickly learned I hadn't been completely abandoned in the hospital. That was just my perception. When she could, Mom came to visit, and when she couldn't, Dad came. A heavyset man, Dad, a former lobster diver, was my storyteller. When he couldn't come, my sister, Jan, accompanied my second mom, Mama. Mama lived across the street and had helped raise me. Seven years older than me, Jan had just been discovered by boys and looked on me as her baby brother. These visits meant so much to me. I screamed when each of these visits ended.

Finally, the day of the operation came. Mom was beside me. I was given an injection and became drowsy. I was rolled along on a gurney and then lifted onto a hard surface. Above me were bright lights. Voices came from every direction. Then a mask went over my face. Then nothing else.

When I woke, I was in a strange room, but Mom was beside me. I lost consciousness again and then awoke in a regular ward. I was surrounded by other children but was unable to see them for I was in a cast that ran from my left ankle and from my right knee up to my chest, and between my legs was a wooden bar. On my left side I could move only my toes and arm. On my right side I could move my arm and my leg from the knee down. That body cast would be my shell for the next six months. Visiting hours were three afternoons a week. The rest of the time I just lay on that cot hour after hour, day after day. Nothing was happening. The hospital food was appalling, and I wouldn't eat except for the Jell-O. When Mama brought me home-cooked meals, I ate those. Just as in school, classes were given, but I wasn't interested. A doctor asked me what I did enjoy, and I said, "Boats!" He surprised me soon after with a stack of boating magazines, and I'd look at the pictures and daydream. On good days they would take us outside. The smell outside was such a relief from the antiseptic hospital smell that was now so central to my life. Those magazines and the smell of the outdoors were all that got me through. I still wasn't eating.

In the next bed was a boy from upcountry, from the wine lands some hours away. I could turn my head and see him, but I spoke only English and he spoke only Afrikaans. Since I had 100 percent visitation, and he had practically no one to see him, Mom and Mama and the little boy soon became close. He snitched on me, telling them I wasn't eating anything. I'd been in there three and a half months, and Mom knew I couldn't survive much longer. She got permission from the doctors to take me home. It took a week to get that approval—the longest week of my life, and at last I was trolleyed out to an ambulance. Mama got in beside me, and Mom followed along in the little blue car. When we got close to home, the ambulance driver turned on his siren to let the neighborhood know I was coming home. When the ambulance door was opened, all my friends were waiting. I was home again with Mom and Dad and my sister, Jan.

Home was in a working-class neighborhood, a suburb of Cape Town called Wynberg. Our house was a comfortable brick one-story home that Dad had built. We had gardens, trees, and lawns. Mama's home was similar and was named "Shalom," which, of course, is the Jewish word for peace. Don't ask me how or why she chose a Jewish word, but everyone was welcome. Our home was named "Amahela." That's the Sosuthu word for welcome. Peace and welcome.

My mom's parents had been extremely hardworking. Her mother, Grandma Stinnie, was a tiny woman who appeared always to be in the process of shrinking with age. Totally headstrong, she accepted no arguments, especially regarding her firm expectations for her children and grandchildren. The lines in the sand were very clearly drawn. In fact these lines were dug out in the sand. She was of Madagascan and Dutch descent, and some of her ancestors were in that great slave population brought into South Africa to work the land. They had survived. No questions. What my grandmother said, was.

Grandmother Stinnie's father had been the footman to a nobleman, and the family first lived on his estate on the well-watered, fertile lower slope of Table Mountain's Upper Wynberg. Lower Wynberg, where my family finally settled, was on the edge of the barren, dusty, and impoverished Cape Flats. A unique spot, our suburb was suspended between economic extremes. It was a quiet and safe community with urban necessities—but my mother's sympathies extended far beyond that neighborhood.

Mom is a force to be reckoned with. She oozes a positive attitude. With this strength, she appears stately, queenlike, someone whom people naturally follow. As a young woman, Mom won renown when she graduated at the top of her class at Cape Town University, and she did this in an era when few women—especially black women—even attended school. Next, she was awarded the International Education Fellowship to Syracuse University in New York, which was a moneyed grant that had never gone to a woman, black or white, before. After graduating from Syracuse, again with honors, she received many offers of employment in the United States, but, despite all its racial troubles, she still loved South Africa and was committed to what she called her "motherland." Returning home, she wrote a series of newspaper articles describing her experiences and was invited to speak all over the country, which naturally caught the attention of the hostile authorities. She was active in politics and in her way was quite influential.

Livingstone High School, which she'd attended and where she taught, was one of the best schools available for nonwhites, actually one of the best, period. And at Livingstone she was constantly around parents, students, teachers, and others who would shape the future of the entire country.

She met my father, Eddie, at the reception that followed a play he had written. He'd had only a middle school education, but a good one in a Catholic school, and had literary ambitions that he would later give up in favor of making a living. They married, and Jan came along, and then seven years later there was me.

Dad's father was Irish and Dad's mother was a Sesotho tribeswoman. Often he would tell me stories about growing up far to the north near the mighty Orange River and how he would swim in the turbulent currents of that river and even cross it—an amazing feat for a boy—or for an adult. I didn't hear classic stories such as "Goldilocks and the Three Bears" or "Robin Hood." I heard about Dad's impressive childhood adventures. Seeing the Indian Ocean for the first time, he was stunned by its vastness and blue color. And the Orange River is just that. Orange. He joined the Royal Navy in World War II and trained as a diver, a profession he would follow afterwards. He'd led this interesting life that was very connected to the ocean, which in turn connected the two of us.

Dad had his own boat, a rowboat, called a buckie, and he'd have a buckie boy to row and assist with the catch. His diving equipment was primitive—a system of filling-station air compressor and garden hose connected to a scuba regulator. Sometimes he'd go up the coast and camp out for a week, hunting abalone, but crayfish were what they caught the most. They're about the size of a Maine lobster only without the fierce claw. Dad eventually earned enough to buy a bigger boat with two outboard engines, which meant he could work offshore, even as far as Robin Island, where Nelson Mandela was imprisoned for twenty-seven years. Out there he'd once witnessed a crayfish migration. Normally it took him an entire day to get a catch, but one morning he came on a piece of ocean floor covered with crayfish, so many that he simply shooed them into his collecting net. In a few minutes he had forty or fifty and by midmorning he'd filled the buckie to the edge of sinking. They took this prize catch in and returned the following morning to find some bits of broken claw and not a single crayfish. He and his buckie boy had had their day of plenty, one to keep hope alive.

My sister, Jan, remembers when there were always crayfish in the house, in the kitchen sink, in buckets. Looking a bit like giant bugs, they frightened her, but back then crayfish was a main part of our diet. I don't remember that abundant time. In fact, Dad sold the boat in 1967, the year I was born. As it became harder and harder to find crayfish, he'd been forced to dive deeper and deeper, and since the compressor wasn't strong enough, he'd just hold his breath below thirty feet. He had no training or scientific knowledge to aid him in this risky business, but he survived and did very well. Then the apartheid government rewrote the fisheries laws and gave the new licenses to white divers only. The black divers had to go to work for the white divers, which meant the independence and really good money were gone. Dad was forced to give up the business. He'd always liked to drink, and after that he drank more and more, so that my later memories of my father are of an abusive alcoholic.

The third adult in my life was Mama, who raised both my sister and me. Mama did have a first name, but we never knew it. To all of us she was Mama. To strangers it was Mrs. Maart. Few called her Mrs. Maart. Originally from an upcountry town called Swellendam, she had cooked in a boarding school for white boys, had retired, and then, after losing her husband, had begun to care for children. Since Mom had a full-time career as a teacher and Dad was a commercial diver, Mom paid Mama to look after us, but money really had nothing to do with the relationship. Mama was a second mother to me, and to several others. She had spare rooms in her house, and a family with two small boys stayed toward the back. In another room, which opened onto the stoop, lived a former prostitute and her little girl, Bernadette. Mama had helped the woman to get off the streets and had found her a job as a scrub nurse. Bernadette was two years younger than I was, and we played well together.

There was also another young woman boarder and her baby boy, Anton. Anton was mentally disabled, and, despite several operations on his brain, he never learned to walk. He was a year younger than I was, but we grew up lying side by side on the same big double bed. He couldn't walk or speak properly. He called me "Neu." He loved matchbook cars and car books and would sit for hours making car sounds. He not only received love, he gave it back with an openness that is denied those of us who are ordinary. In the years since, I've often gone to visit him, and when I approach, he always has a huge smile on his face and a greeting of "Neu! Neu!" A second son, Gary, came not long after. When he was only a few weeks old, the father of the boys was killed. So then there were three of us sleeping in a row on the double bed, and sometimes Bernadette would make that four. We four started out more or less together, and a little later Charlene joined us. She was from the upcountry and a year younger.

For most of the daylight hours this was my home life, and a very harmonious one it was. Mama's household centered around a nurturing kitchen, one which had a wood-burning stove, crackling winter and summer. A wood merchant delivered wheelbarrows of wood, and Gary and I carried it inside. Some nights I stayed over, and I remember Mama stoking that fire last thing in the evening and first thing at dawn. She cooked on the stove, and since she loved to cook, the smell of baking, roasting, and coffee brewing was always present. She'd often give me coffee and a piece of hot buttered bread. Outside the kitchen, in the hallway, stood a tall grandfather clock. That constant ticktock sound, the chiming every fifteen minutes, and the bonging on the hour were always with us, always reminding us of the day's course. Mama loved her radio soap operas, her "stories," and for these we had to be quiet. She might go on polishing pots and pans or cooking, but that was our time to be quiet—an entire hour.

Growing up, we weren't allowed to play in the street, but all of us children could play in our yard or in Mama's. We were free to move back and forth and were welcomed in either house. Mama was devoted to me, and so were my parents. As children we didn't feel those were the only adults we "belonged" to. We respected all the adults around us. "It takes a village to raise a child." That's the way it was.

2

THE DREAM TREE

Upon coming home from the hospital after that final operation on my hip, I was placed in a box in my bedroom. Resting on the mattress of my bed, the box was coffinlike and had been made by Livingstone High School woodworking students, and around its edges were pillows and blankets that kept my body from shifting. Mom slept next to me on a cot. Sometimes I just could not get comfortable, so she worked out a way of holding me. Since I was sore all over, she laid me across her lap and held me through the night. She'd get up in the morning, set me in my box in the front room, and go off to teach school. By then Dad was off selling cleaning products door to door, and Jan had gone to school, so I'd be alone for a while until Mama came from across the street with coffee and buttered bread. Then she'd go home to do her chores. If I needed her, I could just call out "Mama!" She spoiled me. Indulged me! She put sugar in my coffee. I kept asking for more until she built up to six spoonfuls, more sugar than coffee.

There was all kind of activity on the street. Cars came by, and I could hear the old-time floor polishers and the radios playing loud in the neighboring houses. Mama kept coming over to check on me. If she had to go up the main road, she'd tell me and bring back a treat. She'd carry Anton over and put him in the bed beside me. He'd play with his cars and fumble through my magazines and tinker with my toy boats. Then Mama would shout, "I'm back!" After school Jan would bring me things and read to me while Mom sat in the kitchen grading her student's papers—she spent more time on those than at the stove, hence we had many well-done—overdone—and burned evening meals. Still, it was a home of much love, and I was surrounded with care.

Three more months passed, and I was finally putting on weight. The cast came off. A screeching angle grinder spread thick dust into the hospital room as it cut around the perimeters of my body-enclosing cast. Then a mechanical spreader pried off great chunks of the plaster, and all the time I feared they'd take skin as well.

Like a butterfly emerging from a cocoon, I was entering a new life. It was such a relief not to be dependent on others for every movement. However, I still couldn't put weight on the leg. I started water therapy to build up my muscles, and Mom devised a system for getting me around the house. She rolled up the carpets and sat me on a pillow. To get from one room to another, I could slide on my butt on a pillow, my magic carpet. I now had the upper-body strength to manage that and to pull myself up into a chair. My second-grade teacher, Mrs. February, began to come by with my lessons, but my heart wasn't in the work. She would bring her son Rodger, who became my lifelong friend. From time to time other children came to visit. I can't say that I felt disabled, but still I knew I was different from the other boys. That much was obvious.

Mama had a couch on the porch, and in the summer when the weather was nice, she'd carry me out, and I'd sit there for hours. I was improving but still couldn't walk. The porch rail was too high to see over, but the tops of the trees showed, and I could hear all the activities in the neighborhood. Twice a week I would hear the garbage collectors coming down the street. That would be my treat for the entire day. I could hear the truck's engine, the squeal of the hydraulic arm compressing the garbage, and the banging of the cans. The collectors were broad-shouldered men with big smiles. Those men knew I'd be waiting for them. They'd come up on the porch to say good morning and chat with me for a few minutes. I was only six, but they gave me true attention, and I began to tell them that when I grew up I'd be a garbage collector, too, except that my route would be the sea. "I'll take care of the sea" is what I told them—for I already had the notion of being a sailor and that was the only way to imagine the two. And I promised to take them all across the ocean to England.

To build up my muscles, a physical therapist began to give me swimming lessons and to teach me related exercises. That's where I found freedom, a three-dimensional mobility that I lacked on dry land. Even then I was connecting to water—but on a smaller scale. I knew already that I was of water. Every Sunday afternoon Mom would splurge and cut on the hot-water heater. Then rather than a cold rag wash, everyone had a real bath. I always bathed with Dad, and we played this game where I put my head under water and held my breath while he counted. I could hear his garbled voice, "grone, grwo, grhree, grour. . . ." In the beginning he counted very quickly so I could claim to have held my breath for an applaudable length of time. Over the years, he gradually counted slower and finally reached a normal reckoning of seconds. By then I was quite good.

Dad would get out of the tub first, and I'd stay in playing with toy tug-boats and sailboats until the water was cold. When I got out, Dad would tell me stories about diving commercially for crayfish and abalone. When I got crutches and hobbled around the house and the garden, he watched over me, and in the years to come he encouraged me to swim and eventually to dive and to dream—and also to build my own toys.

Mom's father had been a carpenter, and though he died right after I was born, his workshop was still there right up the street and also his now-empty aviary, both priming my imagination. A truck yard was next door, and I'd get packing-crate lumber to build my own birdcages and tree houses.

In the backyard were swaying syringe trees I learned to climb, and the next step was to turn those into a playground for myself and my companions. Only Anton had to stay on the ground in his pram. Sometimes we'd help him take a step or two, but he lacked the muscles for walking and even his conversation was limited to a few words. Besides calling me "Neu," he knew "car," "bread," "coffee," and "Mama." Those were the important things in his life. He stayed below, and I'd climb up into the tree house and read my books about diving and going to sea. Dad gave me one by the underwater explorer Jacques Cousteau, *The Silent World,* and others I got from the library. I was dreaming of the sea, and that tree house emulated the slow, creaking motion of a boat. I came up with the idea of suspending our wooden ladder horizontally with four ropes from my tree, all this three feet off the ground. I had two sticks to row my ladder, and I'd get a motion going that could almost make me seasick. It was our only ladder, and every time my dad needed to do roof maintenance, I had to dismantle my ship's tender.

That became my dream tree. Dad attached an old cargo net to the edge of the tree house, and I could climb that as if going up the stern of a Spanish galleon. And when the wind blew, I'd sit in the tree house and imagine that I was enduring the storms of Cape Horn, that I was sailing the Southern Ocean and exploring the coasts of the Americas, because I'd read about all these voyages. Yet when I made the mistake of sharing these dreams with a few of my schoolmates, they thought I was crazy. They began to call me "the nutty professor" until I was nine and an airplane flight to Europe gave me a new prestige. Dad had never doubted the power of my dreams, though, and despite his increased drinking and the difficult years since, I haven't forgotten that early support.

Before the last operation, I had accepted school as my lot in life. I had a uniform and a little hat. I learned quickly until the second grade and the last of the operations. After that difficult bout in the hospital I lost interest in schoolwork, and my teacher, the one who was also the mother of my friend Rodger, began to harass me. She kept telling me I was certain to fail. I figured, "why bother?" Mom asked me what was wrong, and I explained this to her. She visited the elementary school and was told, yes, I was certain to fail. She said nothing to me at the time, then on the June break she took Jan and me on the train eight hundred miles to the north to Lesotho. A former British colony, Lesotho is a land-locked country in the center of South Africa, and, though politically independent, it was impoverished and depended on exporting to its surrounding neighbor. Its biggest export was men, men to work in the South African gold mines.

Mom made me carry my schoolwork along, for it would be a working vacation and more. My father's mother and cousin that we'd traveled to visit now lived in a city, but they took us back to their former village of Mafaking. We walked over this barren hill (I'd graduated from crutches to a cane), and drifting toward us was the sound of singing. At the crest we looked down on a distant scene of women working in green fields beside a winding stream, women breaking into the hard orange-red soil with their hoes, women singing loudly, with incredibly harmonious voices. Mom wanted us to see this other part of our heritage. Our grandmother had been born in Lesotho, and she and my dad spoke the Sesotho language. I heard it being sung.

We were in these rocky hills looking down on a strip of fertile gardens and on all sides rose the snow capped Drakensberg Mountains, peaks as majestic as the Rockies. I went back with Dad years later and heard the women sing again. When I think of Africa, that vision often comes to mind.

Returning home, Mom told me I was headed to a new school, Rosemead Elementary, which was only a block from Livingstone High, where she taught. She'd graduated from Livingstone, as had her brothers and sisters. Jan and I were both destined to attend. My new class was a huge improvement. I was introduced and welcomed by my new classmates. They'd been told I'd had an operation and walked with a cane, but I was no different than anyone else. Not once did anyone even suggest I would fail. I was told that if I applied myself, I would do well. And when I did, I was praised. On my first big test I scored a 100, and through extra study I soon jumped to fourth in the class. Half of the day one group of children was taught in English, and then in the afternoon the same instruction was given to a second group by teachers speaking Afrikaans. I attended both sessions.

Discipline wasn't a problem. Our principal, Mr. Hector, walked so ramrod straight he seemed to be tipping backwards. He had different canes for exacting different punishments and, to go with that, the sort of persona that put the fear of God in you. When he entered a room, we'd rise to our feet and say in unison, "Good morning, Mr. Hector," and continued to stand until he said, "Sit." This respect was no different than what students had been taught at home.

As with all schools, we had a bully on the playground, and when he got around to teasing me, I tripped him up with my cane; I was forced to fight back on occasion. In the third grade, I met Noel Soloman. He was called "the wacky professor," and because of my good grades and sailing dreams I was still "the nutty professor." Together, we walked the perimeter of the school yard, I hobbled and he walked, and for years and years we did this and talked and talked about our dreams.

When Noel played soccer, I could only watch. Finally I insisted on playing, and even though I couldn't run, I was included. My ambition was to score a goal before I graduated from elementary school—just a single goal. Once, while trying to teach me how to score, my teammates and I accidentally went dribbling and kicking all the way through the school's flower garden. We looked up and there was Mr. Hector. Normally, that was a caning offense, but since I was being taught to score, he pretended not to see and turned away. Years later, he and his wife laughed with me over this. I did finally come close to scoring. But the opposing goalkeeper was just too good, which taught me a valuable lesson. My dream was to score, but his job was to prevent me. What mattered was the trying.

3

BUILDING BOATS

At the end of our road was a stand of pines and a big field. Beneath the trees we'd find the pine nuts, little hard-to-spot seed-pods that we children would spend hours collecting and more hours cracking with hammers to get the delicious, sweet meat. It was the field beyond that gave me the most pleasure. I'd spend hours lying in that grass, looking up at the clouds, dreaming of the boats I would someday sail and waiting for the March winds to arrive so I could fly my kites.

In early January I'd go to the neighbor's yard and, with his permission, select and cut the bamboo I'd need. Then, dried and varnished, this choice wood became the cross pieces for tissue-paper kites, bright kites with elaborate tails bobbing behind, and all constructed to what I figured were the correct aeronautical dimensions. Building them was as much fun as flying them, but, then, I'd always enjoyed building.

I also made boats out of paper. Mom brought cardboard from school and factory wastepaper, and with that I designed and then built paper boats. These were flat-bottom boats with pointed bows, sloping transoms, and raised superstructures. One was over four feet long. When finished, they were painted with watercolors. They didn't actually float, though, except for one that was more like a raft than a boat. Two and half feet long and constructed of wood, foam, and plywood with a cotton sail, this lop-sided creation was launched into a swimming pool (one of Mom's ex-students had made good), for I had to have one that would float and sail.

I did not get an allowance as such. At Christmas or for birthdays, I received money from Grandma Stinnie and others, small sums like fifty cents. All was saved, and a bank account was opened into which I would deposit these gifts. It was toward my future, Mom had told me. I also collected newspapers and sold them to the recycling center. These coins went into a piggy bank. I remember wanting a Monopoly board, and I spent months gathering the resources. Finally I was close, just five cents short, and Dad tossed it in. It was the first item I saved toward and achieved, learning the value of money, savings, and compounded interest. I never stopped playing Monopoly, except today it's with real money and real property and toward financial freedom.

In 1976 Mom, Jan, and I went to Europe. I came home from school one day and found our bags had been packed, and Mom said we were going to visit her brother, Uncle Edward, in London. Dad drove us to the airport, and all the way there Mom seemed nervous. At the time, I didn't realize we were fleeing the country.

A special Gestapo-like branch of the police was arresting teachers that were considered subversive, and Mom, questioned once before I was born, was again under suspicion. However, at age nine I understood nothing that was happening. We made it through passport control and onto the plane and then to London. For me our trip was a vacation adventure.

In London we stayed with Uncle Edward, who was a doctor. We went everywhere, visiting the Tate Gallery and then Westminster Abbey to see the famous graves, and we saw a show at Covent Gardens. While crossing the English Channel, we met a highly regarded male dancer, a black American who looked just like Sidney Poitier (whom we knew from just having watched *Guess Who's Coming to Dinner* on the first television set we'd ever seen). The dancer drove us around Paris, took us to a show, and put us on the Orient Express for Switzerland. Mom had some former students there who showed us the cities and natural wonders. The most impressive sight to me was Charlie Chaplin, who was sitting on his veranda with his wife. As we walked by, we waved and he stood up and bowed to us exactly as he did in *The Little Tramp,* a great event, for his silent movies were still playing at home. While there, we stayed with a farm family in the kind of house where the cattle are on the ground floor. By then I could get around without my cane, and the family's son and I played in the barn and across the fields and sat in the cherry trees, gorging ourselves on the delicious fruit. Then we were off to tour Germany and the Netherlands. Not once did we stay in a hotel. Mom had friends and fellow teachers everywhere, people with whom she discussed solutions to the South African problem. While we played, she worked at building awareness and support for the oppressed people of South Africa.

After six months of travel, Mom enrolled Jan in private boarding school in London, where she'd stay for five years, and Mom and I returned to South Africa. The troubles had quieted down. I came home a hero. No longer was I "the nutty professor," for I was the only student who had flown on an airplane or had been overseas, so, at the age of nine, I became the classroom storyteller. Whenever we had free time, I was called on by the teacher to relate a traveling adventure. Rowing on the Thames, seeing Shakespeare's grave at Westminster Abbey, being bowed to by Charlie Chaplin—I always had a story to tell.

By now, though, I had begun to understand that South Africa had problems not found in other countries. We were unique and in an ugly and irrational way.

Growing out of the Soweto uprising of 1976 was an increasing political awareness and rising political violence. In 1980, when I was twelve, class boycotts were enacted in the Cape Province. At first, this made no sense to me for I knew many students simply wanted to skip classes. Denying oneself an education could only hurt in the long run. Throughout the country, nine weeks of school were lost. At Livingstone, however, learning did continue. In the midst of all of this, I studied at home. More than ever my mother was encouraging me to read. All my family expected me to attend university and to become a lawyer or an academic of some kind, and my mom now became my full-time tutor. Even on Saturdays (after art classes) we went to a classmate's home, where Mom taught us math, sciences, social studies, and languages, which would push us beyond our grade level. By this time, though, my main interests were in boats and diving.

From the time I was the age of twelve on, the solo sailors Joshua Slocum, Bernard Moitessier, and Francis Chichester and the diver Jacques Cousteau were my idols. The libraries were segregated. I was supposed to use "our" one-room branch, but I'd make the painful hobble to the white library. The librarian there recognized my hunger, my ambition, and, being a brave woman, she turned a blind eye to my color and went out of her way to gather up sailing books for me.

The summer before high school, I'd learned to snorkel. Here was a sport that didn't require leaping and bounding around on the land. I also joined a spear-fishing club and excelled. At last here was an adult activity which Dad and I could enjoy together. By then, he was often drunk, and most of our interaction at home was reduced to my avoiding him as much as possible. He'd come home at night, get his supper plate from the warming box, and go to bed. If I was still up, I'd go straight off to my room. There was no way of knowing what his mood would be, whether his temper had the upper hand, whether he'd begin to scream at me for no apparent reason. On one of those nights, he'd lashed out, calling me a "sissy." I wasn't manly enough for him, couldn't do the manly activities which he expected of a son. However, in diving we had a common ground. In the water we didn't fight, but we did compete. In diving I was soon his equal and eventually his better, for I could hold my breath longer, dive deeper, and gather more abalone. I was the better diver.

Finally, the day came, and it happened to be his fiftieth birthday, when this became obvious to both of us. We'd gone out to snorkel at False Bay, a place where we'd often dived, but the currents were strong this day, and we had to battle a chop. He said it was too rough, and we swam in toward the beach until we reached the surf zone. One mark of a good diver was the ability to catch a wave that would surf him all the way onto the rocks of the shore without smashing him on those rocks. Then, after landing on the rocks, he would have to pull off his fins and jump onto the beach before the next wave came. A question of timing. I caught my wave and went to the parking lot to wait for Dad. It took him thirty minutes to join me.

I look back on my father with sadness or at least with a tremendous impatience. He was there for me when I was very young, but when I was older, he was there for me only in a negative way. True, the loss of his fishing license under apartheid had crippled him just as the absence of a hip joint had slowed me. The apartheid laws had thwarted generations of South Africans. Even with those impediments, though, there was still room to exercise our wills. I looked at the choices he had made and knew they were the wrong ones.

In his own way, though, my father struggled to launch me into a better world. When we dove together, he would always remind me that people might discriminate but that the ocean did not. Black or white, the sea was judging you by your abilities—among these, your ability to survive. Also he found books and encouraged me to read, and there was one book that he actually read out loud to me. It took months, but he read me *Papillon*. This is the story of a French prisoner sentenced to life imprisonment on the infamous Devil's Island; it deals with endurance and ends with a triumphant escape. I've since sailed by that desolate island off South America a couple of times, have seen that low cluster of palms on the horizon. Whatever his shortcomings, my father understood what I was facing.

More was involved in our relationship than books, though. I had my father's stories and, to some extent, I still had his companionship. Fishing was a passion of mine, and from an early age I accompanied him to False Bay. We often went as guests on commercial fishing boats, one being the *Southern Star,* which I was allowed to helm—taking my mind off the nausea. Eventually the seasickness passed. Here was the promise of great adventure, but from that vantage point I could see yachts sailing on the open sea, and that was my real dream, to be a yachtsman. Unfortunately, in South Africa there was no such thing as a colored yachtsman, and my Cape Flats roots made this even less likely. When I was twelve years old, Dad took me down to the False Bay Yacht Club, located on an incredible bay lined with mountains sloping to the water, with yachts bobbing in the harbor and, docked nearby, most of South Africa's navy. Dinghies were being launched, and I went from captain to captain, asking to be taken sailing. Finally I was told to check at the club ferry landing, for the sailboats big enough to take passengers were there. I informed the first captain I met that I had read many books on sailing and now wanted to gain practical experience. He said, "Call your father and hurry back." He was a Cape Town lawyer named Bill, and the boat was a thirty-six-foot sloop. He showed me how to hank on a sail and set a headsail. We raised the sails, the sloop heeled over, and off we went to windward. I helmed a somewhat erratic course, with the wind in my hair and the taste of salt spray on my lips, and I was in love forever with this sport.

The following Saturday, after tutoring, Mom dropped me off at the city's other marina, the elite Royal Cape Yacht Club. I asked all day, "Will you take me sailing?" Dozens of boats and no luck. I took the train home. The next Sunday I did this again with the same results. On the third Sunday a skipper said yes. I was told to sit in the middle of the boat and stay very still. I paid close attention to what the others were doing. The fourth Sunday was race day. Crewmen were needed, and suddenly I became a "sailor."

After that, I continued to knock on hulls to find others who would take a "colored" on their boat. I was always there, one of those dock waifs who was always smiling and always ready to lend a hand. I'd begun my sailing career and eventually was enlisted by Colin Farlem as a permanent crew member. Colin was a tall, weedy bachelor who worked as a bank teller. His boat was an old wooden thirty-footer, a Royal Cape One design racer, *Lapwing*. I crewed on her for five years, and, besides the basics of sailing, I was taught all there was to know about keeping a continually disintegrating boat afloat and headed for the finish line, valuable knowledge that I would eventually put to good use many, many times.

My dream was coming true, but many in my community were dismayed. Nonwhite children didn't sail. I might be a deckhand fixing broken gear and cleaning up behind the whites, but I could never become a yachtsman. Since sailing was the sport of the white and wealthy ruling class, even to have such aspirations was suspect. Just by dreaming of such, I'd joined the enemy. That's how many of my fellow students saw my efforts. They simply couldn't understand that my dream was to overcome all this, to sail as an equal to any man. This was a crossroads in my life, and I had decided to fight the fight as I saw fit.

Then I fell in love, which only made things worse. I was thirteen, and her name was Rejane. Her father was a lawyer and would eventually serve in the new South African cabinet. One day Rejane would marry one of my older friends and have children. In the eighth grade Rejane sat two benches behind me, and she was stunningly beautiful. She invited me to her fourteenth birthday, and I danced with her at her party. For nine months I suffered my love in silence and then, in a rash action, professed my feelings for her. In the afternoons I was working in a pet shop, surrounding myself with all sorts of exotic fish and birds, which to me, at least, were the accouterments of adventure. I used the pet shop phone and dialed her. I made small talk and then blurted out my declaration of love and then in my confusion disconnected myself. She never did reciprocate. I'd gone out on a limb and without thinking, cut it off. A year later I resigned as vice president of the politically oriented Pioneer Club and gradually withdrew from the school community altogether, decisions driven in part by Rejane's presence in the Pioneer Club meetings and so many other places. At recess I'd sit alone in the isolated "lover's lane," envious of the couples.

I committed myself to a dream, which in a sense meant I had entered a fantasy, so I decided to write a novel. Not just a story, but an entire book-length adventure. The hero, a young boy exactly like me, becomes a skilled skin diver and battles sharks and rescues those in distress. Then he becomes a sailor, acquires a first-class sailboat, and takes part in the OSTAR (Observer Single-handed Trans-Atlantic Race). And, of course, he gets the girl of his dreams and has access to great wealth. The trick was to make it come true. I wrote this impossible fantasy but never gave it to Rejane. I put it away, only to find it again about ten years later. By then I was the hero of the story, but without the girl.

My parents helped me buy a wet suit, which was necessary for diving in the cape's continually cold waters. It was secondhand and much too large, but I pulled it on over the padding of an old wool sweater and was soon making money as a "recreational" abalone diver and underwater repairman at the yacht club. Spearfishing in False Bay proved to be particularly profitable. This was on the Indian Ocean side; as the waters were warmer, bright red and yellow coral grew abundantly in small valleys. One morning, I'd been swimming these twenty-foot-deep crystal clear waters and for some reason was missing fish with every spear shot. I was returning to the surface for a gulp of air and saw the glimmer of sunlight above striking slowly fanning fins. I was swimming in the midst of a yellowtail school. Twenty of these fish, each close to half my own length, were inspecting me, not realizing that I meant to do them harm. I was stunned. I imagined what it would be like to have such majestic beauty withering on the end of my spear. And then I lowered the speargun and let them swim on. Already I was careful not to kill what couldn't be eaten or sold; the day soon came when I decided I would stop spearfishing altogether.

For centuries Cape Town has been an obvious stopover for round-the-world sailors, and I now began to search them out. They came on every size and type of sailboat—from the sleekest, most modern racer to the most plodding of wooden antiques. They came from every walk of life. Or rather had retired or withdrawn from every walk of life. Few were wealthy. Some dreamers brought their families; others sailed alone, and it was these, especially the single-handed sailors, I wished to join. To my surprise the solo skippers were usually the friendliest and most gregarious of all. Five or six of these sailors would pass through every year. I'd invite a select few home for supper, and we'd be treated to tales of high adventure from all over the globe.

In 1982 the British Oxygen Corporation sponsored a single-handed race that was based in Newport, Rhode Island, with stopovers in Cape Town,

Sydney, Australia, and, after sailing around Cape Horn, Punta del Este, Uruguay. Covering twenty-seven thousand miles of ocean, the BOC race was not only the longest solo-sailing race in the world, it was the longest race of any kind, solo or otherwise. I could do that, and someday I would. When I met those first contestants on the Cape Town docks and found the courage to say all this out loud, they didn't laugh. I stood waiting when the English sailor Richard Broadhead came in, and I caught the mooring line he tossed. He was in third place. He'd been at sea for weeks, but instead of rushing off, he invited me on board, showed me around, and talked to me about the race. He listened to my own dreams of sailing and encouraged them. I made up my mind at that very moment that someday I'd do the BOC Challenge.

Later that same year, Colin Farlam proposed me for membership in the Royal Cape Yacht Club. Some members weren't happy at the thought of a deeply tanned member, but the committee had no problem with the request. By then I was a sought-after crewman. It seemed the sea was a great leveler. Rich or poor, black or white, male or female, such distinctions were of no concern to the ocean. Neither was age. I was fifteen years old. The ocean doesn't know or care. We were equally wet and equally in danger.

The next year, my parents helped me buy a scuba cylinder and regulator. I began to clean hulls, clear fouled propellers, and retrieve valuables that had been dropped overboard and that had drifted to the bottom. For a modest price I did anything about the yacht basin that required an underwater approach. Boats were my life. The water was my living. When the time came, instead of enrolling in the university, I enrolled in a commercial-diving course at the College of Oceaneering in Los Angles. One of the best schools, it was also one of the most expensive, but my mom somehow found the resources.

In one sense, I was already learning valuable lessons. Besides sailing with Colin on his old classic design, I was now crewing for wealthy businessmen when they raced and was able to listen to the conversations taking place on these boats. This was my business course, my substitute for an MBA program. As they became comfortable with my presence, both the owners and their crews (the other crew members were often corporation employees and board members) freely discussed their business methods. Out on the decks and down in the galleys, mergers were formed and new companies started. I recall one German industrialist, in particular, who consistently used his incredibly expensive boat as a boardroom and there was a race-car driver who did the same. It was a way of seeing exactly what sort of team they had. There I was surrounded by lawyers, accountants, financiers, strategists of all kinds, all these members of an elitist white corporate world, and it quickly became apparent that winning the sailboat race and making the big deals weren't so far apart, a knowledge that I've put to good use in recent years.

4

CALIFORNIA

During my last months in South Africa, I was crewing regularly on one of these "MBA" boats, a sixty-five-foot yacht owned by a French industrialist. He was interested in South African oil fields, he was immensely rich, and his daughter, Terry, was immensely spoiled. I was seventeen years old, and she was twenty—beautiful, tall, blond, blue-eyed, and spirited. I thought of her as a "brat." I'd spent hours scrubbing a deck that she then deliberately walked over with dirty shoes. Once she ordered me to fetch some parcels from her car. "'Thank you' is such a small phrase and doesn't take much to say," I announced as she was walking away. A few days later I was sitting alone in the yacht club reading a magazine. "May I buy you a drink?" Terry said in French-accented English. I declined and went back to reading. "For a boy who tries to teach manners, you should have a few of your own." She sat down next to me, uninvited. "I am not a whelp who orders people around and stomps over their hard work," I said.

I got up and went to another table. She called out for me to come back. We were the only two in the lounge. I told her she'd find many men in the bar who would love to drink with her. I kept trying to read my magazine, kept trying to pretend she wasn't there. She kept speaking in this voice of such weariness, of such sadness, and I kept stealing glances. Finally, she walked over and said, "Neal, may I join you?" I put down the magazine and motioned to the chair. "Truce?" she asked. That was the unlikely beginning of a turbulent ten-month relationship.

She asked me out. On our first date I took her for a picnic on Table Mountain. I couldn't have afforded the kind of restaurant she was used to. She was accustomed to men who could commandeer the entire restaurant for a night, for just the two of them. Instead, I gave her an entire mountain. Instead of a helicopter, we used the city's cable car. I showed her what I could afford to show her, the simple things that she'd never experienced. On that first evening, we reached the summit of the mountain, and I found a secluded rocky outcrop, one offering a view of the entire bay as the sun set and the city lights came on. Without speaking, I took a single red rose from the picnic hamper and handed it to her. She blushed. I spread out a tablecloth and served her a supper of lettuce, tomato, and avocado pear salad; cold meats; fresh bread and cheese; and a bottle of sparkling wine.

She told me about growing up all over the world. She had no memories of her mother, who had died long before. She was raised by nannies. Her father traveled the world on business and had little time for her. At nine she'd gone off to boarding school. She'd also had a year of college. She enjoyed parties of the jet set variety, and her father paid for whatever she desired. I say "paid for" because even in this buying, he showed no emotional concern.

Money couldn't have bought her what we were now enjoying—a warm, still afternoon with no sound but the songs of birds. Then came a brilliant, but cloudless sunset, and as a ship slid into the encircling shelter of Table Bay, a new moon rose behind us, and the sky filled with sparkling stars. I put my arm around Terry. She snuggled against me. We kissed. I felt like a king.

Romantic, certainly, but we had so very much going against us. We had no friends in common, no life in common. I'm not sure I can even say that love factored into our equation. Lust certainly did. I won't say love. And, yet, we were trying to love each other. I was showing her the simple pleasures of life because those were all I could afford, but she showed me things that had escaped my notice.

Since I was considered a second-class citizen, a nonwhite, even dating her could have had repercussions for me. Not for her. Nobody at the yacht club was going to risk snubbing her, not with her father's kind of money. For me, there could have been a price to pay. Still, I can't say I gave that a second thought. I assumed she'd get bored with me sooner or later and move on. The time had come for me to take the diving course, and I went off to Los Angeles. Terry wasn't around, and I didn't get to say goodbye.

I was seventeen years old, knew no one, and, after three days in Los Angeles, was incredibly homesick. I searched out a marina and a friendly face. I met Arnold Cook, a sixty-five-year-old former naval officer living aboard his forty-three-foot *Chantey Dragon*. He was amazed that I was allowed to fend for myself at that age, but also understood the strength it had taken for my parents to cast me off. Over a cup of coffee, he made me a deal. He was separated from his wife. He had terminal cancer and was too weak to work. I could move out of the youth hostel where I was staying, and, in exchange for minor maintenance work, I'd have a cabin on his boat. I accepted. Here was my new home. I began classes, made new friends around the marina and, on the weekends, crewed for several different racing skippers, even practicing with them at night. Before I knew it, my first course exams were coming up. This was March 1985.

All the while, Arnold's condition was worsening. I'd come onto the boat and find him doubled up in pain. The doctors wanted him off the boat, but he refused. He preferred to stay in his bunk or, on a good day, make it up to a chair on deck. I kept expecting to come onboard and find him dead. He held on, though, and one afternoon he met me with a shock of another kind. He said, "There's a message for you from a Terry. Who the hell is this pushy woman?"

I was stunned. Terry had come to Los Angeles. She wanted to see me. We met. She was angry. We spent several hours going over how we felt about each other.

That night I returned home to the *Chantey Dragon*. Arnold was gone. He'd been taken to the hospital, where I found him wrapped in tubes and too weak to move. He said, "Look after my boat." I visited him frequently in the hospital, running errands and sharing my boating adventures.

Terry and I continued seeing each other. During our time together, we lived the high life, flying to Europe on her private jet, cruising the Mediterranean in her dad's megayacht, and enjoying the life of the extremely rich. We drove exotic cars and dined in the fanciest of restaurants.

I took my final exams. I passed ten of the eleven. At the graduation party, I found Terry sitting on a stranger's lap. She was high on drugs, and he was stroking her thigh. I was jealous and angry. I yanked her to her feet, and she slapped me. Here was the life I'd been fantasying just four years before, at least the unlimited wealth and a beautiful woman part, except nothing about it was right. The next morning she came down to the boat acting as if nothing had happened. She had an early birthday present for me. We'd happened to walk by a Porsche dealer, and as we were browsing, I asked the salesman about miles to the gallon. He said if I had to ask that, I couldn't afford the car and walked off. Terry had called her father, told him she needed transportation, and then bought the Porsche with his credit card. This was supposed to be my birthday present. I didn't keep it—but did drive it for a while.

Not long after the disturbing graduation party, Terry flew off to Monte Carlo, and I took a backpacking holiday in northern California and returned to Los Angeles. I had just turned eighteen. Terry came back, but she was a stranger. She'd gone down fast. Starting from a few joints, she went to popping pills to snorting cocaine to injecting heroin in less than a month. She had the money to support any habit and the habits of all the new junkie friends she was hanging out with.

When her father flew into Long Beach, I requested a meeting, and I went on his plane, an enormous private jet. I told him about Terry and her drug problem. She had a bodyguard, Max, who loved her like a father, but now he couldn't handle her either. I told her father that. He blew up at me. He said, "All the kids are doing drugs! What's wrong with you?" He threw me off the plane. Not even a year after that, she flew her own plane into the side of a mountain. Her boyfriend was killed instantly, but Terry was kept on life support for a time. Her father remained beside her. Finally he had it turned off and killed himself with a bullet. Max sent me a sorrow-filled letter. But that was a year later.

After graduation, Mom flew over for a surprise visit. With a newly made friend from England, she toured the area. With me she sailed to Santa Catalina Island and camped on the beach. I missed Arnold's company and having her on the *Chantey Dragon* made it truly seem like home.

Next, I tried to take a bus to Alaska but wasn't allowed to cross the border into Canada. My first real encounter with the barriers we call countries. For a South African even to pass through Canada required a visa. I turned back and spent eight "mountain-man" weeks camping in the Yosemite National Park. Except for the brown bears and coyotes, I was camping alone, disciplining myself for the future I was already planning.

Then, with a Greyhound unlimited bus pass, I toured the rest of America in all directions. Those buses served as both hotel and classroom for I was on them day and night and got my Americanization lectures from fellow passengers and sleepy bus drivers anxious for company. Needless to say, I met a broad spectrum of humanity. That trip did have one real destination,

Newport, Rhode Island, where I was to meet Francis Stokes, a great sailor who was preparing for his second BOC attempt. I mistakenly believed he was lost at sea in the 1987 race.

Sadly my immediate loss was my seafaring friend and shipmate, Arnold. A great sailor too, he died in the hospital as I flew home across the Atlantic, to Cape Town.

5

MINING DIAMONDS

T he year of study in Los Angeles was divided into two courses. In the first we learned the theory of diving and decompression. Nitrogen builds up in the body when you're diving to any depth, and, on returning to the surface, a diver must ascend at a controlled rate. Too fast and one gets the bends, a painful affliction of the joints that can prove fatal. We made our first few dives in a large tank where we became familiar with the gear. Then we graduated to the murky harbor where we learned to execute simple tasks underwater and to look after our partners when they were below and we were above. At the end of three months this class had dwindled from twenty-three hopeful divers to eleven. The second course lasted four months and taught us to inspect metals underwater, scanning them with electric current for hairline cracks and discovering metal fatigue with ultrasonic testing.

At the end of 1985 I flew back to South Africa in search of diving work, only to be told I had to have a Department of Manpower certificate. My new American diploma had no value in my homeland, and yet these same companies were hiring American and British divers who had the identical qualifications. I was told that I had to retrain in a South African school; however, if I was interested in diamond mining, I could get a temporary exemption. There was a shortage of divers in Port Nolloth, a small port up north near the Namibian border. I went with a white diving buddy, a South African of Dutch descent, and was soon introduced to even harsher South African realities. The old-line Afrikaner general manager insisted that I sign a one-year contract. I talked over the working arrangements with the supervisor, who promised hard work but good wages. I signed, and only then did I ask about accommodations. They only provided these for white divers. I went outside straight to a public phone booth, called the president of the company, and asked him why this was so. He answered, "You're in

South Africa now, not California," and hung up. Soon after, I was tracked down by my supervisor and offered a room in a house overlooking the harbor, in the colored part of town.

My diamond-diving career began. The equipment was primitive. On the deck a compressor forced air into a regular air tank, which connected to a garden hose that went over the side to a scuba regulator. The hose was attached to a securing rope with duct tape, and, using a carbine clip, this was attached to your weight belt. The regulator went to your mouth. That was it. We had no communications, no hot-water suits, no method of measuring the diver's depth, no lighting, no emergency scuba cylinder if the compressor died—and it would die. Of course, you would have died too, if you couldn't swim that seventy feet to the surface, exhaling all the while. There was not anything or anyone to help you survive underwater. You were on your own.

The mining pump itself was a bit more sophisticated. The diver held a nozzle-tipped eight-foot section of flexible pipe that was attached to a solid lime-green hose six inches in diameter, which ran off to the boat. We were vacuuming the seafloor with this immense vacuum cleaner—hundreds and hundreds of awkward pounds that the diver manhandled. On the bottom you pushed the nozzle forward, picking up anything up to the size of a bread roll. While holding the nozzle, the bigger rocks you pushed away and the very biggest you worked around. You were seeking bedrock. You were looking for diamonds or, more exactly, looking for a heavy black substance called kimberlite, which had washed into the gullies on the seafloor. You'd work forward into the sediment in a two-foot-wide path. You had a system, one that might take you deep into potentially lethal gullies. Also, large swells on the surface could suddenly create an uncontrollable twisting nightmare below. Just imagine a garden hose propelled across the lawn by a sudden burst of water pressure. Then multiply that by a hundred times and imagine yourself not on the suburban lawn but underwater, with zero visibility. Imagine yourself down there blindfolded and searching for diamonds.

For most of the day, I was busy with work, and a typical day ran from ten to fourteen hours. And if the weather was good, we went seven days a week. When the seas were rough, I studied for the Department of Manpower exams that were to be given in September. I didn't know then that my application to take the exam would be refused. It seems I lacked sufficient training. Ridiculous, since the school I'd attended was rated one of the best in the world.

On top of that bureaucratic annoyance was the racial prejudice in Port Nolloth. To celebrate one particularly good day, a diamond jackpot sort of day, the dive team went out to the only restaurant in town. We were a tight group, especially since we'd just made some money together. The white divers and I sat down at a table. Within minutes the manager came over and told the white divers they couldn't bring a "colored" in his restaurant. He instructed me to leave. The humiliation, the outright anger, that I felt was immense. Worse, my fellow divers, whom I considered close friends, just shrugged their shoulders and ordered, as if nothing had happened. I did the same work as they did for the same wages. When we were at sea, their lives were in my hands, just as mine was in theirs. Yet, I couldn't eat at the same table with them.

That was not the last time I would be refused service in the town, and, even at sea, I was surrounded by bigotry. In this out-of-the-way place I was the first educated black man whom many of the whites had seen. Not only that, I'd studied overseas. They were deeply suspicious and would have taken any opportunity to fault my work. I gave them none. Life for the black deckhands was even worse, but they'd spent their lives suffering under this segregation. They swallowed their pride and took their wages, as did the other black divers, who, despite their South African diving-school diplomas, were treated no better than the deckhands. Even from these black men I felt isolated, for they all spoke Afrikaans, and, despite some high school instruction, my knowledge of it was poor. For me, this rural dialect was the language of the oppressor, but as I stayed there, I did learn more. Being shuffled from boat to boat also made forming friendships difficult. I was lonely and depressed. I did the monotonous work, I walked the shore at night, and I studied, and I dreamed of the day I would sail my own yacht past this miserable harbor of Port Nolloth. To fight the boredom, I would make diary entries and write letters. One letter to a friend began, "I hate this town."

After three months, the family I rented from needed their room back, and the harbormaster found me a vacant house in the white section. Actually, I was to live in the servant's quarters, but I had a key to the main house and could use the shower there. This was rent-free. The house was for sale, and I was to show it to potential buyers and keep out the vandals. One afternoon, a particularly rude Afrikaner of middle age took a brief tour and demanded to see the servant's quarters. He turned out to be a former tenant and also the mayor of the town. Not being white, I couldn't legally live in the main house and wasn't, but he and the rest of his white friends didn't want me in that part of town, period. Two days later my electricity was cut off.

Nothing about Port Nolloth was state of the art. An old wicker laundry basket was run up the flag pole to indicate the sea was up and the sand bar couldn't be crossed. I was given a few days off and went home in a rage. I was close to tears, reduced to this by a feeling of utter helplessness. I couldn't quit because I'd signed the year-long contract. Living there was hell. My mother understood all this, for she'd experienced the same. Her gentle advice was to swallow my pride and be strong. Fortunately, on my return, a reprieve was waiting. The company wanted the divers to take a large pay cut, so the contract binding me to them was now broken. They paid me off, and I gladly left Port Nolloth.

After trying in vain to find diving jobs around Cape Town, I took a temporary diamond-diving job with a small company located twenty miles down the coast from Port Nolloth. I was given decent accommodations on the white side of this new town, and there were rumors going around of diamonds as big as your thumbnail to be picked from the face of the bay's red cliffs. These supposed pluses were offset by the company's even laxer safety practices. In fact one diver was soon killed. Also, shortly after my arrival, the mayor and aldermen objected to the presence of a black person in their section of town. The company moved me to a shack some distance away, an accommodation that had no toilet or cooking facilities, not even drinking water. A mattress had been tossed down on the bare gravel floor. I had no choice but to accept. If I were to realize the dream of having my own sailboat, of racing solo across the Atlantic and then around the world, I had to make money, a great deal of money. I swallowed my pride.

In a way coming home to my forlorn shack at night was preferable to being in that wretched town. On the bad weather days I would sit on the rocks and watch the sea pound them, the spray flying futilely across those unyielding surfaces, my situation exactly. To describe my own anger and frustration as a volcano, though, would have been a more fitting comparison, a smoldering volcano ready to erupt. At least there was the release of doing the best job possible. On the boats I was given more and more

Underwater diamond mining

responsibility, and though my white supervisors got credit for my work, I did take pride in being a lead diver. Toward the end, I even got on a boat where my skills were openly praised.

I went to work for Wally, a wiry little Scotsman who drove his crews and himself hard. Nobody wanted to work for Wally. He lived by example. He'd work faster than anyone on the boat and do his job twice as well. He didn't expect you to keep up. He did expect you to work at least half as fast as he did and to be half as effective as he was. From the minute you stepped on the boat until you stepped off, you stayed busy. Most guys said no, for the same reason I said yes. That was my work ethic, as well.

Wally's boat was small, only forty feet, but he carried five divers. Still, this was inshore mining, which meant that violating the boundaries of a mining concession was easy to spot. But if there was a heavy fog, we could be certain that at the last moment our captain would turn back toward shore and drop the anchor just inside his legally permitted grounds. Then we'd pay out a hundred yards or more of anchor line and begin to poach until threatened with discovery.

Twice Wally chose to mine the other side of the boundary while I was on the bottom. I was working away and suddenly the nozzle began to leap about. It went berserk in my hands and then, clinging to it, I was given the ride of my life. I knew that up on deck the crew was yanking in the extended anchor line, keeping it free of the spinning propeller, as Wally ran the boat forward at full speed, dragging me and the hose behind. We had six or seven minutes to get the operation legal, so as soon as the hose halted, I had to open the nozzle once more and pretend to be hard at work. A minute later came the inspecting diver in scuba gear. I waved and shrugged at the small amount of work so far accomplished, showing him I wasn't much of a miner. All that morning I hadn't found a decent spot to work. The Academy Award–winning shrug had to say all that and disguise the fact that we'd just managed to raid a couple of hundred carats from the illegal concession.

Even as Wally was borrowing diamonds from his neighbors, he and many other captains were being treated the same way by their crews. Up on deck the raw sediment was dumped into a system of revolving screens that washed the coarser material back overboard. What remained was dumped into a pan where it was very quickly but very gently shaken. This was like panning for gold, except that diamonds have a very high specific gravity so they settle to the bottom of the pan. The pan was flipped and the diamonds picked out, and occasionally the sorters (who were the topside divers) would stick the diamonds in their mouth in order to have both hands free to work. Some divers would forget to spit out the larger stones. It wasn't hard to figure out who was doing this. When you walked out onto the parking lot, they were the ones driving Porsches. This did annoy me, for not only was I not making enough to buy a Porsche, since we were paid by shares, the honest divers were helping to make these car payments.

Stealing from your coworkers was one thing, but I still couldn't work up much sympathy for the De Beers family's pilfering problems. (A portion of the De Beers enterprise eventually did help me go sailing.) This billion-dollar operation had mines ashore surrounded by great electric fences. Their fear that diamonds might be smuggled out in used equipment caused them to abandon unreliable bulldozers and earthmovers by driving them into the ocean. We'd pass the yellow, house-sized pieces of almost new machinery that the surf was breaking over, on the way to the mining concessions (granted by the government to its major individual supporters).

On shore the miners worked in uncomfortable camp conditions, staying six months at a time, working seven-day weeks and twelve-hour days. When they left at the end of the six months, they'd be x-rayed to prevent the more obvious forms of smuggling, swallowing them or, as the Paul Simon song suggests, slipping "diamonds in the soles of [their] shoes."

After a few months with Wally and on another small rig, I was finally allowed to take the Department of Manpower's exam, which, not surprisingly, was easy to pass. Exam notification in hand, I walked into the office and resigned. Never again would I be reduced to living and working under such conditions.

Immediately, I went onto the four-hundred-foot, fire-engine red *Trident Cape*. This seaworthy, comfortable vessel was equipped with the latest mining technologies and used the latest diving-safety measures. She stayed three miles offshore in a hundred feet of water, and she remained there, once not coming into port for four hundred days. Supplies and crew members were ferried out. The overhead for a week was in the millions, and, to show a profit, we'd have to bring even more millions on board. Tough to do, but in addition to commissions, we divers were fortunately on salary, high ones. Each of my contracted tours of duty was for twenty-eight days at sea and fourteen ashore. I was so happy with the money and the quality of life, though, that I stayed eighty days, then came in for my two-week break and stayed for only one of those. I was quickly promoted to lead diver and given extra responsibilities. The whole two years I never worked a normal schedule and usually spent my time ashore researching and designing the sailboat of my dreams.

Our principal investor was one of those rough and ready types who showed up in South Africa during the 1950s. He had come with the shirt on his back and an engineering degree. He had been responsible for the chemical processes that removed the gold from the ore, as he thought the old method was wasteful. He quit, formed his own company, bought the leftover "tailings" of others, and, using these throwaways, ended up as a multibillionaire. Still, he wasn't hard to approach, and during his visits I felt free to offer my opinions. He wanted the divers to study geology. I suggested to him it would be easier and less expensive to teach one geologist to dive. That type of contact with his employees had helped to make him very rich. His Afrikaner general manager must not have thought so, though. He had a real problem with black employees, especially ones who were good at their job. We butted heads on more than one occasion. He wanted to manage the flow of information. He was paranoid and wanted total control.

In April of 1986, I flew to London and took the train to Plymouth, where I sat through the two-day theoretical exam that would allow me to dive on the North Sea oil platforms. I passed and took the rigorous five-day survival program, which included being strapped into a simulated helicopter, inverted, and then violently dropped into a swimming pool. Underwater and unaided I had to unstrap myself and make it to the surface. That completed, I went looking for work and found none. The divers on those rigs hung on to those coveted positions. What I found instead was work washing dishes in a Bengalese restaurant in Aberdeen, Scotland. A step up from the diamond mining in Port Nolloth, but when a chance to dive for scallops came up, I headed off to the island of Arran in the Firth of Clyde. Working alongside my skipper, Tom McKlusky, I managed to make a living and was welcomed (occasionally with open arms) in the small villages along the Scottish coast. Still, after an enjoyable year, I'd had enough of cold water and of missing my family. I returned to South Africa and my old mining job on the four-hundred-foot *Trident Cape.*

Unfortunately, this particular mining venture was doomed, for the concession our investor had been given was poor. Politics decided all that. I recall that we found one diamond the size of a thumbnail, twelve to fourteen carats, and on the same day recovered two thousand carats in smaller stones. A day like that meant a few thousand dollars as a bonus for me and months of operating funds for the corporation. However, that was the only day like that, and the company eventually went bankrupt. For our employer, I don't think this project had been much more than a hobby, but it was far more than that to me. With what I'd saved and a handsome severance package, I could begin to build my boat.

6

THE GIFTS

I n 1988 I commissioned a dream-filled, would-be designer—Dutch mathematician Marinus Goolouze—to formulate the hull shape for an oceangoing sailboat. Since a mold was required, to build completely with fiberglass was too costly, and the resulting boat would not be particularly strong. Instead, we bent a veneer of okoume, a type of mahogany, over a cheap wooden skeleton, then with a layer of epoxy we secured another layer of the veneer on a forty-five-degree angle to the first and a final third layer at a ninety-degree angle. Fillers were laid into any gaps, then laboriously sanded smooth, and a final coat of fiberglass went on both inside and out. Then the hull was flipped over, the bulkheads and ballast tanks were laminated into place, and the deck went on. I moved onto the boat, using the deck for a roof. I painted the hull red, and, in years to come, I'd call her "my little red monster."

This was all happening in a boatyard in Mossel Bay, South Africa, 359 miles from Cape Town. I had accomplished so much, yet when a journalist and I tried to have lunch in the Mossel Bay Yacht Club, I was refused service. I said I was a member of Cape Town's Royal Cape Yacht Club. The Afrikaans-speaking manager pointed to a sign that read "RIGHTS OF ADMISSION RESERVED" and motioned to the door. On the way out I heard the bartender remark, "It's a sad day when a club allows colored people privilege to their sport."

My mother's other brother, Uncle Victor, lived right behind us. Like my father, Uncle Victor was an alcoholic, but his wife wasn't the strong person my mother was. Uncle Victor's family was raised differently. The importance of education wasn't stressed, and my uncle was not the kind of man to set his children dreaming—he was the kind who had let himself be beaten by the apartheid system and all of life's other inflictions. A newspaper article came out describing my boatbuilding, and the following Sunday

Building the hull and deck of the Stella-r *in Mossel Bay. Photograph courtesy of Rodger February.*

morning Mom sent me next door on an errand. Uncle Victor laid into me. "Who do you think you are? Who do you think you are trying to be? A yachtsman?" he screamed. He threw me out of his house, and it was years before I went back. At that point, he'd had a stroke and was lying on the sofa with a copy of my first book, t.s. *No Barriers,* on his lap. He couldn't speak, but he showed me the book and went thumbs up. That was his way of saying I was right to dream. But that approval was to come twelve years later.

I needed additional money to keep construction moving, and since a continuous quest for sponsors had achieved nothing, I agreed to deliver a sailboat to Texas. Stopping off in Brazil, I bumped into a Brazilian friend on the dock. He took me home to eat with his family: ten people in a shack made out of mud and tin, one of thousands in this squatters camp. They happily shared what they had with me, and they refused what meager offers of charity I could make. I'd grown up in a brick house and enjoyed privileges this family could barely imagine. Just one thing contrasted with the squalor of that camp. My friend had a sister, Maria, who was sweet, smart, and the most stunningly beautiful woman I'd ever seen. I fell in love with her instantly and wanted her to come on the boat. She laughed and said she was going to stay in her community to give medical care to her neighbors. She was determined to make a difference and exchanging her mat on the dirt floor for half of my bunk wasn't part of the plan. The night before leaving, I went to dinner again, but Maria did not show up. Later I learned there was only enough food for ten. Because she liked me, she gave up her bowl of rice so that I might dine with her family. That's one of the most memorable gifts I've been given, ever.

An interesting experience and a learning experience, this crossing took a detour when I put off a disruptive drug-taking crew member ashore, and it ended when I went into Mexico for repairs and was forced by the immigration officials to leave the boat as I did not have a visa. Flying on to Houston, Texas, I found work in the Gulf of Mexico, laying and repairing underwater-oil pipelines around the offshore drilling platforms. Once again I was soon made diving chief, and Andy, my buddy from the diamond coast, was my diving partner. He was probably five feet, one inch, tall at the most and stocky. Andy was all muscle.

Those divers were tough: they knew they had to depend on each other, and even then they would still need luck. We believed that "You see old divers and you see brave divers. You never see a brave, old diver." That meant if you took chances you'd get killed, but the truth was you didn't see many old divers on those jobs. This was a high-risk, high-tech game, and the divers were usually young and, despite their rough appearance, highly trained.

In the summer of 1989, we were using diving chambers in the deep waters. The equipment was state of the art and included my favorite diving helmet, the Superlite 17. We'd used the same helmet on the *Trident Cape*. It was constructed like a double-decker toilet seat combined with a motorbike helmet that had a rubber flange attached. The seat and hinged flange were pulled onto your head so that the rubber seal closed in under your jaw. Then the helmet containing the fighter pilot–like face mask and communications equipment locked onto the seat. The breathing mixture was pumped into that. The entire helmet weighed about forty pounds, and if you were on deck, you had to crouch with shoulders hunched just to manage the weight. But in the water it felt like five pounds, it was easy to manage, and you had the assurance of an emergency air supply and an earphone connection to the rest of the world. On the ship above someone at a control panel watched over your breathing mixture and depth. Within shouting distance of him, your personal tender was feeding out your umbilical cord.

Once suited up, you traveled down in a metal cage that stopped twenty feet short of the seafloor, for if swells were running, this protected you from being banged to pieces on the bottom. I loved it when the water was clear. I'd pull all the hose I was going to need out of the side of the dangling cage, then climb onto the railing and do a swan dive into that remaining twenty feet. I'd be gliding, falling like a plane toward the runway, and when I got close to the bottom, I'd arch my back and land on my feet. I felt like I was Neil Armstrong walking on the moon. I would look to the distant surface and see daylight as a faint glimmer and the shadowing hull of our ship like a space station orbiting above.

In really deep water we'd use a diving bell instead of the metal stage. On this particular job, we were working around 230 feet, breathing mixed gases. Theoretically this was a safe system and, compared to many places I'd worked, a very safe system. Like any system, in the end you have to depend on other human beings. Though still in the gulf, this platform was beyond U.S. jurisdiction, and Andy and I had a foreign employer who used many untrained personnel. We were working out of a wet bell, taking turns in the water. It was my turn to go out, but the engineer sent word he had only one last cut for us to make. It would take ten minutes to get Andy hoisted through the hatch on a block and tackle and undressed and another ten to return me to work, so Andy said, "Let me go and finish it."

He did. But the rookie engineer had us working on the wrong pipe. Andy cut into this misidentified "riser" with the torch, struck flammable gas, and there was an explosion. He was killed instantly, and the bell was damaged. I lost all communication and was yanked to the surface. That ended my diving career. The damaged bell went up too fast, and I got the bends, which meant if I were to dive deep, I could easily get them again. These were the most serious type-two bends, and the danger to me personally was compounded by the fact I had a reconstructed hip joint. Each time you're bent, you're that much harder to treat. And even without Andy's death as a warning, I knew I had to stop while I still had two legs and a brain. I've used a scuba set once since then and that was to scrub the hull of my boat.

I can't say I ever felt any sort of "survivor's guilt" when Andy was killed. Every diver knew that when he went down, he might not be coming back up alive. We lived with that notion of when your time is up, it's up. I let Andy's death be my final warning. Collecting my remaining two paychecks (both bounced), I went out to California to visit a friend. On this trip I met two solo sailors who would change my life.

At the boat show at Long Beach, California, I was admiring the Monitor wind vane on exhibit and met Mark Schrader, a stout six-footer with a prematurely gray beard and a confident smile. Mark had not only completed the BOC Challenge but was now the race director. Mark encouraged me to enter the BOC and sent me off to Chicago to meet Bill Pinckney. Bill would soon be the first black man to sail around the world alone. A semiretired business executive and old navy buddy of the comedian Bill Cosby, he was now indulging his first love of sailing. Like me, he'd had to face the opposition of a sometimes-hostile white yachting world, and he'd had to prove himself not only good, but better than most. From Bill I would learn to tie racing sponsorship to the education of children and inspirational speaking. With encouragement from these two sailors, whom I'd eventually host in South Africa, I flew home to finish my boat.

The owner of Central Boating, a boating supply company, gave me a 40 percent discount on deck fittings and electronics; another supplier, Manex Marine, gave me rigging at cost; and North Sails also came down on the price of sails. I often was turned down along the way and even had one company executive ask me, "What does a black man know about sailing?" By that time, though, such questions only fueled my resolve. For a nominal fee, a new manufacturer helped me build an aluminum mast. The bulbous keel was modified from a larger BOC design that was given to me free. I hired a mold and poured the lead.

When I was home, Mom was feeding me. Dad offered encouragement and sometimes drove me the 350 miles to Mossel Bay. With the deck on, I installed a gas burner for cooking and a bench that was a worktable during the day and a bunk at night. Over the years a few small improvements were made, but each truly competitive racer is spartan but spartan in different ways. Some are stripped below deck to save weight. Mine was stripped below deck because of budget.

I elected not to have portholes in the cabin superstructure, but not just to save money. They often leak and, worse, in storms can actually break out. I chose to live in a "mole tunnel." And I was never to have a toilet for that was just an expensive, bad-smelling leak. A bucket would not block and could be used for other purposes. The bunk, like anyone else's, was just a place to grab a nap, and for a rough-weather berth I could slip in beneath the cockpit deck. This cubby hole also served for storing my usually meager food and spare parts for they went in the cavity beneath the mattress and bunk boards. Soon I added a chart table, which became the nerve center of the boat. All decisions concerning navigation were made there, and in the beginning they were made only with paper charts and my one and only instrument, a sextant. Gradually, I added computers, radar, and satellite navigation systems. I started with short-range VHF radio, and I would eventually move on to single-side band radio and satellite telephone. These improvements came with time. In the beginning I was equipped little better than Joshua Slocum in 1895 or, for that matter, Columbus.

The time-honored method of trial and error had brought me this far, and in arranging the deck I stuck with it. Rather than work from drawings, I figured out what hardware I could actually afford (with the 40 percent discount) and bought it. Then, sitting in the cockpit, I spent five whole days envisioning what should go where. If I was on the high seas, what would be the safest and most convenient arrangement? I'd sit a winch in one place and consider it for an hour, move it, and repeat until satisfied. Finally, I'd mounted each piece where it fit my hand, and each line for hoisting or lowering sails was led back to the safety of the cockpit. Because of its simplicity, I chose a tiller over an expensive wheel. From the beginning an electronic autopilot would assist me with the chore of steering, but when I could afford it, I intended to add a famed Monitor wind vane.

That sort of as-you-go customizing usually worked out pretty well, but in the months to come I would still face many problems. There was much trial and error. People looked at my hull and said, "That thing will never float."

In October of 1990, the keel was delivered from Cape Town. Finding that the attachment bolts had been distorted by heat, we widened the holes in the hull. The person making the mast could not complete the job in Mossel Bay, so I delivered the boat by truck to Cape Town, and without fanfare she was slipped into the water. The mast was completed and raised. We saw that the mast base would need further support. The stress at the point of attachment needed to be spread further across the hull, and it appeared that the same was true of the keel. In fairness to my critics, I should admit we had seriously underestimated these forces and the hull and rigging had weaknesses. In fairness to myself, though, even after these defects were addressed and the boat had survived races that sidelined and even sank many, many others, the naysayers continued to belittle both my boat and my efforts.

The boats of the third BOC Around Alone were coming into the harbor, and I took off several days to help the English solo racer Robin Davie, then returned to my own project, for the time had come to launch officially. Mark Schrader provided a special bottle of "BOC" champagne and presided over the affair. I popped the cork and in front of the sixty-odd spectators announced to my mother that the boat was named *Stella-r*. In the crowd was the girl of my childhood dreams, Rejane, along with her husband and six-year-old son. In a moment of privacy, I confessed that the "r" at the end

Dad, Mom, and me with Mark Schrader, launching vessel. Photograph courtesy of Rodger February.

of *Stella-r* was for her. She was flattered but also embarrassed. The affection I'd felt for her back in high school still caused her unease.

The next day I went with a crew on a shakedown voyage, an ideal day, a brilliant blue sky, a gentle breeze, and majestic Table Mountain for a backdrop. We traveled without incident at a steady six knots, and, on returning, I signed up for a regatta that was two weeks away. Then I fine-tuned the boat in expectation. However, in the excitement of the first day's race, I made a false start, and after a wide circling came in last out of the sixty entries. The second day brought far worse disappointment. On the way to the starting line we met with rough seas, and the metal support beneath the mast sheared a weld, the rigging went slack, and the hull cracked open enough to leak. Then in making for the harbor, a sudden gust of wind forced me to push against the fiberglass tiller, which broke. We shortened sail further and used a timber to steer.

Christmas was spent with the *Stella-r* out of the water. The crack had to be sanded down and new wood and fiberglass laminated smoothly into place. The resin didn't cure properly. I had to borrow money from my mother. My dream had turned into a nightmare, and worst of all were the negative comments. One of the yacht club's wealthy sailors had this advice for his "fellow sailor." "You should sell your heap of junk." He insinuated that I should get what I could out of it and accept the fact that I would never have enough money to race my own vessel. Looking back on that comment, I had to wonder at the man's sad lack of compassion, at his inability to come up with a word of encouragement for his "fellow sailor." And he wasn't alone. Too many times some yachtsman was telling me that I couldn't do this, that my dreams were impossible. They were trying to steal hope, my hopes and dreams. If one loses hope, the future is not worth living.

I relaunched the boat, passed a new set of sea trials, and abandoned my own yacht club for the False Bay Yacht Club on the far side of the cape. In that happier and more positive environment, I again fine-tuned, raced the boat for a month, and made ready to sail up the coast to Port Nolloth, my first stop on the way to England and participation in the OSTAR, the solo transatlantic race and training ground for many BOC sailors. This race had started in the 1950s with just five participants and grown now to include over a hundred. It was the first race of its kind, and I don't mean just solo. This was the first transocean event for "amateur" sailors—even on crewed boats. It fired the imagination. This race made you. I knew I had to participate.

The farewell was emotional. A goodbye to my almost-tearful mother, my proud father, and Mama, who presented me with a fresh-baked cake. Oddly enough (or perhaps not), I slipped the lines from the same dock I'd made my first sail from as a child. The club fired a three-gun salute to see me off. At last, I was sailing solo.

Rough weather, fog, and calm followed as I entered the harbor of "the diamond capital of the West Coast." Nothing had changed in Port Nolloth. The same racists kept me out of their only restaurant. On board my boat, though, I could entertain my old diving friends.

After a week, I sailed 150 miles farther north to a port in Namibia, and I received both a welcome and part-time employment as a navigator, but an odd sort of navigator. The government was seizing foreign fishing boats found towing their nets inside the 200-mile territorial limit. I made good money, for we were paid out of the trawler's catch, and since they were stealing, it had to be worthwhile fishing. A helicopter was used to place soldiers and a few of us crewmen on board. This was paratrooper stuff. We hit the deck hard and were certainly uninvited. I stopped after four or five trips. By then I'd made enough to pay my bills—and I'd grown uneasy about our methods. My last time out, I was in the cockpit with the pilot and co-pilot. The pilot radioed for a violating trawler to hold steady and prepare to be boarded. Instead our target altered course and steamed away. They were only 70 miles off the coast. The pilot radioed the base for instructions and was told to blow the vessel out of the water. A few shots across her bow and the warning that a missile was aimed at their engine room were all it took to halt our quarry. I ran into the pilot a few days later and asked him if he would have actually sunk the evading trawler. He said, "Sure." He was a soldier, and those were his orders. In his country's war for independence, he'd been firing missiles against the South African Defense Force. This was just another part of his job, but I couldn't equate our boardings with war. If we'd sunk the trawler, her crew would most likely have been lost. It was time to move on.

Before leaving, though, I took some walks along the dunes. I watched a lone rhebok enter the sea until only his head and antlers were above water. I followed the tracks of wild horses. These lived on a few blades of tough grass and "drank" the dew. I didn't know it then, but a time would come when a drop of dew on a blade of grass would have seemed a godsend.

With Mom and one of her former students, I half-sailed and half-drifted north to Walvis Bay. My sister, Jan, flew up to join us. We had breakfast and went to a church service at the Seaman's Mission, the first we'd attended in years. We are not a religious family. My father was educated by Catholic priests but indifferent to that faith, and my mother felt with justification that the churches in our country had sometimes held the people back. Still, we are a spiritual family and do see ourselves as being ultimately in God's hands. We said our prayers. After church I telephoned my father and said goodbye. I shook hands with those I'd recently met and at last parted with my mom and sister. Again I felt the tears welling up in my eyes, and in Jan's were the shine of tears also, but we would not let them flow. Only when I was enjoying the privacy of the sea did I begin to weep.

My mother had not wept. As usual she was strong, but I didn't realize just how strong. For several years she had been struggling with breast cancer. I knew this. What I didn't know was that as I was sailing away, she was headed into surgery. She kept this from me. What could her sailor son do? This was her struggle. That was her reasoning, and, in fact, she did have many substitute sons and daughters that could and did come to her rescue. All those years of teaching, of dedicating herself to others, now paid off. The doctors and nurses who tended her were her former students, men and women whom she'd obtained grants for and struggled to place in the race-restricted medical schools. Only much later would I learn that there had been an operation and that it was a success. Resolute, she had stood on the dock with Jan and waved me on my way.

7

FIRST SOLO CROSSING

Tethered to my boat by a safety line and very much alone, I celebrated my twenty-fourth birthday. I missed them all—friends, family—but the routines of the day helped to fill that void. I read a few pages of *David Copperfield*. "Will I be the hero of my own life?" Charles Dickens asked. It's something I've asked as well. I ate a meal, and as the last sight of the southern African shore passed away, I took out my book on celestial navigation, the one I'd just purchased with the last of my funds, a handful of rand. With a decade of marine work behind me, I was familiar with satellite navigation systems but couldn't afford those, and on my own boat I had been relying on landmarks and ranges of the shoreline. Now the shoreline was gone. I would learn the celestial navigation as I went. With a sextant I measured the angle of the sun to the horizon, applied the proper trigonometry formula, and was dismayed to find myself sailing a thousand miles away in the Indian Ocean. Frantic, I went over the calculations again and again, getting the same results. Finally, after ten days of continually returning to the instructions and with new sightings and further calculations, I understood the process. Still, I never did feel comfortable in using the stars. Usually I'd shoot the sun at noon with the sextant and just try and envision a finishing port. I discovered faith can carry a brave man.

Shooting them or not, the stars of the Southern Hemisphere are dazzlingly bright. Although I'd named my homebuilt boat *Stella-r* (the star) after my mom, I also had the evening star to remind me of her. From her small kitchen window in a Cape Town suburb, she could see it rise. Each night, I'd watch for it as well. We shared that "star." My connection to my father was the Southern Cross, for he'd told me that was the starry emblem that made him "aware of his place on the planet." At age twenty-four I was sailing away and watching with sadness as it gradually disappeared. I crossed the equator, and it was gone from the night sky.

People had called me crazy for dreaming the dreams I dreamed. A once-disabled, black, working-class young man had no business owning a yacht and sailing the oceans of the world. Fellow yachtsmen in the apartheid South African community had declared my boat unseaworthy, saying that she'd sink on leaving port. Thirty-eight feet and built of laminated wood and fiberglass, she was my own creation and by no means fancy. Below she was spartan, a bunk and worktable and a two-burner stove. But my ambitions were grand. Not only did I want to be a yachtsman, I wanted to be a solo sailor, and not only that, but a solo-racing sailor. From the age of four-teen, I'd been told this was impossible. I was not buying. Here I was on my way to Plymouth, England, to enter a single-handed transatlantic race, the famed OSTAR race.

Sea Fever by John Masefield has the line "A star to steer her by." I had more than one star. I often referred to the compasses mounted on each side of the cockpit. I'd glance at the compass, glance at the sails, return below to the unrolled charts, make my decision, return on deck, and alter course, and then sails set, I'd glance once more at the compass. These were cheap compasses with no illumination, and at night the flashlight's beam would be bouncing from compass to sails and back again. The other three dials to watch were the depth finder, which I could now ignore; the speed indica-tor, which read in knots; and a wind-speed and direction indicator. I should say apparent direction, for at sea there are no fixed reference points except for the compass, which required another glance.

Each region of the world has its own trade winds, winds that are con-stant in speed and direction, and these can be assisted or opposed by a vari-ety of ocean currents and other weather patterns. Early sailors utilized these to shift cargoes from continent to continent, thus the name "trades." Natu-rally they influenced my passages, as well, and by first swinging west into these southeast trades, I was making good progress. On the sixth day out from Walvis Bay my new petrol generator failed. Thus I had only limited power for the electronic autopilot, and, unless napping or eating, I'd have to helm—an inconvenience partly off set by the absence of the generator's roar and oily exhaust. Then the pilot failed altogether. I disassembled it, found nothing wrong, and put it back together. It worked. I decided to put into St. Helena to repair the generator but overshot the island. Three weeks out, I finally sighted another vessel, a large factory ship, the sort that pro-cesses fish catches at sea. I couldn't make radio contact. Frustrated, I watched it pass over the horizon. Attached to the stern, I had a thirty-horsepower outboard motor but only a small amount of emergency petrol and making futile chases wasn't an option.

I crossed the equator, accompanied by a school of eight curious and potentially delicious bonito, but none curious enough to bite on the fishing lines that trailed behind. I ate the last of my bananas and canned vegetable curry. That meal was the exception, for usually, I found flying fish on the deck each morning and also had good luck catching tuna. If too small or big the tuna were returned to the ocean. Fish or not, I enjoyed my meals. In calm weather I fixed elaborate pastas with onions, garlic, and canned tomatoes fried in fruit chutney. In moderate weather it was potatoes done in a pressure cooker and topped with melted cheese. In rough weather I didn't risk cooking at all. At the equator the weather was blistering hot, and I dreamed of ice cream.

I had music: one of the taped songs of the Beatles, the Police, Neil Diamond, or Michael Jackson was usually blaring away. On this particular day, I think it was the Beach Boys. I was wearing a harness, sitting naked, peeling the last of my oranges, and tossing the biodegradable peels overboard. I stood up to search the horizon for a ship and realized at once that the boom was swinging my way. I tried to duck, but I was struck hard on the head and, if not for the harness, would have been knocked overboard. As it was, I landed on the far side of the cockpit and, trying to stand, found myself reeling instead. There was blood pouring from a cut on my forehead. For some time, I sat there weak, nauseated, and with head pounding. Then I managed to get below, where I cleaned the wound with salt water and examined myself in the mirror. My left eyebrow was swollen and that eye closed. I squinted and looked closer—and almost passed out again. At the eyebrow the bone was showing along an inch-long slit. I really was frightened. Obviously I needed stitches, but the nearest port was seven hundred miles away, and I had yet to make radio contact with anyone. Tears came to my "good eye." I imagined myself losing the eye or even bleeding to death. There was no way I could stitch that gap shut while looking into a mirror on a rolling boat, especially with a thick, rusty sailor's needle. The first-aid kit consisted of a handful of Band-Aids, a crepe bandage, and a few aspirin. That was it.

Then I remembered that if you applied pressure to a wound, it would stop bleeding, so I took out a clothes peg, the kind of pin used to place laundry on a line and, after cleaning the wound as best I could, pinched the split lumps of eyebrow flesh back together with the clothes peg. The bleeding stopped. Yet even after the swelling began to go down, any dramatic facial expression would dislodge the pin and start the bleeding. And, of course, I had to sleep on my back, for any roll in the bunk and I was bleeding again. Still, I managed to keep the wound clean, and by the third day my eyebrow had knitted itself back together. The headaches still came around, but by the time I reached the Cape Verde Islands a scab had formed. A medical doctor in the anchorage pronounced me healthy enough to continue on but recommended a psychiatrist. Also in the anchorage was a sailboat called *Playboy* where a photo shoot of sparsely clad Bunnies was taking place. Stuck-up girls, unfriendly and full of thunder, but a welcome sight!

By the time I reached the Azores, I'd forgotten the pain, was well healed, and ready to enjoy an island festival and the company of an American sailing family. After sailing alone for months with no medical attention, it seemed comical that both husband and wife were medical doctors.

Though I didn't realize it at the time, my first big test as a solo sailor had been passed. "Resourcefulness," race director Mark Schrader calls it. You have to know a bit about everything, and when that knowledge fails, you invent. Navigator, meteorologist, seamstress, plumber, carpenter, surgeon! Whatever the moment calls for is what you are. And "humility" is another of Mark's crucial ingredients. Pride and self-esteem have their place, but you have to learn pretty quickly that the ocean owes you nothing. If I didn't know that now, I would learn it in the weeks to come.

The fourteen-hundred-mile leg on to Plymouth, England, should have been quite literally "a breeze." Even with contrary winds, I was averaging a hundred miles a day, but on August 19 I sat becalmed. A Russian factory ship appeared on the horizon and steamed close enough to toss me a half bottle of vodka, a girlie magazine, and two liters of ice cream and to tell me a cold front was approaching. The barometer showed nothing, but my hip was aching. Freshening winds soon had "white horses" capping the growing swells, and *Stella-r* was screaming down the face of these, surfing at up to 12 knots. Night came on—a moonless but radiantly starlit sky shared by a cloud or two, an occasional streaking meteor, and gusting winds that now pushed the boat to 14 knots—and then 15, 15.1, 15.2, 15.3. The spray was stinging my face, and my heart was pounding, such a rush of adrenaline, such a sense of freedom, the glow of the instrument panel held me mesmerized. Careening down a wave, the boat reached 15.5 knots. Then, with a heart-stopping sound, the motion changed, and in an instant the boat was at 1 knot or less. The great waves were passing by, the sails flogging. I'd been thrown from the tiller and for a moment lay stunned in the cockpit.

"All hands on deck!" I shouted to no one and scrambled to my feet. But before I could tend the sails, the genoa shredded, and, worse, water was rising on the floorboards. With a bucket I began to bail and soon saw that I'd survive; bailing every few hours would keep me from sinking. Next I lowered what remained of the genoa and examined the rudder. The rudder had snapped, tearing out the bearing as it went. I went below and slept a fitful six hours. In that time, there were no magical improvements. The barometer fell another ten millibars, the sky turned to a leaden gray, and the wind screeched louder through the empty rigging. And water was again sloshing over the floorboards.

Obviously, I had hit something, and I suspected the culprit was a semi-submerged ship's container. As big as a small freight car, in bad weather these steel boxes are lost overboard and the foam wrapping inside can keep them floating at sea level or just below for weeks. More and more, they're a threat to navigation, and when I finally did pull out, the scars on the keel suggested I had struck one. Whatever the object, the damage was great. I could see that supporting stringers were broken, and the keel had loosened and might even separate from the boat. That couldn't be helped, but perhaps the rudder could be replaced. Perhaps I could fashion a steering oar from one of the bunk boards and the spinnaker pole. Two hours was spent on that task. Then I spotted a ship on the horizon and radioed her. After hearing of my condition, the captain offered to take me on board if I wished to scuttle my boat. Without hesitating, I declined.

The Azores were six hundred miles behind me, and Plymouth was almost one thousand ahead. In the log I wrote, "Good sailors do not go backwards." In part this was plain bravado, but also I reasoned correctly that the repairs would be much easier in England. Plus, in turning back, I'd miss the start of the OSTAR, the transatlantic race I'd set my heart on. For repairs I had to find a port closer to the starting line at Plymouth. Better still, I had to make Plymouth. Fine. I'd decided. The food locker held only enough provisions for a straightforward voyage, and, worse yet, two of my fresh water drums had broken from their lashings in the gale and leaked away. I would have to cut my water intake in half. A second ship passed, but the seas were too rough for water to be sent over. An hour later the skies turned blue, and by afternoon the swells were gentled. For the first time, I extended the makeshift tiller into the water and with a manhandling effort was able to point the boat in the direction of Plymouth. After only an hour the lashings holding the bunk board gave way. Despairing and with night approaching, I lowered the sails and got into the bunk.

I dreamed that people were chasing me. They wanted to chop off my toes, and I was running but not moving. They were closing the gap. I awoke in a cold sweat, and each time I slept the nightmare returned. Even with my eyes open, that and other nightmares came on, and combined with these were my legitimate concerns for survival and, beyond that, for raising the money to repair the boat and somehow enter the race. At sunrise the wind died. Drifting beneath a blistering sun, I couldn't find the energy even to hang out my damp sleeping bag, fix a meal, or bail the boat. For three days I hadn't bothered to brush my teeth, which I usually do religiously. I sat on deck and gulped down a glass of water. I had a second and a third and was attempting to pump a fourth when the container ran dry. In just three days I had used up half my ration. My school friends were right. The critics at the yacht club were right. I was crazy to be attempting this voyage.

As if to lift my spirits, Nature answered on cue. From the western horizon, hundreds of dolphins came leaping toward me. Flipping, dancing on their tails, in groups of ten and more, they passed by on both sides of the boat. Surely, a sign, and the majestic red ball of the sun sinking into an orange sea raised my spirits further. Why not steer with the sails? Dinghies can be steered that way. Hoisting both the main and the stay sail, off I went at a seven-knot clip. Except that I was going in the wrong direction. Shaking my head, I went below and for the first time actually bailed the bilge empty. I had completed a job. I felt better. I contemplated the bucket. Why not steer with the bucket?

Attaching the spinnaker pole perpendicular to the stern, I ran ropes from each sail winch to its ends and then tied both to the bucket, which I tossed over. By pulling on one line or the other I could move the half-submerged bucket to either side of the wake and through this friction control the direction of the bow.

It worked. I trimmed the sails and set off in a northeasterly direction. And as a bonus my bucket toilet was now being sterilized.

Thirty miles on my first day. A swallow landed on deck. It accepted a taste of my precious water and perched on my finger before heading off to the west. On day sixteen of what should have been a fourteen-day passage, I was deep into reading Conrad's *Lord Jim* (about a man who definitely regretted giving up the ship) and eating the last of the nuts and raisins. With a startling snort, a huge barnacle-encrusted whale breached beside me, followed by a second. Both a dozen feet away and both longer than my boat, they continued to circle about for several hours, treating me to the smell of their fishy breath and terrifying me with the notion that they might suddenly attack. They were only frolicking in the sun-blessed ocean, though, and with a final flip of their tails they departed.

Again the barometer plunged. In forty-knot winds I took down the sails and rolled aimlessly through rough seas. I still hadn't fixed a proper meal and now returned to a feeling of numbed and uncaring loneliness. The wind shifted and I raised the sails. I ate my last piece of chocolate. During the night my kerosene supply leaked into the bilge, a stinking oily mess that would take weeks to clear out. Looking over the side hardly offered a better view for I'd begun to spot floating rubbish, plastic bags, salt shakers, bottles. Everything of plastic made in the world seemed launched upon this sea, which in one way was a good sign. I was approaching civilization.

Running through my mind were the continual questions, "What am I doing out here? Why? When will it all end?" I was down to one glass of water a day, supplemented by the liquid drained off of canned fruits and vegetables, and years later I would still have a hard time with canned peas. On the twenty-fourth night at sea, I sailed through a spectacular lightning storm—bolts crashed down on every side, but none struck the mast. I shook out the reefs and continued to the northeast. Thick tongued and miserable, I awoke the next morning in a blanket of fog, dampness everywhere, still nothing to drink. Finally, that afternoon I made contact with a ship, and, after hearing of my predicament, the Filipino captain steered close. He hoped to pass me drinking water, but the swells had my mast scribing broad circles in the air and the danger of collision was too great.

Then barely clearing that same pitching mast, two white jet fighters roared overhead and banked toward Ireland—both so low they frothed up the ocean beneath. I could see the pilots' faces. I was one hundred miles off of Ireland and had set a course to Scotland. Ireland is an island southwest of Scotland. That's all I knew about Ireland. Two cups of water and three cans of peas remained. I considered the bottle of champagne Mark Schrader had given me, but the alcohol would only dehydrate me further. I'd save that for crossing the finish line in Newport—someday. A fishing boat passed in the distance. I failed to reach her on the radio. Frustrated I went below and slept. I woke to the thudding of a propeller and, through the patches of fog, saw a fishing boat trawling. It was time to use my precious petrol. I started the Yamaha, motored beside them, and was thrown a line.

"Cook him a steak," the solid captain, Tony Flaherty, instructed, and to me he added, "Take a shower." Even by fishermen's standards I needed a bath. Then with clean-up and a decent meal behind me, I babbled on about my last twenty-seven days at sea, the gales, and my fear of losing my sanity and my dream of entering a solo transatlantic race; he and the crew listened with smiles. They had no petrol or spare charts. They could fill my water jugs but questioned if I should go on. As I sat in the galley, drinking milk, Tony made radio contact with the Marine Rescue, and I was allowed to call home to South Africa and assure my mother that I was well and almost to England. Marine Rescue had other ideas, though, and at their urging I was towed by a naval vessel into the port of Galway. That was August 1991, and a new phase of my life was about to begin.

8

IRELAND ·

At first glance Galway appears inhospitable. The sky can stay a pewter gray that rains or threatens to rain much of the time. And being on the westernmost bump of Ireland, the harbor entry meets with an often-hostile stretch of ocean and requires massive gates that are opened and closed with the tides. Like Cape Town, though, the community has long served as a stepping-off place and had a well-grounded nautical tradition. Before setting sail to discover America, Columbus heard mass in the port of Galway. These were people who understood both the sea and sailors.

Nevertheless I was surprised by the reception. Waiting at the dock, were not only sympathetic navy personnel, but a crowd of television, radio, and newspaper journalists. I was a celebrity, the young solo sailor who had been rescued off the Irish coast. I took exception to the word "rescued" but not to the welcome itself. The custom officials were concerned that my limited medical kit might contain narcotics. Other than that formality, I docked in Ireland and was embraced by wide Irish arms.

Still the Irish people aren't the kind to impose themselves on a stranger. They'd ride by the berth to have a look and wave, but it was the second afternoon before I was invited to an Irish pub to try a glass of Guinness. I might as well admit now, I never learned to enjoy this expensive dark ale. I did grow fond of hot port, though, and Irish pub life did require that adjustment on my part. Except for celebratory occasions, I'd left home a teetotaler, which is an Irish impossibility. Fortunately, I found nursing one or two hot ports could get me through an entire evening, one or two and no more, for not only was I the son of an alcoholic, but I had only pennies to spend. That's what I was doing on my first visit to an Irish pub, spending pennies, and in the process I met Malcolm Goodbody, who invited me home to do my laundry, get a bath, and have a good night's sleep. He said to call him "Paddy" and gave me a front-door key. I stayed on with him for two years.

At a relatively young age Malcolm had sold his business and now dedicated himself full time to kayaking, sailing, and flying and, above all else, to chasing women. His six-bedroom Victorian house was always filled with people. Each time I put the key in the lock, I could expect to meet new company on the far side of the door—sometimes even East Germans, Romanians. Malcolm collected people, foreigners usually, who could be certain of a comfortable bed, a bath, a roaring fire in the kitchen hearth, a bowl of hot porridge, and a cup of tea, and, somewhere along the way, Malcolm could be certain of finding great romance.

My first week in Ireland I'd also met John Killeen, who was involved in a youth sailing program, and he suggested that, to fix her, I put the *Stella-r* ashore in his large storage shed. Arrangements were made with the Galway Bay Sailing Club for "lifting," but their schedule was tight, and in the confusion my boat began to dry out beside the dock in the outgoing tide, and as the boat floated lower and lower, the keel threatened to come through the hull. Then, once the *Stella-r* was suspended in the crane's sling, the keel was unbolted in order to separate it from the hull. Only the leading bolt had sheared off. The operators decided, despite John's objections and mine, to lower the *Stella-r* onto her side. Down she went. The hull splintered, and the keel was torn free. Here was my home, my dream of ocean racing, ruined beyond repair. I was certain she'd never sail again. John took me to Malcolm's, where I crawled into bed and cried myself to sleep.

I had underestimated the Irish people, though, or, rather, I didn't really know them. John had the seemingly unsalvageable hull transferred to his shed and delivered an entire truckload of tools, a bench planer, an industrial band saw, a lathe, and a huge circular bench saw. I began to take away the splintered wood, cutting thirty centimeters out of the hull to find what was solid. I cursed the whole time. With careful lifting all this could have been avoided. Still, the hull had needed strengthening. The real problem, of course, was funding. I had none. But help was coming from a surprising source. De Beers Industrial Diamonds of Shannon donated a sizable check and did it with practically no fanfare. Slowly I began to stitch the hole shut, meshing mahogany veneers, epoxy resins, and fiberglass sheeting to recreate the hull area around the keel. John Killeen was helping in his spare time and brought Peter McDonagh, an aluminum welder, on board. Peter was not a sailor. Directions of "port" and "starboard" were lost on him. Still, he managed to devise a sturdy aluminum frame within the hull that handsomely distributed the weight of the mast and keel. Also a new rudder of aluminum and fiberglass was built and installed. In the end over forty different people would volunteer their time and skills. I was dreaming again.

Malcolm was a true adventurer. I was working on the boat and giving motivational speeches during the week, but on the weekends we'd kayak or go caving or fishing together or visit his castle. Malcolm was in the process of restoring a true twelfth-century castle, replacing vandalized windows, doors, and floors. Stone walls rose over a hundred feet, and on all sides was a forested vista.

Ireland is the stuff of tourist brochures and more. Villages of clustered whitewashed cottages dot the coast. The roads, often single lane, are lined with stone walls that divide sheep pastures from peat bogs. All is green. Green, green, and more green. Except along the rocky shores, where it's windswept and gray, gray, gray.

The outside was our playground. Evenings were always spent in pubs. There are no other people like the Irish, a people so generous and open. Coming from a country such as South Africa, I was overwhelmed by this sudden friendliness and wholehearted support. The pub for the Irish is like a giant living room, a place for conversation and connecting, and a place to get an inexpensive lunch of soup and bread—and for some to meet beautiful Irishwomen. Low ceilings, small windows, thick tobacco smoke about your head, you hear music played and songs sung and discussions that run from the nineteenth century's potato famine or the ever-present fairy tales to the latest in technological advances and world politics. Often children were present. Occasionally someone would have too much to drink, getting loud and stumbling. In our crowd, though, both men and women sipped at their drinks, so the one or two hot ports and several coffees could easily get me through an evening. I was welcomed. I was a celebrity. I'd get slapped on the back and greeted as the "black Irishman." I was "the mad idiot who'd sailed across the Atlantic." My friend Eugene Walters called me "Sunshine" and claimed that this admiration from his countrymen all had to do with luck. A solo sailor has to prepare very, very carefully, but still an element of luck is involved. "Neal," he explained, "the Irish are very big on luck." The pessimistic Irish thought I was lucky in some sort of mysterious way. Much of their folklore involves people being "thrown up by the sea," and I did qualify in that regard.

Soon after my arrival I'd begun to speak in the Irish schools and also in the prisons, the universities, and the yacht clubs. I never turned down an engagement, and through word-of-mouth advertising I did stay busy. Children were my biggest fans and biggest boosters. I could walk through any village, and someone would wave and say, "My child heard you speak." The pay was minimal and the arrangements informal. I'd receive a meal and a bed in a local home. Five pounds was usual, but I might receive a hundred. After one television spot, I was up in Dublin dodging the Christmas shoppers, when a student tapped me on the shoulder, put the equivalent of five dollars in my hand, and vanished even before I could shout thanks.

In the years since, I've spoken to tens of thousands of children, and if I were to count the e-mail conferences, then I can't say how many more, but what I found of the Irish children is true of all children. They ask questions because they're curious. They don't have an agenda, not some point of their own to make. And hence the hardest questions are from the children; the younger they are, the harder the questions are. The children think about what they're about to ask, ask it, consider your answer, and then ask another. They can tell when someone is truthful. Their response is intuitive. If they're bored, you can see it quickly. Children don't mask their responses.

Ireland wasn't completely the Promised Land. Besides speaking engagements, I was also paying expenses by delivering yachts up and down the coast, once on an ill-prepared boat that almost took us down with it. And another time I was approached by the Irish police when customs discovered that I'd never officially entered the country. Still, I was not, as one newspaper reported, "an illegal alien."

Work proceeded on the boat. The keel was reattached, the bolts sliding into their holes with a single millimeter to spare. I fitted on a new Monitor wind vane, tidied things up, and prepared to launch. The people of Galway had made this possible. With a crowd of a thousand on hand, a real Irish Claddagh king's blessing, and a guitarist strumming sea chanties, the mayor swung a pint of Murphy's stout against the bow and relaunched *Stella-r*. I was the city's official entry in the OSTAR race. It was at this festive occasion that I briefly met a girl named Gwen.

After practice sails in the bay and the installation of new satellite-directed distress beacons, I was ready for the starting line—and the finish line off Newport, Rhode Island. A week before departing, I returned to the boat to find a sprig of heather and a short note and poem in the cockpit. The poem read:

Dark man
with Gypsy locks
and vagabond breath,
Pirate of hearts,
set me as your figurehead
and I shall scan the seas for you.
Dark man
with beady gull-like eyes,
your gaze a slippery fish to hold,
stare past and beyond out to sea
a glimpse of merman
scaling dreams.

There was a signature, but the handwriting was undecipherable. I had a fan. Who was she?

Goodbye to Galway Bay. Then five miles beyond the last well-wishing vessel, came a shout out of nowhere. Malcolm had missed the farewell party and paddled out in his kayak to have the last word.

"You were down below sleeping already," he shouted. "With no windows, that boat's like a mole's tunnel. You can't see me coming, nor the rocks, as you feel your way along in your burrow!"

A pleasant four-day sail to Plymouth, a pleasant burrow, I should say.

Ten days were left to the starting gun with plenty of chores remaining, but a festive atmosphere settled on the racing community. One sailing couple teased me about what I'd like on my approaching birthday. As a joke, I said, "A spinnaker in a sock." The husband, Tim Halford, wrote me a thousand-pound check. No British sailmaker could deliver in time, but a South African one did.

I passed the safety inspection. Now, for the first time, I was able to walk the docks unhurried and size up my competition. Several entrants were using this race as their qualifier for the Vendée Globe, a solo race nonstop around the globe. All I could think of was just finishing this event. Owning one of these sixty-foot rocket ships was beyond my imagination.

Four days to go, and there was such a crowd of well-wishers on the boat that I could get nothing done, which was their intent. They'd come to give me a surprise birthday party, one complete with a cake and twenty-five flaming candles, masterminded by my Irish friends, Rosie, and solo racer Harry Mitchell and his patient wife, Diane. Wearing his baggy shorts and sandals and beaming his mischievous grin, Harry Mitchell hugged Diane as they sang "Happy Birthday" to me. A longtime competitor, Harry was looked up to by all. He was one of my idols, had become my mentor, and was quickly becoming my very good friend. I had first read about Harry, then I met him, about two years earlier. Three days to go and congratulations arrived from the False Bay and Royal Cape yacht clubs as well as a generous eight hundred pounds from the South African Ocean Racing Trust.

Finally, in early June, with Rosie and friends singing in the distance, the gun fired, and I was bound for America. The tall-masted towboat followed for a bit, then with the Eddystone Light looming, she gybed away. Several powerboats and helicopters with cameramen stayed close, one helicopter so close that when I raised the new spinnaker and shot forward, my mast tip almost plucked the panicked pilot from the sky. He beat a retreat, which collapsed the sails for a confusing moment. Harry Mitchell on his *Henry Hornblower* was still in sight—but ahead.

I turned inshore in search of less tide and more breeze, and the fog rolled in, leaving me inside the ferry and shipping lanes, where I endured a terrifying night filled with muted horns and engine sounds and an endless fog-shrouded parade of rapidly passing running lights. Fog amplifies and disperses sound, and, of course, the imagination does the rest. I stayed on the radio, constantly giving out my position and my becalmed state.

Daylight came and with it a breeze that carried me south around the Bishop Rock lighthouse and kept the spinnaker big bellied until late in the afternoon, when a loud "thump" was heard at the bow. The boat slowed for a moment, then surged forward again. Floating in my wake was a large plank. I hung over the bow. No apparent damage. During the night the first gale brought with it mountainous waves that either broke over the bow or had the boat slamming down into a trough. I pumped the bilge dry and lay down in the bucking bunk for a nap, a fitful doze that ended completely

Repairing the hull

when I came to for a moment and heard sloshing. Water was well over the floorboards. In bare feet and flannel underwear, I frantically pumped the bilge dry. Three minutes later the water had risen to the same level. With the motion of a washing machine, the debris-crowded water was sloshing about my ankles. I checked the intake to the ballast tanks and the keel bolts. All sound. Between the next pumpings, I went into the forward compartment, and I discovered a square meter of fiberglass and veneer was delaminating where the plank had struck the bow. I raced on deck and put a third reef in the sail. I'd done this still in my underwear with no safety line and in the dark. Going below, I outfitted properly and returned to examine the damage from the bow.

Obviously I wasn't going to make the two thousand miles to Newport, but could I sail even the minimum of 150 miles that separated me from land? I checked the charts. Though the Irish ports were further than my English options, I could make it on one tack, and I'd be certain of speedy help from the Irish. I set my heading accordingly and by late morning was able to reach John Killeen on the phone. He suggested Baltimore, the Irish Baltimore, and since others were privy to the call, I soon had several offers of tools, materials, and labors. After arriving, with the boat dried out against the slipway, the wounded area was allowed to dry in the sun. Then two

Irish artisans did a rapid fiberglassing job with quick-drying hardener, the interior done even as I was being towed clear. Eighty pounds paid out for the glass. Labor free. And while they'd worked, a broken weld in the aluminum bracing was patched, and I even caught a short nap. After twenty-seven hours for repairs, with the race class leader 550 miles ahead, I went banging off again into the Atlantic swells.

The next two weeks passed without mishap, a steady rhythm of catnaps, nondescript meals, and weather bulletins to be analyzed. For this race John had helped me get a laptop computer with weather fax software that connected to a shortwave radio. Even before my hip began to ache, I had a weather prediction. I'd made a first step into the technological world many competitors took for granted. Of course, the knowledge of bad weather did nothing to dissipate it, and midway between the two continents I entered conditions normal to that region.

I'd chosen this extreme northern route to take advantage of currents, but here where the Labrador Current met the Gulf Stream a drop in water temperature coupled with relatively warm air produced a constant dense fog, one that reduced visibility to only three boat lengths. Still, a light breeze from the south demanded that I raise my new bright red, blue, and yellow spinnaker. I was now of wind and water. *Stella-r* jumped forward, and alongside her bow a school of dolphins began to leap. Below decks their happy squeaks and squeals were my serenade until dark came, and they abandoned me to that cold and foggy ocean.

At first light and with winds still freshening, I was eighty miles closer to Newport, but the fog lay even thicker. Throughout the day the water temperature continued to plunge. I had entered the Labrador Current in earnest, entered into a game of Russian roulette, for icebergs were certainly ahead. Still, two of my rivals had already come this way, so it was onward, rapidly onward, until the halyard chaffed through and the spinnaker collapsed into the sea. To be competitive, I'd have to climb the mast and replace the halyard. I dreaded this. With a two-purchase block and tackle hoisted to the mast top, I sat in the boson's chair and hauled myself hand over hand to the first spreaders and rested. Then I rose to the second spreader, where I hung exhausted, slamming against the mast as the gentle swell below swung me in a wide arc above the ocean. Then with eyes shut tight, I finished the climb, opened them, and replaced the halyard. Once on deck, I sat weak-kneed and allowed myself to contemplate the eerie possibility that with me hopelessly entangled above, the boat might have sailed on like the tale of the *Flying Dutchman,* racing the Atlantic forever as a warning to other solo sailors. Instead, I was headed on to Newport, Rhode Island, "the Sailing Capital of the World," and a port that had figured in my racing dreams from childhood.

Nineteen days out brought an even deeper fog, an actual blanket of fine water droplets in the morning, but finally the sun began to burn though. Hundreds of terns and a handful of gannets circled above. Sunshine, ten knots, and from above the sonic boom of the Concorde, an intrusion heard daily.

I crossed onto the shallower waters of the Grand Banks, and the seawater was close to freezing. This far north, I decided to give up my nap schedule. I'd expected to see fishing boats but didn't. What I did see when the last of the fog raised was a giant, shimmering blue-white iceberg. Less than a mile away, it was lying directly in my path. Since seven-eighths of the ice is below the surface, I expected at any moment to hear the crunching sound of a collision. I helmed the boat hard away. That caused the spinnaker to collapse and flap violently against the mast. If not doused into its sock, the sail would tear. In a few frantic seconds, that was accomplished, and I raced back into the cockpit to organize the remaining retreat from danger. Suddenly I felt a bump and heard a "thunk." The boat slowed for a moment and a lump of pure white ice appeared drifting in the wake. I had hit what's called a "growler," a very small iceberg—in this case the size of a family car. I rushed below in search of damage and found none—fortunately—for I was out of radio range and in this cold could not have lasted more than two or three days in the raft.

Discovering only on the following morning that a crack was slowly flooding the forward compartment did little to lift my spirits. The fog settled in again. I raised the spinnaker and altered my course to come close to Newfoundland. In the shallow water, I'd be safer from the icebergs, and I'd be closer to a port and could reestablish radio contact. Still, this did mean harder pounding from the waves and so more-frequent pumping of the forward compartment.

Figuring I'd reached the fabled fishing grounds of the Grand Banks, I reestablished radio contact. I made a ship to shore call to BOC race director

Mark Schrader in Seattle. He listened to my recital of woes and encouraged me to keep racing. I'd come a long way since we'd first met beside the wind-vane display, back when the boat was only imagined. Spirits up, I headed on down the Nova Scotia coast. More birds and now dolphins to keep me company, but the aluminum space frame had cracked further, and on a starboard tack the chain plates (fixed plates on the deck that various aspects of the rigging are attached to) were being pulled from the deck. Reducing the sails, I tightening the shrouds by once more pulling myself up the mast to the spreaders, a wildly swinging operation I still dreaded.

Twenty-one days out and another hundred miles closer to the finish, the wind rose to forty knots and the number four headsail tore along its seams. I tacked toward Halifax. By radio I sent word to my parents that all was well. In the night I passed the reassuring beams of two lighthouses. Then the reflected orange of a city's lights glowed in the cloud bank. Too close to the coast and badly in need of rest, I tacked off shore into an increasing lumpy sea, with growing winds, some thunder and lightning, a freezing rain, and seas breaking over the length of the boat. I was very, very cold.

July 3 and only 266 miles to the finish line. The wind dropped, and the tide was strong. Three cruising whales easily passed me by. The wind rose, and it was my turn to pass by—a fleet of working fish trawlers. On the radio with one, I heard a familiar complaint. The banks were being overfished, but if the fishermen stopped fishing, being fishermen, they'd be out of work. I was also told that François Bourgeouis was only twelve hours ahead. And I was offered a fish lunch. To accept would have been "receiving outside assistance while racing." The next day brought news of other racers. Simon van Hagen had finished in an amazing seventeen days. Colin Chapman and Bourgeouis weren't far ahead. If I was willing to risk a crossing of the Nantucket shoals, I might beat them to the finish line. I pulled out the chart and set my course through these narrow doglegged channels, where I sometimes slowed to a half knot, leaped across sandbars to find deeper water, and fought the swamping overfall of cresting waves that rose where conflicting currents met. A single mistake and I'd be aground with little from the tides to float me free. I trusted the charts and my skills and went.

Ten hours and I'd crossed the shoal. Seventy miles to the finish and the wind on my beam. I piled on the sail, and the fog descended. At that point I wasn't about to let the two other boats beat me. Still, I had to find the finish in all that fog and tide, a nerve-racking concern that passed just before dawn. I had done it, completed the first dream of my boyhood. On the rain shrouded dock was a small crowd of spectators and competitors. Forty-four boats had beaten me here. Seventy-eight started. I'd finished seventh in a class of nine, taking twenty-eight days. I wasn't far behind the larger-than-life Harry Mitchell.

9

BACK TO IRELAND

A presentable placing and one dream accomplished. I had raced across the Atlantic Ocean. I was a made man. I had completed my first OSTAR. And, believe me, I celebrated. Ecstatic, I jumped about the deck and patted the hull as if that boat were a living body, and once in the berth I shook the hands and accepted the hugs of well-wishers. Yet, oddly, I was soon depressed and worried, occupied by the repairs that had to be done. Members of the Newport Yacht Club came through with tools and materials and encouragement.

I was at work when Mike Richie sailed in on the *Jester*. He'd taken forty-five days to cross and came in last, but this was his twenty-first solo crossing, and many friends and journalists were on hand. When asked what his best-ever solo-racing finish was, he answered, "Last." The question was repeated. "Last," he repeated. "I am always last. When the going gets tough, I lower my sail and read, eat, sleep and drink. I'm in no hurry."

Mike was seventy-five-years old, and he and I were the last foreign competitors remaining in Newport. A dinner in Mike's honor was given by the Rhode Island State Yachting Association, an incredibly delicious and elaborate meal followed by the presentation of a medal and the Key to the City of Newport to Mike for being the oldest man in sailing history to cross any ocean single-handed. And then a second set of medal and key was presented to "a recipient (who) came from the furthest destination, and against the odds." There was more. The young man had "set an example of what courage, determination and dedication is, and has been an ambassador for his native South Africa and for his adopted country, Ireland. Most of all he has been an ambassador to sailing. . . ." The Key to the City of Newport was given to me. Overcome, I took several minutes just to compose myself. Then I thanked them all, everyone, especially my parents, who had offered me encouragement along the way. "Thank you, all!" And still today, I thank you all.

The return sail to Ireland was rough and contained a solid week of forty-knot winds and cresting seas. But the Monitor wind vane allowed me to stay below deck and let the icy winds howl. Twenty days out, I reached the Porcupine Banks, two hundred miles off the Irish coast, and even steeper seas that tossed me and the bunk upside down when the *Stella-r* took a hard, heart-skipping, breath-held knockdown. She righted herself, though, and with only the loss of navigation lights I managed to slip through the Galway Harbor gates just ahead of a forecasted force nine gale. Twenty-one days to cross from Newport. I met my friends, talked to reporters, and settled in to search for further sponsors and resume my speech making.

October came, and I'd moved back to Malcolm's house. One morning a knock came on the door. There stood Gwen Wilkinson, the pretty girl I'd met some months earlier when we had relaunched my boat. Back then I had invited her out. She stood me up. I was happily surprised but at the moment busy finishing a chapter of the book that would become *No Barriers*. I left her to watch a solo-sailing video and returned to the computer. Those were the first minutes of what would become our first date.

Gwen had slipped into my life. She was Malcolm's cousin and the roommate of his sister. She was bright and Irish in her manner, her movements, her stubbornness, all perfect in their Irishness, except for the dialect, which had been tempered by a prestigious boarding-school education. She was small, or thought of herself as that. "Petite" you might say, but I wouldn't dare. She had a dry humor and all sorts of talents. She had incredible chestnut hair that swayed behind her as she walked. She was shy until she got to know you. Soon we were living together on the boat, living under the most spartan of conditions, no shower or toilet or even heat, and only the most primitive of kitchens. What money there was went for the repairs. We'd spend the equivalent of perhaps seventy dollars a month on ourselves. More than once we'd literally scraped through the bilges, looking for a few pence. "Tea money."

We'd been on the boat together for some months and were on our way to her family home for the weekend. I was working on my book when I mentioned this poem that had been left on my boat, one signed with an undecipherable signature. I recited the first verse. She finished with the second.

She had written the poem and left it with a sprig of heather. The heather means good luck and come back to me. From that clue, I should have guessed. Here was the woman who had promised to be a "figurehead" on the boat and "scan the seas" for me.

After returning from Rhode Island, I'd begun in earnest to make inspirational speeches. Without deep pockets or sponsors, it was necessary to exercise what solo sailor Bill Pinckney calls my "Gift of Gab." In one five-month period I spoke at thirty venues, mostly primary school groups. I showed slides of myself diving among the bright fish and brighter coral, the *Stella-r* swinging at anchor in some sunny exotic spot or dolphins leaping clear of the water. Those images would be shining on the snug white plaster wall inside, and outside was the usual cold rain. These pink-cheeked, blue-eyed children, every one of them bundled up in a heavy wool sweater, would be hypnotized. Then I'd click on a slide showing a sea turtle caught in a plastic six-pack holder or a gull ensnared by monofilament line. "What can you do about this?" No answers. I definitely had their attention. "What can you do to clean up the environment?" They'd stare back. I'd take a step down the aisle and pick up a piece of trash paper from between the desks. "This is how you start cleaning up the environment. You start with your classroom and move on to the beach." It's simple. The earth is four-fifths ocean, and by one estimate four-fifths of the garbage floating in it comes from the land. I'd point to the poor turtle or the ensnared gull and then ask, "Do you want to be responsible for this?" No! They definitely didn't. The trick is to let them see they have choices.

As mentioned, the Irish are not the most optimistic people on earth. Like many Europeans they tend to see optimism as an American disease, but, at the same time, you don't find that arrogance that may be the true American disease—or is that only self-confidence? In a softer voice, I'd tell the children that I grew up in a working-class neighborhood not much different from theirs. I'd tell them how I was born without a complete hip joint and couldn't run, that I could barely walk. I'd tell them, "But I dreamed of something better. I read books and I dreamed. I told my parents that I was going to grow up and be a solo sailor, that I'd build a sailboat and sail by myself to distant places. They didn't understand this. Not at all, but they encouraged me to dream, and now I'm here standing before you. You have choices. You can make a difference in this world."

Those were the messages. Make this world a better place. Dream, aspire, believe in yourself. The children were the best of the audiences. University students tended to shut me out, not curious about me or apparently about anything else. One way or another, adults could be a surprise. I gave one series of presentations in Portlaoise, the maximum-security prison where most of the prisoners are in for subversive crimes, mostly IRA and INLA (Irish National Liberation Army) members. I was uncomfortable with this group at first and not sure I wanted to be locked in with them. After they'd cracked a few jokes, though, I relaxed, and after a good lunch in the staff canteen even went off to the cellblocks to meet some of them in person. Sentenced from ten years to life, these men had made headlines around the world for their bombings and related destructiveness and were kept separated from the ordinary prison population. They wore everyday clothes. They expressed no hostility toward the staff. In the months to come, I continued to meet with this "captive audience" and lectures that were meant to last an hour would always run to two. For centuries Ireland had been treated as an English colony or worse, so I wasn't surprised that the inmates would ask me about South African politics. Yet, most of their questions concerned how I dealt with prolonged isolation, my fears and difficulties, and the reason for taking on the solo challenge. Solo sailing has been compared to doing time in a prison. They could relate. Looking at these men, it was hard to imagine them masterminding acts of violence. As a confirmed pacifist, I found it particularly hard to imagine. They were ordinary human beings, the kind you see sitting in a pub or even babysitting children.

From years of addressing groups, I'm able to make distinctions. When the audience is composed of children, the more affluent they are, the less interest they show and the shorter their attention spans. And, as mentioned, regardless of wealth, late teenagers and people in their early twenties are the worst. The younger the children, the keener they are to ask questions, to comment, and to make contributions. These men in the Portlaoise Prison were like those youngest children. They had that sort of vigorous curiosity but at the same time retained the intellectual depth of well-read adults. They were the perfect audience.

I'm going to leave out the Jesuit priest who insisted in Gaelic that I address his students only in Gaelic (I declined) and the Detroit school principal who insisted I address his students from behind a bullet-proof shield.

(I walked around in front of the shield, and they listened to me without incident.) What I'm leading up to is an encounter with one particular not-so-perfect audience. I had been invited to a community discussion on the topic "Ireland: A Third World Country on a First World Planet" and somehow the problem of "the Travelers" came up. I raised my hand and volunteered, "From the sound of it, I am a traveler, and I don't think you're being fair." The speaker said, "You're not a Traveler. You're just somebody passing through." I answered, "I live on a boat and travel the oceans of the world. I'm the same as these people." Of course, I had no idea that the word "Traveler" was used in place of "Gypsy." When this was explained to me, though, I still felt the same.

The Irish Gypsies have a bad rap. They're proud to the point of arrogance and not the best of neighbors, but in part that's because they expect to be criticized no matter how they behave. In the old days they lived in horse-drawn caravans and traveled the country, working as tinsmiths. That's where the name Travelers came from. Trucks now pull the caravans (the horses they keep to trade among themselves), but these days it's useless to go door to door repairing leaking pots and sharpening knives. Plastic housewares and electric sharpeners have doomed that livelihood. They simply move from place to place. They don't care who owns the property where they set up, and if you're the landowner, you can expect your property immediately to drop in value. They cut down the trees for firewood, throw trash and rubbish about the site, and have a reputation for stealing. To make matters worse, they mock the efforts made to help them and consciously head their children toward a life of the same.

The police do their best to ignore them, to let them settle where they want and, at least, inside the camps, to let them police themselves. Most pubs don't want their trade, and if they enter a store of any size, security personnel follow them up and down the aisles. The parents discourage education, and the mostly illiterate children are often put on the streets to beg, dozens of kids between ages five and ten coming at you going, "Change! Change! Change!" Also from their mouths come such words as I would never have believed, but then the Gypsies are very good with all words. It was an ugly situation that was centuries old, and in recent months the camps and the communities around them had reached the point of open violence. One camp had been burned to the ground and some Gypsies killed. There were threats of reprisals.

I'd been working with one of the outreach programs directed toward the poorer Irish children, and over lunch a group of politicians and businessmen suggested I give the same lectures on the importance of education and the power of a dream to Gypsy children. In this community the government had built a trailer park that accommodated forty to fifty Traveler families, and the conflict between them and the local boys had been increasing. I'd had boys from this same housing project already working on the boat. Communication between the two groups had broken down completely. Would I go into the Travelers' camp and speak? I agreed.

Gwen declared that I was asking for trouble, that I was inviting a public-relations nightmare and risking both our positions in "polite" Irish society. For all her relaxed ways, she was definitely a part of that aristocratic society. She said, "If you go to that camp, you might not be welcome at some tables." There was real friction between us. I said, "In South Africa I was told that the blacks are no good and worthless, and I am black. Gwen, people didn't want to be with me because it would keep them from being welcome at some tables." This was absurd, really. I couldn't let the prejudice of others stop me from doing my duty. I said, "If you care about me, you'll support me in this."

She cared. She'd never even been in a Travelers' camp and decided to see for herself. On the announced evening, we were driven there, to the site of this "other" culture. The children were very direct. They started out asking Gwen how old she was and then how many children she had. When she said, "none," they wanted to know why. She said, "Because I'm not married." They said, "Are you going to marry Neal?" All interesting questions, questions that cut right to the bone. Yes, an interesting evening. If anyone disagreed, they'd just yell over the opposition. Mayhem! The more excited people got the higher the volume and pitch. And when shouting and arguing no longer got the point across, they began to beat on each other—both children and adults. The children, especially, lashed out in this way. I was so saddened. I'd never encountered this form of expression within a supposedly coherent community, a form so anchored in aggression. At the end of the evening, I asked, "Are there any questions?" One of the girls asked if they could they come see the boat. I said, "Of course."

Gwen just about died, for the visit to the camp hadn't overcome too many of her misgivings. The boat was dry docked in that large shed, and we were living aboard her. The Gypsies would be there in a couple of days. Gwen shouted, "You can't bring them here!" The shed covered a good one-fourth acre, and it had great high ceilings and roll-up garage doors. John, the generous owner of the shed, had an old Rolls Royce, a Mercedes, tools, and another boat stored in there as well. Gwen insisted the Gypsy children would attempt to carry away these expensive toys, at least in pieces, and then return with their parents for what remained. Still, I couldn't act according to her perceived image of these people. I said, "Gwen, I walked into that camp with my wallet. Everybody warned me not to take it, but when I walked out, my wallet was still in my pocket." Gwen insisted I clear the visit with our landlord, John. It wasn't my wallet that was going to be at risk. John was concerned but trusted me to see that nothing happened. I also talked things over with a barrister friend, a no-nonsense, self-made man who was well placed in government and respected by the aristocracy. He agreed with Gwen that my actions could bring social reprisals and cost me sponsorship dollars, but, on the other hand, being non-Irish, I had a unique opportunity to diffuse this ugly situation.

Led by a group of nuns, two dozen of the children showed up at the shed. I showed them around the boat, but, of course, they were hard to contain. The cover was pulled off the Rolls Royce, and if I hadn't locked the cars, the children would have been inside them. I did have my hands full, but at the same time I couldn't help but marvel at all that energy. Perhaps the nuns were reading my mind. They asked if I needed help. I had the local boys on the weekend, but other than that Gwen and I were on our own. If the nuns could find two Gypsy boys to work with us, would we accept them?

I saw this as a great opportunity for I'd be helping to heal a rift in the community, reach out to these two young men, and get some much-needed work done at less than rock-bottom rates. Fortunately, the nuns would even provide for their transportation and food, for Gwen and I could not even transport and feed ourselves. I agreed.

Gwen said, "No way." She said, "Neal, they will rob us blind and damage the boat. Don't do it." I said, "Well, from the beginning you've been saying, 'don't, don't, don't,' and we've yet to have a negative experience." "Don't do it," she said. "Anybody could steal from us," I said, "We need the help and really, look around here. What do we have to lose?" I'd pledged to look after John's automobiles and other toys, but aside from the boat, all

Gwen and I risked were the clothes on our backs and several cases of Mars chocolate bars.

Attending a boat show, I had met an executive of Master Foods, the makers of Mars Bars, and as a result I approached the company for sponsorship. The reply was that if the Irish soccer team failed to qualify for the World Cup playoffs, the company would shift its support from that to my sailing. For that critical soccer match the entire country was glued to the television sets, and Gwen and I were the only ones in all of Ireland rooting for the opposition. Ireland won and as a consolation prize Master Foods sent us a note that read "One a day!" and a large box of giant-sized Mars Bars. Three hundred and sixty-five chocolate bars were what we lived on, and so when the two Gypsy boys, Paddy and Willy, came to work for us, they were allowed to eat all the Mars Bars they wanted.

They'd need them to keep their energy levels up. The great shed was impossible to heat, and whatever the temperature outside, it was ten degrees Fahrenheit colder inside. We had the Mars Bars for calorie heat and several layers of clothing, but in order to fiberglass an extra two feet on the stern, it was necessary to build a tarpaulin tent around the boat, heat that, and cure the epoxy.

By then we were determined to enter the BOC Challenge for 1994, which meant sailing soon in their preliminary race, The BOC Atlantic Alone. Unlike the OSTAR, this single-handed race would be from Falmouth, England, to Charleston, South Carolina. This was the qualifier for the big BOC Challenge, also known as the BOC Around Alone. I'd been considering not racing at all and simply making a solo circumnavigation, but Harry Mitchell had convinced me to qualify my boat by adding on two feet to her existing thirty-eight. Working with Gwen and our Gypsy lads, we did that, and we also added two mandatory watertight compartments, paneled the interior, and painted the hull and deck, which translated into sanding, grinding, patching, and painting for many weeks.

"Man's work," as the boys saw it, and they weren't shy about expressing the Travelers' chauvinistic ethic to Gwen. Every day we'd stop for lunch. They'd unpack the cold meats the nuns had sent, and in the beginning Paddy and Willy would tell Gwen to make the sandwiches and put the kettle on for tea. These were not jobs for men. Of course, Gwen was having none of that. She said, "If you're not putting the kettle on, you can just

71

Me with Paddy and Willy, the two "Traveler" boys

watch me drink my tea. If you're not making sandwiches, you can watch me eat mine." Quite a revelation for the two boys, this first contact outside their community and it was with a modern Irishwoman, but this was an education for Gwen as well.

Over the months I happily watched as these opposites nudged closer and closer together, watched as they went from "You stay away from me, and I'll stay away from you" to tolerance and from there to respect, and finally to friendship. None of that overnight, though.

The boys were ages seventeen and nineteen. When they disagreed about how the job should be done, they beat the hell out of each other. I'd hear wood go smashing as they struck each other with planks, yet once the argument was settled, they held no grudges. One minute they'd be in a vicious fight, and the next they'd be doing a jig together or singing an Irish song. Singing? They never knew more than the first couple of lines of any song, and these they would sing over and over and over, which drove Gwen and me insane. Gwen, who knew the lyrics to most every song, at first refused to tell them more until the four of us finally joined together as a family. Then she taught them all the words and even sang along.

Repairs finished, Gwen painted (with an artist's oils and brushes) four Irish scenes in the saloon. Wherever I sailed, a bit of Ireland would be going along. We renamed the boat *Protect Our Sealife* and prepared to launch. Jim Fahy, an Irish television journalist, sailor, and great supporter, interviewed Paddy and Willy and me, and in the resulting program pointed out that these two Traveler boys were no different than any other recruits for they were honest and dependable. Which they were. Left to clean up the shed on their own, they made it spotless. Every tool was accounted for. They were dedicated craftsmen who needed no supervision. In short, I'd happened upon the perfect support team and at the same time opened up a much-needed line of communications. The dialogue we began way back then is still going on. Paddy and Willy have moved on, but the two communities remain on speaking terms.

10

A FAMILY CHRISTMAS

Gwen's dad, Paddy Wilkinson, was an engineering graduate of Trinity University, and the Wilkinsons were an ancient, moneyed family. One day, he just turned his back on all that. For a while he'd owned a pub and then exchanged that for a canal barge, and with wife and child he took off on a floating campaign to save the Irish canals. Already polluted, there were plans to fill them up altogether. Gwen was quite young and grew up on that barge until her father decided to build a house. He bought a large piece of mountainous land, moved everyone into a tent, and constructed a traditional Irish house in the traditional efficient manner. He even planted a small forest to replace the trees used up in the house's construction. They had no neighbors, and her father had become an "almost" hermit, a man who'd had his fill of society and what passed for culture. The very mention of media mogul Rupert Murdoch would put him into a fury; the fare on television did the same. If you counted my solo sailing, we were both "almost" hermits and got along great. We both wanted the best for his daughter, and, even without marriage, I thought of him as my father-in-law. Gwen and he were close. I suppose I reminded her of him—in the aloneness and the adventuresomeness. She told her father that what I called "determination" was just "plain stubbornness."

Gwen's mother, Ann, went back to college in her fifties and now heads up an environmental group. Like her husband, she wasn't happy with how the world was going and said so. I can't say that she and I saw eye to eye when it came to Gwen. I think she wanted more for her daughter, but since her daughter loved me, she opened her home. I was tolerated because she didn't want to alienate her daughter. Gwen had been educated in the best of boarding schools and was scheduled to go to law school until she took up with this South African Gypsy.

Gwen saw her parents as being different. She'd been raised differently. In a sense the jump from a canal barge to the belly of a sailboat wasn't all that great, at least, not the way jumping from a townhouse or country mansion would have been. Still, it was a pretty good jump. Growing up in that way had given her one disadvantage. She was very shy—well, at first. Then she was the opposite, a challenging woman, who could discuss and argue. She was well read and could ride horses, paint, and cook with professional skill. What she hated were dinners and parties where you were expected to make small talk to strangers for an hour or two. She could get through those for my sake and my sake alone. Of course, the attention that surrounded my sailing dreams—the interviews with the press and the photographs and radio and television interviews—were her absolute worst nightmare come true. She did them for me and eventually became quite good at getting us the attention that sponsors required. In exchange I showed her the world, even if we did travel on a shoestring and in the direction the wind was blowing.

For our first Christmas we went to her parents', and on display in Gwen's bedroom was a bit of a surprise. Riding trophies, ribbons, and photographs, everything in there was related to being a horsewoman. I understood then just how passionate her attachment to horses was. Yet, oddly, she was allergic to horsehair, and without medicine a simple trip to the stables would leave her wheezing for breath. Eventually we'd ride together everywhere in the world but Ireland, and, looking back, I think the horses had more of her heart than I did.

That Christmas was perfect. Outside a light dusting of snow had fallen, while inside Gwen was cooking chocolate cakes and chocolate truffles and a wonderful boneless duck. As in many Irish homes, the center of the house was the warm kitchen, more specifically the wood-fed Aga stove. In the evening Paddy had his Newcastle brown ale, which he drank as if it were the first or the last he would ever enjoy. Gwen and her mother had their red wine and I my hot port. No television except videos. We'd play vicious games of hearts and friendlier games of scrabble. There was a flight simulator on the computer. We'd take turns flying. All of it so different from the Christmases I'd spent with my own dad.

The house had a long narrow hall with the kitchen on one end and on the other Gwen's bedroom and next to it the guest room. I'd go to sleep in the guest room and wake up there, but don't ask me about the in-between.

Her parents didn't either. And this Christmas arrangement was eventually extended into frequent lengthy stays. In the autumn of 1993 I was completing *No Barriers,* and Gwen wanted to be home. I'd sit in the study with the laptop, writing away. Gwen would run from her bedroom to the kitchen, and I'd hear this pitter-patter of steps. It was as if she'd slipped from being a self-sufficient woman into being a seven-year-old girl racing from room to room. Pitter-patter across the hall to the washroom, pitter-patter to the kitchen, pitter-patter back to the bedroom.

For a break we'd take the High Nellie bicycle into the neighboring village of Boris. Gwen knew the people, but not well, and, even in the pub, I don't recall the usual sort of camaraderie. It drove Gwen crazy when we'd walk to the boat along one of those twisting Galway lanes and I'd stop to chat with everyone I knew, which was everyone. The two-block walk could take an hour. She accused me of having ulterior motives, of being friendly in order to gain financial support for my sailing. She was right. I did see the general public as a gigantic sponsor and did court their approval, but eventually she realized I'd talk to people no matter what.

Luckily for her, this nearest village to her parents was eight miles away. She and I would go off cycling or walk down the empty road from blackberry patch to blackberry patch and tease each other about how many got eaten instead of going into the basket. We were always holding hands. All over the world we'd hold hands. Even horseback riding we'd hold hands. We were like two magnets: no matter which way we'd face, those hands would lock together. Walking or sitting in the pub we'd hold hands.

The BOC officials wanted to get publicity for the event in South Africa, and so they arranged for me to fly down. I could look for sponsors, and the race would have a visible presence, a South African racer to meet journalists and promote the event. Gwen wanted to go, too, and since I was finishing up *No Barriers* and working on the boat, she went down two weeks ahead. There were complications. A right-wing group carried out a public execution—nine dead. Times were tense, so tense and potentially violent that Mom was nervous about me appearing in public with a white girlfriend. Also, while we were staying in her home, Mom did not want us sleeping in the same bed. Like Gwen's parents, she was from a less-permissive generation, but, unlike them, she wasn't going to turn a blind eye to my slipping down the hall after the lights were out. Added to that was my family's desire to handle my publicity campaign in South Africa. By this time Gwen had committed herself to meeting with reporters and all the rest, and that's what she did. When I finally arrived, we took rooms in a hotel.

We did succeed in getting some positive press coverage for both the BOC race and my own campaign, but I failed miserably in getting support. Three sponsors were interested, and I invited these individuals to come and hear me speak at the Royal Cape Yacht Club. The commodore, John Levin, requested that I fax him personal information to use in introducing me. I told Gwen to skip that, for I was to meet him four hours before the keynote address and could tell him in person. Except at that meeting, he angrily accused me of speaking ill of the yacht club, of going to the government and complaining, and I responded in kind. That night when he introduced me, he said, "Neal Petersen should get no help from anyone. He is unprofessional. He ignored my inquiry for information and deserves no help." This he said in front of my would-be sponsors.

From others in that yacht club and from the larger South African sailing community came a continuing barrage of criticism. My boat was unseaworthy. She was a floating coffin. She could never stand up to the Southern Ocean. It was criminal for the BOC officials to let me participate. "He has to be judged by his results," said one critic, who most probably had been given everything he ever had. "He can't expect other people to pay for his dream." No danger of that. I had approached fifty South African companies. One company gave me three hundred dollars. The rest said no. Not much had changed for a child of color. Gwen and I flew back to Ireland even poorer than when we arrived, if such was possible.

In fact, after we'd moved the boat over to Falmouth, England, for the BOC Atlantic Alone start, Gwen and I came very, very close to giving up. I had enough money left to buy her bus ticket to her parent's home. That was it. We needed to find Saint Regis, the saint of impossible dreams. What lay ahead looked like an impossible dream. We had only seventy-two hours until the signal gun fired. The satellite communication equipment and the radar with its perimeter alarm system were still in their boxes waiting to be installed, and we hadn't even found or could afford a single-side band radio. To pass the BOC inspection and reach the starting line, I had to have all three in working order. We were beaten. We had no place to go and were so burnt out on the boat, we just started walking the streets of Falmouth. We walked for hours. It got cold and started to rain. We had a couple of pounds between us, so we went into a pub and got two coffees. We were sitting there nursing those, and the wife of the owner of the local ship chandler, the Bosun's Locker, must have seen us hanging our heads, because she came over and asked if everything was all right. Gwen burst into tears and fled to the bathroom.

The woman followed Gwen, and her husband came over and asked what was happening. I told him we were pulling out of the race, that we'd be going back to Ireland in the morning. You know, it's strange. For years I couldn't remember the names of that Bosun's Locker couple, and yet I could see their concerned faces and remember what the woman said as if she'd just spoken. They were the Hoptons, Lyn and Alan. Lyn came out of the restroom with Gwen in tow and announced that we were going to spend the night at their house. She said, "Finish your coffee. In ten minutes a taxicab will be out front. He'll take you to our house, and the guest room will be ready. You're not going back to the boat tonight. You'll have a hot bath, lock the door, and make love. Forget about racing and boat problems. Tomorrow morning you'll be rested, and we'll put a game plan together."

We did. That was the first time in three weeks we'd slept off the boat. When we came down to breakfast, Alan phoned an electronics installer. Then he asked how much I had left on my credit card and was told some ridiculously low amount. He made a list and left. I went down to the boat and helped the installer mount the radar and the satellite communications. Then my Bosun's Locker host took me off to an old Marconi dealer who pulled a radio off a shelf, dusted it off, and sold it to me for little more than the installation cost.

If it hadn't been for that husband and wife from the Bosun's Locker, we wouldn't have raced. If Malcolm hadn't shown up and lent Gwen the bus fare back to Ireland, she would have been stranded in Falmouth forever, which wouldn't have suited her at all.

The day before the start I had another boost. South Africa had a brand new flag, swallow tailed and with bright colors to represent all the people of that new nation, and this was the first international sporting event to take place since it was adopted. But we were so poor that we couldn't afford this flag, and South Africa had shown no intentions of donating one. Somehow Sebastian Coe, a member of the British parliament and former Olympic gold medalist heard of our situation and donated one. Actually, he did more than that. Coe, who had begun his running career at the age of twelve, shared my belief in the importance of both self-discipline and goals. His

1981 record for the eight-hundred-meter sprint would go unbroken until 1997, so at that time he was literally "the fastest man in the world," and he came in person to assure me that I, too, could realize my dreams.

That night a bon voyage party was held. The Blue Angels planes were to do a flyover; there'd be fireworks and a band. The BOC Race Committee had brought in top clients. This party was not just the talk of Falmouth, it was the talk of England, and its purpose was to wish us sailors well. An hour before the party, Gwen threw a major wobble. She wasn't going. We were dressing at the apartment of Nigel Rowe, a fellow solo racer and BOC corporate director. We argued. She argued that she hated parties, that she hated having to make small talk to strangers. I argued that we both had to attend. This turned into one of the major fights of our life together. In the end she went.

11

THE BOC ATLANTIC ALONE

G etting the boat relaunched and ready for the BOC Atlantic
Alone and the BOC Challenge to come had been a major
nightmare. But through sheer determination and a bit of
luck, we . . . I say "we," meaning Gwen and I, but actually
there is another "we" involved, and that's the boat and me. A boat is a living creature. It has a personality, it has a spirit, and with a boat you can definitely have a love-hate relationship. After all, the boat is a she. Forgive this
chauvinistic notion, but I'm not alone in this assumption, at least, not yet.
Though "Jane's Fighting Ships" recently abandoned "she" for "it" when
referring to ships, the venerable insurer Lloyd's of London is sticking with
"she." They understand.

A boat is a she, and when something on board breaks, there's the hate of
your relationship. Then comes a begging request, the hoping that things
stop breaking, because "if she quits on me, I'm swimming." And next comes
gratitude. When you finally spot land, you reach over the side and give the
hull a pat like Gwen would to a good horse and say, "Thank God, you got
me across." Sometimes, I'm not even sure who's been more determined to
cross the ocean, the boat or myself. Of course, comparing a woman to a good
horse, might not set too well with the non–horse lovers and, to do this love-
hate analogy true justice, I should mention the romantic connection to the
boat, the nights at sea under starry skies and the incredible sense of companionship that grows out of all of this, which I suppose does greatly compli-
cate any sailor's relationship with a flesh and blood human, that inevitable
triangle. Of course, I'm speaking here of the male sailor, and male solo sailors
specifically, and since more and more women are taking up the sport, maybe it's best to abandon this analogy altogether.

For the first time ever, I felt guilty about leaving someone behind, someone worrying about me and missing me the way I'd be missing them. The

ocean was my life. Gwen accepted that. Still there was that bit of nagging guilt, on top of the many normal worries. From the starting line on, I was patching and switching sails. Along with a brown envelope containing a hundred pounds, I'd gotten a complete set from a competitor, generous Robin Davie. They were a bit ragged but better than my own, so off I set matching and patching and keeping the boat moving. Then a week into the passage, the regulator on the propane tank burst, filling the cockpit with noxious fumes that the wind pushed straight down into the saloon.

I was battling to screw the tank shut and the lazaret open, all the while the propane was freezing my hands. And I'm certain that some piece of electronics down below is going to generate a spark that will turn the boat and me into a quite impressive ball of fire. At the same time, I'm coming to terms with the fact that if I don't end in a ball of flame, then I'll have no warm food from here on. No more cups of hot chocolate, no hot meals. There's not going to be hot anything. With fumes finally dispersed, I went below and studied the pantry. What was on board that didn't require cooking? The answer was about a ton of canned peaches, about a ton of canned potatoes, a tiny bit of chocolate, and a handful of raisins and a mouthful of nuts. Everything else needed at least boiling water to become edible. Would I turn back to England? No. If I was going forward, I decided that a more southerly course would take less out of me physically. I'd gone hungry at sea before, and there's a distinct loss of energy involved. I veered slightly to the south.

Cold peaches. That sounds good, but there are only so many times you can eat them with enthusiasm and the same is true of half-cooked potatoes, and, believe me when I say that you're going to eat a mixture of peaches and potatoes together only once. (Gwen's suggestion, I should add.) I was cold, I was tired, I was hungry, and, after a storm blew through and ripped up most of the sails, I was exhausted. I had nothing more to give. I went below to catch a nap, a nap that should have lasted no more than an hour, but as now and then happened, I slept two, and when I woke, I sensed the motion of the boat had totally changed. Even asleep, you're usually aware of a change, your body shifts in the bunk and you wake. But not this time. I slept on, and when my eyes did pop open, I could hear the wind howling through the rigging. Obviously a raging gale was occurring out there, but the boat was sailing smooth and steady as if she was set upon a swimming pool. In order to rise, I put my hand out of the bunk and my hand dipped into water. Almost level with the bunk was ocean water, and it dawned on me that my boat was sinking. My boat was flooded. I was actually sinking. A whole psychology is involved in the act of sinking. It starts with "Oh, my God, there's actually water in the boat." Denial time is very short. Very. It's not a purely scientific term, but the word "overdrive" comes to mind. For me, not the boat. From having a bellyful of water, the boat was sluggish, it's the weight of water that was keeping her so steady, and now I was plowing through the saloon's calf-deep water. The boat had three semiwaterproof compartments, the one I was in, another major one forward, and a smaller one beyond that. As I was connected to those two by a hatch, I immediately slammed that down and bolted it shut. Then I hit the button on the emergency electric bilge pump and was relieved to see the water I was standing in sucked away. Which, of course, meant that my leak was in one of those forward compartments. This also meant that as I continued to pump, the stern was rising and the bow was being pushed further under.

I charged up on deck to take down the sails and realized that not only was the bow lower, it was already beneath the approaching waves. With sails down, I remembered to send out a notice of distress. I scrambled below, typed out a satellite fax to Race Control saying I was sinking. Then I called Portishead Radio, for no matter who I spoke to, it would be patched through that communications center. England was a thousand miles away, but the signal reached there clearly. "This is the vessel *Protect Our Sealife*. My position is . . . Will you please relay this to Race Control?" Of course, my satellite communication system immediately started flashing. Race Control was coming back wanting a status report, and I had a close friend, Simon Rabbit, with the Marine Rescue Coordination Center, who was also calling. MRCC would be coming to rescue me, but right then being rescued wasn't my major concern. I'd built this boat myself. This boat had no insurance. I'd already decided if she's going down, she's going down kicking and screaming. I signed off and, grabbing a flashlight, headed back on deck.

It was dark by now. Not pitch black but early evening, the sun probably setting but no setting sun in sight. No stars shone either. Just a gray, grim sky of low clouds streaming by overhead and wind still screeching through the rigging, and below an entire ocean of gale-driven waves that the bow was determined to enter. Where's the leak? I opened the forward hatch and climbed in. As in my diving days, it was like climbing into a wet chamber, except I wasn't wearing a wet suit. It was like lowering myself into a very chilly swimming pool, one where I know the water's cold, and I slip my toe in and then my foot and so on, until I have the courage to take a total plunge. It was like a swimming pool, except the water was closer to freezing and I was by myself, a thousand miles from the nearest shore, and now the bow was settled to the point where the forestays were underwater.

She was going down. I took a deep breath, not to withstand the shock of freezing water, but a deep breath as in "let's deal with it." Forget swimming pool, this was Daniel in the lion's den. I dropped through the hatch. I was up to my waist in the freezing water. In emergency situations, this compartment was served by a manual pump, and I grabbed the handle of that and started pumping. And pumping. And pumping. Each stroke was supposed to clear out a pint of water, but despite my efforts the water continued to rise. It's up to my chest. Taking the flashlight I dove and searched the hull for some sign of a hole, a gash, some sign of a break. Nothing! I dove again, and guiding that circle of light across the entire hull surface, finally realized that the water was flowing in not from the bottom but the top. Between this compartment and the one most forward was a small, high channel way that handled the cables. The water was entering through that, which meant the leak was beyond the bulkhead and that the compartment was completely full of water.

The forward-most access didn't enter from the deck, but from that common bulkhead, and it didn't hinge or bolt. It had to be unscrewed, which required screwdriver and wrench, which I scrambled off to retrieve. I was assistant mechanic now. Also chief mechanic, chief diver, and chief motivator. Bear in mind, there wasn't any "Hey, pass me this." Or "Hold that." And bear in mind that of all those mentioned, I was by far the most frightened for I was the one who was actually watching the very real waves rolling even higher over the bow.

Hatch off, I dropped through the narrow opening, one so narrow my shoulders barely squeezed through. I still had a good six feet of black, freezing water to swim through, and no room to turn around. That hardly seemed a consideration now. I held my breath, set off, and in an instant was seeing the problem. A clamp attaching a hose to a through-hull fitting had come adrift, the hose had popped off, and though the resulting inch and a half hole was relatively high, the pounding waves had gradually filled the forward compartment to the point where the hole submerged. All the while the water was also leaking through the cable channel toward the stern. And since the missing hose in question was connected to the manual pump of the middle compartment, when I pumped I was frantically recycling from one compartment to the other.

What a relief. I knew what the problem was. I jammed the hose back in place, and now all I had to do was pump the boat level. Except the boat was on a forty-five-degree angle with the Atlantic Ocean a foot or so from the center hatch, and water was actually over the pump handle, so far over that I had to hold my breath in order to pump. I began. Though, by then, I was literally turning blue from the cold. I was shivering and in a state of minor hypothermia, but the act of pumping was certain to warm me, which it did. That loss of energy could easily be replenished with plenty of good hot food and liquids, which, of course, I had none of.

Underwater and pumping, though, I was not exactly bemoaning the missing luxury of a cup of tea or hot chocolate. When you're dealing with survival, a future with hot tea does become pretty irrelevant. You focus on the task at hand, the one that has to be accomplished or else you die. In a sense, I'm not even sure that the skills required of a competent seaman are the same as those required by a competent survivor. The second are far more a matter of instinct, and my instincts were telling me to pump and keep pumping, which I did. Eight or nine strokes with breath held, catch another, down again, and so on, until my nose was above water and I could pump slower and feel confident that we, this boat and I, were possibly going to make it. After an hour of this the water was finally down to what I was certain was a survival level, and suddenly I remembered to radio Race Control with the news that I'd found the leak.

Simon at MRCC was waiting on the line and said he had a ship two and a half hours away. I told him not to divert them and to downgrade me from "a situation" to "I'm dealing with something onboard." He said he'd call back in half an hour, and I returned to the forward compartment and began again to pump, pump, pump, but with a firm resolve to make my promised radio to Simon who, in turn, was reassuring Gwen. By then I had no concept of time. In the hole it was black, quite dark, and time was now measured by how many strokes I had going up and down before I was out of breath again. My immediate goal was to dry that compartment so I could move on and dry the other one and then to go on and finish the race. Yes. I was already considering my position in the race. My mentor, Harry

Mitchell, though much to the north, wasn't far ahead and venerable Floyd Romack was just behind but further to the south.

Every forty-five minutes I ran to the radio and patched a call through to announce, "I'm beating this one!" and the dangerous pronouncement of "Nothing worse can happen!" Of course, something worse can always happen, but in this case it didn't. The boat began to bob over the waves, and I began to tune into a more ordinary state of the world. I put up more sail and pointed her to the finish line. I went below and realized how cold I actually was and how emotionally drained. During this crisis I'd taken several phone calls from Gwen, Simon relaying both sides of the conversation. We'd decided from the beginning that if I had a problem, he would notify her immediately. No matter how bad the situation, Gwen would have the facts. Then if I could make a phone call, I'd contact her myself.

The vessel would survive. Now to worry about me. I had to get warm, which in the absence of hot food and drink, left me only the sleeping bag. I stripped off and crawled in. Given what I could afford, this bag was nothing special. I pulled a blanket over me as well. I was entitled now to a little rest.

A night's sleep did wonders. I checked in with everybody and kept plugging along, bow pointed at the finish line, nothing to eat but cold peaches and potatoes, all the sails shredded, and credit cards maxed, but I was back in the race. For about a week, anyway. Then I broke a chain plate just about through. Only a thread of metal held it. That had to be replaced with a bit of sail track held in place by screws removed from the deck and a strategically placed piece of rope. As a result the entire mast was out of column, twisted like a drunken debater, and in such a sorry state that a port tack could be taken only with a minimum of sail.

In this shape and with this wind, I had little choice but to divert to Bermuda for repairs and make an almost ninety-degree turn to the south. Pretty soon the weather was warming, and I was actually taking pleasure in sailing. I spent hours on the deck just soaking up sun, and the layers of clothing started coming off. Then the wind shifted and reaching Charleston was easier than reaching Bermuda. I flopped over to my "good" tack, put up every scrap of patched-up sail, and kept her there for several days. I was racing again! The wind was pushing me closer and closer to Cape Hatteras, which meant I had to beat my way down to Charleston. Somewhere over Ohio a depression had formed that could bring with it northerly winds. So forgetting Charleston, I pushed the boat straight at this system, and ninety miles off of Hatteras received my reward, a squalling, cold rain and a wind that pointed me to the finish line.

Night came, and with the shoal not far off and the mast held up mostly by faith, I should have shortened sail. Still, figuring I had worked too hard to get here and being just two hundred miles from a cup of hot chocolate, I poled sails out to each side of the boat and, with forty knots of northwesterly behind me, went humming along through the dark. The lights of Frying Pan Shoals made their appearance just before dawn and from the lee of the shoal a Coast Guard cutter came bearing down on me. They were patrolling out of Charleston and suspected me either of smuggling drugs or being completely insane, but on hearing I was finishing a transatlantic race and intended to take part in the BOC Challenge, they pulled alongside and greeted me with a friendly interest. "We'll see you in Charleston" was the sign-off message.

The winds were due to shift. Twelve more hours. That's what I asked for, begged for. I was tuning in the Charleston radio stations, getting local music, news and weather, getting my first real feel for the Carolinas. I'd passed through once on a Miami-bound Greyhound bus and another time on a night-shrouded Amtrak train. What I knew of Charleston, South Carolina, is that the first shot of America's great Civil War was fired from or at a fort in that harbor. That was it. Will the people be as generous to poor sailors as the Irish were? I could only hope so.

12

CHARLESTON, SOUTH CAROLINA

The finish line. Thirty-eight days at sea. A couple of the entries had arrived two weeks earlier, but I was happy to be there. I was especially happy to be towed into the harbor, for this treacherous entry is a maze of flashing buoys mixed with radio towers, a jumbled mess of lights, and the way in was bordered by rock jetties and extensive shallows. I was treated to a moonlight harbor tour. First came a great mass of low gray masonry, the famed Fort Sumter, and beyond was a surprisingly low skyline punctured occasionally by church steeples, and finally a great parade of pastel mansions that appeared white in the moonlight, all close to the harbor's edge. That was the Battery, a collection of wealthy homes to which Gwen and I would soon be invited and where we would most thankfully be eating some substantial meals.

At 3:30 in the morning I stepped ashore at the City Marina. An all-night party was apparently just breaking up. With Gwen already holding my hand, we stepped gingerly over a couple of fallen partygoers. We were headed for a borrowed beach house on nearby Sullivan's Island. Just one stop to make. My host driver pulled into a Piggly-Wiggly supermarket, the likes of which I'd never seen. Apparently, this was a poor neighborhood, but just how rough could it be? Four in the morning and cop cars were everywhere. Cops on patrol inside. Cops outside the store. I got my groceries and got out of there. I'm thinking, "So this is Charleston?"

We slept late the next morning and lay on the beach in the afternoon, trying not to think about the boat. The next day we did the same. And then it was time to make repairs. Just six weeks to the start of the BOC Challenge, we still had no money and no credit left on the cards and thousands of dollars worth of damage to be repaired. First of all the boat had to be hauled out and a leak stopped, so I was towed up a good length of tidal river, to one of the few available boatyards.

The countryside around Charleston? It was August of 1994 and every day the temperature reached close to a hundred muggy degrees, with bugs, mosquitoes, and stinging flies like I'd never seen. I had no energy left. I weighed just 140 pounds when I reached Charleston. I was skin and bones, and things I once did in a heart beat now took a long time.

Still, the boat was out of the water. The keel had to be dropped. That's where the leak was. After thirty-eight days of sitting in the cockpit, I was standing all day and working overhead. The heat and humidity were crippling. I actually looked back with fondness to those shivering, hungry days in the North Atlantic. I really did. This quiet, easygoing guy kept stopping by the boat to offer tools and lend a hand. His name was Ken Bonerigo, and he worked in the yard. He was intrigued by the notion of my entering such a high-tech race with this homebuilt boat, and pretty quickly he realized I was broke. The boatyard owner soon realized this as well. He complained that Ken's time was worth fifty dollars an hour. Not to Ken, of course, but to him. "I can't do that," I willingly confessed. "I've got no money." That honest response got me ejected from the boatyard almost immediately, but by then the leak was fixed. I'd patched on the boat during the day, and, to pay the haul-out bill, I'd lectured and sold copies of *No Barriers* at night.

The boat was back in the city marina, and Ken would come by after work and lend a hand. Of particular value, he built a dodger to shield the cockpit, a fighter plane type of screen to keep the expected Southern Ocean waves from swamping me. He built it with scrap, and it's kept me dry for years and probably even saved my life a time or two–a good friend. There were others about to lend Gwen and me a hand. We were given rides and meals and encouragement, and even lent money, because my dream of racing a boat such as mine in such a grand race did appeal to a good many. Royalties from *No Barriers* arrived just in time to pay half the entry fee. Friends lent the rest.

Henry Hornblower was berthed straight ahead of me and onboard was her skipper, Harry Mitchell. That meant I could spy on him, see how hard he was working or not working; he could see me watching and always flashed his mischievous grin.

I'd first read of Harry in 1980. According to the article, this fifty-six-year-old Englishman was preparing for the twenty-seven-thousand-mile solo yacht race held every four years, the famed BOC Challenge. I remember thinking that I could do that, I could enter that race. I was fourteen at the time. Harry's first Around Alone attempt had ended badly when he fell asleep off of New Zealand and his boat went onto the beach. He hadn't given up, and in 1990 I'd actually met him as he was preparing for another BOC attempt. He was stocky, no more than five feet, six inches tall, and by then he definitely had the look of what he was—an old sea dog. The devil's own grin, a well tanned and squinting countenance, all he lacked was a single gold earring, and he planned to add that honored accessory when he made it around Cape Horn. He walked up to me at the BOC press conference and greeted me. He said he had a girlfriend in South Africa and would I give her a call and say he was thinking of her. His beautiful wife, Diane, was standing right beside him. She was grinning, too. I said I would, and we three were soon wandering through a boat show and making plans for future races.

I don't know how Harry made his money. Some sort of motorcar dealership, I believe. Though we asked, nobody ever really knew his business background. He had plenty to say about seagoing adventures, though. He was one of the last merchant marine cadets to train on a square-rigger. He'd grown up before the mast, that is, as a common sailor, and did represent that transition from the old days to the modern era. We were "you youngsters," and he was "chairman of the old farts' club," yet he readily accepted computer literacy and all the rest as the necessary tools of racing progress.

Harry was a most generous and likeable competitor, a sailor who had "host" families all over the world, not just a South African "girlfriend." Sad to say, he didn't make the 1990 race, for while crossing the Atlantic to reach the starting line, his boat was hit by a freighter and dismasted. I'd sent him a note of sympathy then, and he'd replied, "There's always 1994." There was, but now, at age seventy, he felt time was running out, and he was determined to round the Horn alone. Harry's prompting had gotten me into this race, and now here we were together. We were well matched. In the two times we'd raced across the Atlantic, he'd beaten me by one day and then by five hours. The gap was closing.

There was one other racer who in years to come I would also be matching myself against. Minoru Saito was Japanese. A thin weed of a man, I'd met him in Cape Town in 1990, when I'd helped out by climbing his mast. He didn't speak much English, but we would eventually learn to make ourselves understood on the radio and compete with a very friendly feroc-ity. His boat, the *Shuten Dohji II,* was ten feet longer than mine. The boat name translates as "Son of a Drunk." Though I only learned that recently, perhaps we had that in common, too.

Charleston was starting to take on a certain charm for we were experi-encing southern hospitality. Gwen and I were invited into homes and fed often in the downtown mansions of the wealthy, high-calorie, tasty meals served on banquet tables in high-ceilinged, many-mirrored dining rooms. If I had a speaking engagement, we could at least count on a buffet of some sort there. One good meal a day, that was all we asked of life—of the Charles-ton citizenry. For the rest we would snack. I started to gain weight back.

We paid down the credit cards and then maxed them again. I worked on the boat, and Gwen, shy as she was, handled the publicity and did it well. There were busy and still desperate times, but I'd started speaking to the local schoolchildren and, being my mother's child, that seemed as im-portant as all the rest.

Fourteen days to go. All the competitors were tied up in their berths, with frenzied activities on the dock. Race management was conducting safety and equipment inspections. Each skipper was given a laptop com-puter with sophisticated communications and weather-routing software that we could customize to each individual vessel. Linked by satellite, a weather map is transmitted to the laptop, where it merges with our current position, our desired destination for the next couple days, and the boat's pro-grammed abilities and then spits thousands of potential routes. Then the skipper inputs the sail configuration and expected performance, and the machine suggests an optimum route. Ninety percent of the time this didn't work for me, but, unlike most of the others, I'd designed the boat and lacked technical specifications required by the program. For weather changes I still had to depend on the ache in my hip joint.

The race management was offering this instruction and technical sup-port, but by now I actually had a support team of my own. Besides Ken and his associates, a Dutch friend, Vim de Koening, flew in from Ireland and said, "What can we do?" A workforce! But still no money. Then completely by accident, Dr. Pierce Lyons of Altech, the corporate boss of my Dutch friend, spotted the Irish flag (and the American and South African flags) flying from the boat. He donated one hundred dollars and in return was given a copy of *No Barriers,* which he read flying out. The next day he contributed enough to get us to the starting line. We had our first substantial sponsor. Except we still needed sails. Ten days to go and nothing on the boat but the secondhand patchwork I'd left Ireland with.

Still, our mountain-high problems had melted down to half a mountain high. We could stop scrounging for everything, and, once some Charleston restaurants generously began to give free meals to the racers, Gwen and I could eat more than one meal a day. We were happy and due to get happier. A groundswell of support was building in Charleston for us and the entire BOC project. Doors were opening, not just metaphorical doors but real doors. Then the September issue of *Outside Magazine* appeared on the newsstands.

Months before, a journalist, John Grant, had spent ten days with Gwen and me in Ireland. To Gwen's dismay he'd wanted to know everything about us and our dream and the boat—everything. Now came the article, fourteen very complimentary pages with photographs. Suddenly we were truly famous. People in Charleston were pointing and saying that's the guy in *Outside Magazine.* The prices of materials dropped to very cheap and sometimes to free. From around the world came encouragement, from Cape Town and especially from Ireland, where the government ministers and cabinet members sent words of support and where the schoolchildren were collecting "Pennies for Petersen." (According to the same Irish friend who called me "Sunshine," this was a version of the old missionary plea of "Pennies for Black Babies.") Still no sails, though.

Then a fax arrived from Cape Town. "Where do you want your sails sent?" Reading of my plight, a company down there had rush-ordered a complete set of sails, and South African Airlines would deliver them for free. I actually thought this was somebody's idea of a sick practical joke. I called North Sails in South Africa, collect. Yes, I had a sponsor and the sponsor was Gilbey's, a large, well-known brandy company.

Here I was addressing schoolchildren about the power of a dream, talking about the options in life and how they could do as I did and choose not to take drugs and not to drink. Plus my father was a chronic alcoholic. His downfall as a family supporter, financially and emotionally, had been alcohol. I was expected to sail around the world with the gigantic name of a brandy decorating my spinnaker and mainsail.

Gwen and I retreated to a friend's house and talked it over. If I accepted the sails, I was caving in to what I felt was a wasting influence on the world. If I didn't accept, I wouldn't make it to the starting line, much less, around the world. Gwen suggested I telephone the company. She said, "Have a heart to heart." We sat down, drew up a list of my concerns and dialed the number. I got the manager and after thanking him for his generosity, explained that to accept meant compromising much that I felt strongly about. I said, "I don't know my father as anything but a drunk, and I don't see how I can accept these sails without supporting you, and I really don't see what can be done." He answered that the sails were mine. They wanted me in that race and that if I would fly the spinnaker as I came into Cape Town, they'd take photographs and that would be the payment. As a company they always urged the responsible use of their product, and, of course, I could continue to make inspirational speeches to children in any form I wished.

This seemed fair. After all, if I didn't attempt the race, my value as an inspirational speaker to schoolchildren would be diminished. In any event, I reasoned it so.

The sails arrived, and, from Chicago, Bill Pinckney arrived. As previously mentioned, Bill was the first black man to sail alone around the world. I'd met him several times, looked up to him. He was the fast talker who had told a reporter, "Petersen has a gift for gab." He'd told the same reporter, "Neal has a certain naïveté that works for him and against him. But the key thing is that he just goes through life. The stuff that sticks on other people just sort of slides off of him." Kind words, and he was a great help, but as soon as he arrived, the journalists seemed to forget I was there. More postrace trauma, the sort of thing he claimed slides off of me.

What does twenty-seven thousand miles of sailing do to the human body? Five of us challengers were examined, weighed, and measured down to the last drop of muscle and fat. The lead doctor pronounced us amazingly "fit" but warned that it's not unusual for a sailor to lose fifteen pounds for every three thousand miles traveled. During the trip we were to keep a record of our diet and body measurements. At the end we would be examined again. Food! I was taking two chocolate cakes and three precooked meals along. The first days I'd be banqueting. After that, it would be the usual rice and pasta spruced up with fruits, canned meats, vegetables, and handfuls of garlic and herbs.

The crew was bolting gear onto the boat even as she was towed to the starting line. The fleet was being assembled. One wag described the variety of entries: "There they are—the brave, the broke, the absolutely destitute." Yes. Absolutely destitute from start to finish. That morning was chaos on an even grander scale than I could have imagined. A light chop on the sea, hundreds of bobbing boats to see us off. Altech, a sponsor, had sent a film crew. They were on the boat and would be filming from a plane as well. Of course we weren't ready. Yet there we were. Nineteen of the world's best sailors and myself. Six were sailing in the fifty- to sixty-foot Class I division, the most advanced and most expensive of the boats, million-dollar Kevlar sleds with towering carbon-fiber masts, space-shuttle electronics, and extensive shore crews to handle any complaint, and, above all, they had deep, deep pocketed sponsors. I was sailing the equivalent of a Volkswagen Beetle, and these were Ferraris, an analogy that applied particularly to speed, handling, and comfort. Broad enough to be nicknamed "aircraft carriers," with twin rudders, deep keels, and towering masts, these vessels have a directional stability and sea kindliness. The ride is comparatively smooth, and the demands on the skippers less exhausting, for their speed enables them to break through the calms quicker and sail around unsympathetic weather, and thus they are at sea for much less time. On the other hand, when traveling at twenty knots an hour, a skipper's reaction time is less, and when things go wrong, they go wrong in a quick and ugly way. In the simplest sense, speed is dictated by the length of your waterline and the amount of sail—the more, the better. It's all proportional. More boat, more stress, more money, more support equals more speed. By then I dreamed of having one. Not to do the BOC Challenge, but to race around the world someday nonstop in the Vendée Globe.

The remaining entries were in the forty- to fifty-foot Class II division, and even in this class we had some state-of-the-art boats and superstar skippers. My boat was the smallest and close to being the slowest. Also, my boat was home-built and probably the least comfortable.

It was an intimidating situation even without the attention I was receiving. Worst of all, I was leaving Gwen behind. Except for my thirty-eight-day crossing, we'd been together night and day for the last two years. At this point she was my family. We reached the starting line. It was goodbye to my support crew, who'd been bolting down gear up until that very moment. I got a hug from my boatyard pal, Ken. "Here," he said, "here's a

Me and Gwen

list of repairs that still have to be made." What else could we do but laugh? As always the last from the boat was Gwen. We held each other, unable to speak, just snuffling away tears and nodding. Then she stepped onto the towboat and was sped away.

There is a chaos to any race start. But at least before the starting gun there's an area reserved for the racers alone. Here they do their prerace maneuvers—while waiting for the first of three guns to go off. The first gun is the ten-minute warning. Then five minutes later a second warning —when the major jockeying for position begins. Finally, the starting gun sounds, and all the bows are heading across. That's when the major chaos begins. You have spectator boats coming in for a close look, the press boats to dodge, and, of course, your fellow competitors to maneuver around. No bumps in this race—but that's not always the case. I was racing again.

13

RACING TO THE SOUTHERN OCEAN

Twenty-seven thousand miles to go, with four legs and three stopovers. We'd be traveling west to east, stopping in Cape Town, Sydney, and Punta del Este, Uruguay, and then we'd head home to Charleston. The winning time is on an accumulative basis. That is, the leg times are added together, so it was possible to do poorly on one or two legs and still win. Emergency repairs can be made on board, but with no outside assistance, or they can be done in any port with or without assistance.

Already I was breaking the course down into manageable blocks. Get across the Gulf Stream, catch the northeast trade winds down into the Caribbean, get through the Doldrums, and so on. In my mind I could imagine an entire strategy. Three days out from Charleston, and my forestay broke: my imagined itinerary was scrapped. I would have to turn back or detour into Bermuda. Receiving permission from Race Control, I diverted to the island, and with (as often happens) the unsolicited and enthusiastic efforts of local yachtsmen I was rigged anew. In exchange I spoke at a local school, which led to television interviews. Hang onto your dream, I told the children. To the television audience I said the same. Twenty-four hours later I was being towed seaward, back to my own dream.

I was well behind. The lead boat was a thousand miles ahead. Nothing to do but claw my way down the coast of Africa, though "claw" isn't quite the right word—at least not at first. I began with passable ease. With trades filling the brandy-bottle spinnaker, I was into a groove, one filled with flying fish, a full moon, starry nights, and increasingly warm temperatures. Then came the Doldrums, that windless region where the northeast trades cancel out the southeast trades. The Doldrums came like a physical blow:

temperatures of one hundred degrees, me a puddle of perspiration in the cockpit, drifting on a sea without a ripple.

Crossing my arms was like standing before a fire. I stopped eating almost entirely. In that heat, how I could face lighting the stove? I did eat one thing—chocolates. The boat sat in place, the sails managing an occasional flop. I watched the horizon for any cloud. I searched for shade beneath the sails. The clacking of the halyards against the mast took on a tortuous note. Suddenly a single black cloud formed, growing darker and darker. A squall was coming. I reefed in the sail, preparing to go from no wind to forty-knot gusts. Then there was pelting rain, a lightning strike or two, and three minutes later I was dead in the water again, totally windless but with a miserably cross sea tossing me about. Again up went every scrap of sail, and I waited for the next rain to form up. Night was worse, for the squalls came in the dark without warning, and if I fell asleep even worse was in store. I woke in the night to a careening boat, and by the time control was gained, the longed-for wind was gone.

Six days of such, and then on the horizon was another sail. Minoru Saito in the *Shuten Dohji II*. I'd caught up with him, and Harry Mitchell was also close by. Floyd Romack was well behind us all. Floyd's another old-timer, and in the months ahead, I'd come to know him well. Remember, we were linked together by the length of our hulls. A sixty-foot with the proper hull design could pass through a windless stretch like this at ten times the speed, and some of these had already arrived in Cape Town weeks before. The Frenchwoman Isabelle Autissier had even broken the previous record, beating her nearest rival by days, all before I was halfway across. That didn't mean we three couldn't compete against each other, and, of course, we did. Slowly I began to pick up speed. From an average of .9 knots I quickened to 5, and set a wide course to catch the Atlantic high, a high-pressure zone. I did not pass Minoru, but I did overtake Harry Mitchell.

Harry and I spoke every four hours on the radio, discussed problems, and in that sense were not sailing alone. Floyd Romack checked in, too. He and Harry went back a long way and were accustomed to sailing at the rear of the fleet, calling themselves "the tailgate Charlies." I was initiated into the membership, and I entered into the betting books for who would be buying dinners. To see Harry on the horizon, which I did for over a week, made the ocean seem much smaller. Still, I was determined to pass him, and, being younger and capable of around-the-clock effort, I finally did.

Far behind us both was Floyd, in a heavy boat that the Doldrums continued to hold prisoner.

In the middle of nowhere, two sparrows arrived on deck. At first they were apprehensive, but as the hours passed, we grew accustomed to one another. At sundown they went below and explored for a roost, and there accepted a drink of water. The next day they flew on and off the boat, and one eventually hopped on my finger. By the second evening all I needed to do was hold out my hand, and the sparrow came to perch. Two days later, a huge freighter passed close by, and the sparrows flew in its direction. They jumped ship for a faster vessel, one with better prospects of reaching land. I hated to see my companions leave.

Of course, seagoing chores continued. I swapped a torn headsail for the spare, and, managing to stuff only half the canvas into a sail bag, pitched it below. While this consumed much of the cabin, the damp material also created a nestlike place in the heeled-over vessel. Then to make instant mashed potatoes, I boiled a kettle of water, which added to the already-sweltering temperature. What was I doing stuck out here? Perspiring and despondent, I yelled out "this sucks!" after a few spoonfuls of the gooey, textureless mush, and I returned below, where I curled into a ball on my headsail beanbag and dreamed of Gwen until I slept the foul mood off. As luck would have it, I had recorded that small bit of comic outburst on a videocamera supplied by the BOC, and it was highlighted in the BOC Challenge's Emmy Award–winning film of the race.

I'd estimated fifty-two days for a crossing. My Dutch friend had flown down to help but could wait no longer. Gwen, too, had arrived on the fifty-second day and was struggling with fund-raising and with helping out the sailors already in port, those that hadn't slipped away to other continents for holidays and promotional events. Theirs was a different world of racing entirely. Yet, my own racing had rewards that such highly financed captains could not know. For one thing, Gwen and I were now sending and receiving nightly messages of mutual longing, and for another I was coming home.

A hundred miles to Cape Town. Four years since I'd sailed away, and now I was in home waters, waters I'd quite literally grown up on. I was navigating from the same local charts I'd left under. Fifty-five miles from the finish line my inbound track was crossing my outbound, only that was just lines on paper while ahead were the lights of a fishing fleet. Dozens and dozens of Cape Town boats and Saldana Bay boats all fishing for snoek, and fishing for snoek was something I'd done as a child with my dad. One boat was directly in my path, and, to make sure he saw me, I went on the radio and announced, "This is the vessel *Protect Our Sealife.*"

Suddenly, every captain out there started coming on the radio. "The hometown boy is coming home!" All those excited congratulations, all that pride in what a colored South African could accomplish, what an incredible feeling that was. Sixty-seven days from Charleston, South Carolina, pretty much alone, and here I was dodging my way through an entire fishing fleet. They were motoring toward me, honking horns and shining spotlights on my sails so that over my head were these glistening triangles for banners, and the sound was better than any brass band. I was thinking it can't get any better than this, and then the moon rose in the east, and I had my first glimpse of Table Mountain, the famous backdrop to Cape Town.

For five centuries Table Mountain has been a welcoming landmark for ocean-weary sailors, but for me at that instant it meant so much more. On the slopes is Kirstenbosch, one of the largest botanical gardens in the world, where as a child, I'd go each Sunday with my family. We would walk up to Skeleton Gorge, and after recovering from my last operation, managing that walk on my own was a major accomplishment. From far down in the garden, you could hear the roar of the gorge's waterfall, and once there, if you sat quietly, the baboons would call to each other and eventually put in an appearance. Then, in later years Rodger, my old school friend, and I had explored the caves of the lower slope. Taking only a flashlight, on our backs we would wiggle and worm our way into tiny tunnels, noses scraping the ceiling, and somehow manage to exit at some distant hole we had actually planned to reach all along. I'd spent many happy days on the side of and inside of Table Mountain, and here, at last, was that dark, majestic monument rising above the sparkling lights of surrounding city, and at that very moment, rising above the mountain was the moon.

I was on the radio with Race Control and estimated a finish-line crossing of late morning or early afternoon. Inside the bay where I'd learned to sail as a boy, the rescue boat was finally approaching. Gwen and my family were on board. Gwen and race director Mark Schrader transferred to an inflatable and headed toward me. It was a perfect sailing day. Bright sunshine. Full sail up. The spinnaker was big bellied, and dolphins were playing in

Sailing home waters at Table Bay. Photograph courtesy of Rodger February.

the bay, and that incredible mountain was in the background. Finally I heard the crack of the gun, and I passed the finish line. Gwen was on board. She was fighting back tears, for as the head of my support team she didn't think it proper to cry. I gave her a big hug, the kind that says, "I've just spent sixty-eight days at sea, and I've missed you every minute!" and she gave me a kiss that said the equivalent plus "Thank God, you're alive." As a bonus out came a quart of chocolate ice cream. The rescue boat tossed me a line, and now I was close enough to see my parents and others cheering from her deck. I was being towed into the harbor, and ahead were two tugs with their fire hoses forming a tremendous arch of sparkling water, and eight or nine boats, both power and sail, were cruising alongside. Still, nothing, absolutely nothing could prepare me for what was waiting in the yacht basin.

I could see people on the docks, thousands of people. And then as we came closer, some of these people began to sing. My entire high school (both present students and old classmates) was waiting there in the basin, and they began to sing the school's alma mater, which contains the lyrics "No ocean is too big to cross, no mountain too high to climb." I had come a long way from being a fourteen-year-old boy, dreaming, to a being a solo veteran just like Richard Broadhead. Who was going to be the boy on my deck?

Incredible. Not just to be greeted by thousands but to go from being completely alone to being completely surrounded. What's more, all this was being filmed. Television cameras were on the dock, and they were filming live when I stepped ashore. My parents gave me my first official hug and then friends crowded in. So much to catch up on, but I had only forty-eight hours until the restart. Work needed to be done on the boat, the mast especially required attention and had to be pulled and reset. So many demands on my time, and the race was about to begin again.

South Africa was changing. As one reporter remarked: "To see a man of colour sail into his South African home port, taking part in an elite world-class sailing event and kissing his white girl friend on the dock was a scene virtually inconceivable when the race last visited in 1990." What hadn't changed, though, was the criticism I was getting from some well-known South African yachtsmen. My boat was still "a floating coffin," not strong enough to survive the endless pounding of the Southern Ocean. My boat was unseaworthy. Something else hadn't changed. We still had no money.

My family's relationship with Gwen didn't help matters. There were awkward feelings left over from our BOC promotional visit, when we'd ended up in a hotel, and they still wanted to run my South African campaign. They'd never done fund-raising or set up interviews, and Gwen had. Though she might not enjoy public scrutiny, she was used to it by now, and she had experience. When an invitation for lunch came from the minister of sports, Gwen wasn't invited, and my family was. Gwen almost left both the race and me over that. I felt I had to attend for I was given ten thousand rand by the minister. Gwen didn't leave the race—she didn't leave me.

My father had begun to drink again—which was almost a relief, since the expectation that he was going to start drinking kept us all walking on eggs. Race time had come, and the mast still wasn't reset. The fleet went without me. Harry Mitchell had finally sailed in. Two days later, an hour after my mast was secure, he and I decided to sail out together. The mast rigger and a friend came along to the starting line, for that was to be my shakedown cruise, as well. We debated and decided the shrouds were tight enough. They dropped into the inflatable. I held Gwen in my arms one last time. We kissed and she, too, was gone. Over the radio Harry Mitchell said, "Let's go, youngster. I'll race you to the starting line."

Off we went. "At last!" I thought, "I'm out of here, I'm done, I don't have to come back to Cape Town for a couple of years, maybe longer." All that remained was to clear Cape Point and head into the Southern Ocean and finish sailing around the world. Except I was exhausted, far more drained than any distress at sea could have left me. I didn't realize that until I made a tack inshore, lay my head on the cockpit rail for just a moment, and, without meaning to, fell asleep. What woke me was the motion of the boat being picked up by swells. The rocks were maybe four boat lengths ahead. I'd gone out of fifty feet of water to eight feet. Immediately I tacked and punched a way through the breaking seas. With the boat pounding her way clear, I thought, "Gee that was close."

I quickly realized that all that Cape Town emotional baggage wasn't going to allow me the luxury of an easy passage out. I spent the remainder of that day short tacking and, with each maneuver, felt my energy level sinking even lower. Gwen was flying out that night for Perth, Australia. She was to visit an aunt and uncle there while she waited for me to arrive in Sydney. Even thinking of the moment of her takeoff was a drain. We'd survived a homecoming. What worse could happen? Never, never ask that question.

Finally clear of the cape, I caught a nap and then had a good chat on the radio with Harry Mitchell and another with a fan from a nearby hake-fishing trawler. A good week of steady sailing followed and then crackling over the radio was the news of a bad storm. Here was my true introduction to the famed Southern Ocean, a stretch of water so open and lengthy, the swells can mount to the height of six-story buildings and the winds can blow with an equal force. I checked in with Harry, set the wind vane to do the steering, and went below for a nap. So far nothing but smooth sailing.

Suddenly, I woke with the boat surfing the crest of what must have been a considerable wave. A glance at the instrument panel told me I was traveling at a reckless twelve knots. I already had two reefs in the mainsail and not much headsail, but with a fifty-knot gale blowing I went on deck and shortened further on the headsail. That put me surfing at about ten knots. To escape the cold, I went below again and was lying in the bunk listening to music when I felt the boat again surfing a crest and then surfing down and then came a sudden change of motion. She wasn't coming back on course. She was trying to screw around to the windward. The mainsail crash gibed over, but she was still on the face of the wave. She'd turned sideways.

Feeling as if I was in slow motion, I rose from the bunk, felt the wave break, and felt the boat being picked up, and over and over and over she went.

I couldn't move because I was lying on the hull, against the side of the hull, and she was still going over. The cabin was pitch black. I had no visual references, only felt ones and the sensations of motion and the force of gravity. I felt this pressure more and more. I was lying up in one corner between the hull and deck with my entire bunk—bunk boards and mattress and sleeping bag—and my food lying on top of me. I struggled free and moved toward where the cockpit should be, and I tripped over the wires that ran along the cabin ceiling, so, at least, I was oriented. The boat was definitely inverted.

We'd capsized. Was she going to come back up? Every motion I made seemed a delayed response, as if I was reacting a second too late for everything.

Finally I just stopped and waited for her to come upright. But she did not. Water was flooding into the saloon; the hatch was open. She and I were finished. I was terrified. No other word describes that sensation. Then suddenly she began to right herself. She didn't roll completely over but returned the way she'd come and with a quickness that had me running over the hull like a hamster in a cage and all the while gear was tumbling along with me and hundreds of gallons of water. She popped back upright. The wind vane was attempting to reset the course, but she was still sideways to the sea, and I felt certain the next wave was going to flip me back over. I had to get on deck. I had to get my sails down. I had to get the boat pointing down these waves, to get control.

All I had to do was wade through this calf-deep water and untangle myself from the floating debris. I realized that the contents of the chart table had been thrown onto the starboard bunk, which meant my laptop computer had gone underwater. I could dry the charts, but without the computer my communications system was knocked out. Yet I knew that what was on deck was far more important than anything below. Hand over hand I went up the ladder and into the cockpit, and at once I saw problems —at least one colossal problem. As a result of the knockdown, the mast had buckled, and now, with the lower shrouds still holding, the upper mast had broken free. This broken section of the rig was scribing a wild arc through a sky of screaming black clouds. Depression began to settle in.

I managed to furl the headsail, but the kink in the mast meant the halyard couldn't be released. Which meant I'd have to climb the mast, cut the halyard, and then gather the sail in by hand, all the while watching the section of rig over my head spin violently. I shimmied up the mast. No harness. No time for a harness, and nothing to attach it to. I was tossing back and forth through the sky, just going hand over hand with the rig above disintegrating and the hull beneath gyrating through these house-size waves and with the wind at fifty knots. Chaos, complete chaos occurring hundreds of miles from nowhere. Finally the sail was down and lashed. Nothing more could be done topside until the mast finished off its spin by breaking in two. It did occur to me to tilt the boat. I pumped water into the starboard ballast tank and heeled her over slightly, so that when tumbling mast section came down, it wouldn't fall directly onto the deck. Then I pumped the bilges dry. Only when that was complete, did I feel secure enough to make radio contact with the outside world.

Surprisingly, the radio seemed to be working. I couldn't reach Cape Town, though, and Harry Mitchell wasn't scheduled to contact me for another three hours. Still, hope springs eternal and I kept trying the radio every few minutes. Not that I wanted to announce a full-scale distress. I just wanted to tell someone somewhere that I had a problem on board.

I kept trying the radio, without success, and started putting some order to the sodden mess below; all the while I was waiting for the upper half of the mast to come crashing down—which it did a couple of hours later. And when it came, it came violently, smashing into the side deck and hull with such force that the base of the mast ripped off the mast step and one of the remaining stays snapped. Held by a great tangle of ropes and wires the broken mast was laying part on deck and part in the ocean. From down below I could see daylight where the deck and hull join. Where the mast struck there was a gash four feet long and six inches wide, and now every swell was dumping gallons and gallons of water back into the cabin.

I covered the gash with my sleeping bag. That just left the broken mast section banging against the hull, attempting to puncture her further, and of course, one end was still swinging free and apparently aiming at me. Anticipating this, I had a piece of line tied off and ready. Waiting until she came off a swell, I reached over into the water, took a wrap around the mast and scrambled back to the cockpit, where, using the winch, I cinched the whole mess as hard as I could against the hull and lashed the remaining loose rigging to the deck. I was exhausted.

I went below, and on the radio I could faintly hear Harry trying to reach me, and with my antenna down I couldn't reply at all. Connecting one end of a power extension cable to the antenna terminal, I climbed the mast stub with the other, and created a makeshift antenna. I tried the radio again. Still no luck with Harry Mitchell, but Floyd Romack responded. Floyd was still in the Atlantic, still approaching Cape Town. I asked him to relay word of my dismasting and my position to Race Control. He could only read a portion of this but understood the basic message. The mast was broken, and I was okay. He e-mailed this news to Cape Town, and in less than a minute the location light on my communications system began to flash.

That flash meant I'd been found. A satellite passing some twenty thousand miles above was busily beaming word of my position to Race Control. I knew that they're trying to reach me, which they would normally do by e-mail, but since the computer was destroyed, I did not have that option. I just had to hope that radio transmission would eventually improve and that at least my position and condition were known to the outside world. In the meantime, there was nothing left to do but get back on deck and begin to cut, pull, and shift the collapsed rigging into a more orderly arrangement. Except now the winds were gusting to seventy knots and the seas building. White water was everywhere, with waves breaking continually over the boat, and giving up that project I returned below.

Finally, a tremendous sense of disappointment took the place of simple depression. Australia was six thousand miles away. I wasn't going to drift there. I had only one choice, and that was somehow to reach the continent of Africa. Anything else was suicide; that was a certainty. With those unhappy thoughts of failure in mind, I was finally able to reach Cape Town Radio. I explained all to Race Control and then asked to be patched through to Gwen in Perth. The call had to be collect, and as it also was the middle of the night, she had to be awoken.

"I won't be keeping our date in Sydney," I said.

"Where are you, Neal?"

Already, I could hear fright gaining over sleepy confusion. "I'm okay," I said perhaps stating the obvious, but it was necessary to put some good news first. "I'm alive, but the boat flipped, and the mast broke in half. Gwen, I'm going to patch together a jury-rig and turn back. I won't make it to Sydney."

No need to add that our dreams, what the two of us had been working for all these years, were over.

In response she gave a cry, almost a moan, "Oh, Neal, that's so . . . ," but already she was switching gears. "Neal, if you got back to Cape Town you could set a new mast and get back in the race."

"I'll try, Hon." I knew the chances of that happening were slim to none, for once there I'd have to stop and raise the funds for repairs. And I guess she knew that, too.

"You're alive," she said. "You're alive, and the boat is floating, and, Neal, that's all that matters. I'll see you soon."

No. I had already asked far too much of her. I told her that I couldn't give her the life she deserved. She replied that she cared about me. I told her to forget me and build her own life. "No," she said. She would not abandon me. "Not after all we had been through" were her exact words. In all our time together, this was the closest she'd come to saying out loud that she loved me.

Whatever happened, we'd be together. We had a blueprint for the future, a blueprint of sorts. In the morning, with the seas beginning to run down, I climbed up the mast stub and secured it with rope shrouds, then strengthened it further by running another rope from the mast to both the bow and stern. That accomplished, I hoisted the storm trysail for a main and turned the staysail upside down, raising that as well, and, so arranged, started plodding back to Africa.

I'd heard from Floyd and finally got through to Harry. English sailor Nigel Rowe radioed his condolences as did several other competitors. Though the BOC had grown from its early "sailing family" beginnings, there could still be, on this level, a strong sense of kinship.

Four days later another violent storm came through, this one with winds gusting to eighty knots. I took down the makeshift sails, but the twelve-foot stub of mast created enough windage to drive me eastward, and the accompanying seas were so steep, I almost capsized a second time. Gwen was making plans to join me, but in the meantime she would have to seek encouragement by phone from her father and Ken Bonerigo. I was beyond all but the most expensive radio contact, and unless I was losing the boat, she would have to depend on e-mail bulletins posted by Race Control. I now had regular radio contact with my sister, which cheered me up, and cheering up was much needed since I'd received word that my father, on learning of my troubles, had gone on a drinking binge and disappeared. My mother was having to deal with him.

At that point a journalist asked over the radio how I felt about having to drop out. "I'm sad," I answered. "I'm disappointed. Someday I'll return with a high-tech boat and a sponsor and someday I'll complete this race. I am a competitor."

What was I really trying to say to him? Once signed off, of course, I could actually come up with a proper answer. What I'd meant was that instead of focusing on the loss and what it had already cost us in time, energy, and money to get this far, instead of focusing on the notion of a failed dream, I knew I could count on Gwen and on the majority of my family and that I still had many supporters, but I also understood that my future as a racer was to be decided only by my own vision of that future and how I dealt with my present. While my racing career might hang in the balance, a favorable tipping of that balance was my responsibility and mine alone. Someday, I would race again.

14

THE EARTH IS FLAT

Ten days later, in Port Elizabeth, South Africa, and with a good night's sleep courtesy of some friends of Mom's, I can't say that things looked better. I went down to the boat the following morning, and, oh, what a sorry sight—the boat lying on the dock with rigging all over the place and mast in pieces. Someday I would race again but for the present my sailing days were over and done, and that "someday" seemed very, very far away.

With the help of a local yacht club, I got the remains of the mast pulled out and went to work untangling the mess, but I was only going through the motions. Then a surprise visit from Floyd Romack gave me a boost. He'd finished the first leg too far behind and had to drop out as well, but he had a proposal to make. I should get the boat repaired and back to Cape Town, and then the two of us would sail across the South Atlantic and join the race in Uruguay. We'd finish the race unofficially but with the blessing of the race director. I took heart in that suggestion, for I did owe both myself and my supporters a finish to the race. How could I tell the children of the world not to quit if I abandoned my dream? Floyd said, "Salvage what you can, and leave the rest behind." Of course, he wasn't just talking about the boat.

Now, you could hardly argue with a man who had made four attempts to complete the race, without ever crossing the starting line until the last try, and now had been forced to drop out after only one leg, a man who had survived numerous near-fatal heart surgeries and named his boat after one of these, *Cardiac 88*.

I got serious about floating the boat and following his plan. Gwen, too, was excited, but she was stuck in Australia until Christmas Day, for only on Christmas could she fly at the cheapest possible rate. Even that was being paid for out of Floyd's generous five-hundred-dollar Christmas present, the balance of which was going toward a new mast. How to get the remainder financed? How to get the Cape Town–built mast to the boat or perhaps the boat to the mast?

I didn't have answers. I decided to fly home. This was on my mother's birthday, and I planned to surprise her with a hug, the only present I could afford. My sister, Jan, met me at the airport. She and Gwen had had a stormy relationship for, as mentioned, both thought it their place to run the South African publicity campaign. Over lunch we talked at length. For the first time in our lives we were drawing close. At least, the dismasting had done the job of officially connecting me to my sister and vice versa. At last we could deal with family matters we'd been avoiding for years. Through the radio conversations, she'd come to see me as something other than her kid brother. I was her brother, plain and simple, a brother she needed to encourage and support and one who would and could return the favor. All right, then, we knew the most important problem facing the family was not getting me around the world, but the two problems were connected. To circumnavigate I would have to stop in Cape Town, and when I stopped, I'd always be faced with Dad's heavy drinking and all the emotional turmoil that brought with it. Our new partnership of brother and sister would deal with that.

Two days before Christmas, I asked Dad to come to lunch with me. We ate, and then I leaned across the table and explained as calmly as possible that when I was in the middle of the ocean fighting for my life, I didn't appreciate the additional problems he caused. "Mom is trying to hold things together and you go and get drunk," I said. "I am going to be home for Christmas and for just once in our lives, I would like to see you sober. Do you realize that Jan and I have never had a Christmas when our father was sober?" I said, "Get yourself together, clean yourself up. For once, don't make life worse for the people around you."

He apologized. Over and over he apologized, but I knew that such remorse would last only for a short while and he'd go back to his old ways. Still, for Jan and me this was something that had to be said. For our peace of mind, if nothing else, we had to express out loud the pain we felt and as a result, we did get one good Christmas.

That afternoon I flew to Port Elizabeth and met Gwen, and that night we were lying in bed, holding each other. The joyous, loving part of reunion was over, and we had to face the fact that so much we had strived for was coming apart.

I said, "I can't say exactly where we'll be headed, but I want you on the boat with me when I leave."

She said, "Yes." Just that one word.

"Anyway," I teased, "we don't have the money for you to fly."

She rose up on an elbow and, grabbing my arm, gave it a good shake. "You can't know what that was like. To wake up in the middle of the night . . . to be six thousand miles away in Australia and have you on the telephone, telling me you had flipped upside down. And . . . and then not to have the money to fly here, to have to wait until Christmas Day. Neal, you can't know . . . how helpless that made me feel."

I held her in my arms again, and we made a plan. Together we'd work on the boat and somehow get it shipped to Cape Town, where a new mast would be waiting. Then together we'd sail to Uruguay and from there I'd finish the race alone, unless there was no money for her plane ticket, in which case she'd finish with me on the boat.

The next morning we started preparing the boat for transit. A friend phoned around the shipping companies and found a ship headed for Cape Town. I quickly started building a wooden cradle to put the boat in, for this ship ran on a weekly schedule and was about to depart. Gwen and I would have our own cabin on board. The crane operators agreed to work for free, and so did the stevedores. We had all this cooperation from the unions and the companies. Perfect. When the boat and cradle were lifted, though, the cradle broke, and the ship had to leave without us. Still, the captain promised that he'd pick up a sturdier cradle in Cape Town, drop it off the following week, and pick us up the week after.

The shipping company executive who was coordinating all this invited Gwen and me to spend the night. He said, "We'll sit around the swimming pool, have a barbecue, and talk sea stories." We did, and I couldn't help but recall the reception an earlier around-the-world sailor had had in Port Elizabeth. A hundred years before, when the first solo circumnavigator, Joshua Slocum, had passed this way, the government officials had warmly welcomed him and then treated him to a lecture on how the world was actually flat. All this, of course, seemed completely ridiculous to a man in the process of circling the world, and he could credit it only to the ignorance of a few, until the following month when he had an audience with the country's president, Mr. Kruger. "I am sailing around the world," Slocum announced. "The earth is flat" was Kruger's reply. "You don't mean 'round the world. It's impossible! Impossible!" In the years since, I have sometimes used that story when trying to explain apartheid to audiences. Only willful blindness can make such an unlikely and unlawful system work.

I was reminded, too, of my dad's trip to Port Elizabeth when he was a boy. It was here that he'd first seen the ocean and realized that what he'd heard was true. The ocean was indeed endless, and it was indeed blue and not the orange of his Orange River. Here at Port Elizabeth these poetic discoveries had propelled my father out into the world for he'd eventually joined the navy and become a diver.

Actually, that happy and idle week Gwen and I spent in Port Elizabeth was memorable in itself. We went horseback riding with another couple. Gwen ended up on a retired racehorse and was in her element. The horse was for sale, and she fantasized about buying it and about our staying on here and living in the broken hull of the boat. The racehorse still had some life in him. Gwen had considered being a jockey at one time and might have succeeded for she had that genuine talent for riding. She'd ridden with the Irish Hunt Club and won numerous medals. She loved fox hunting. She loved the adventurous chasing of the fox, not the bloody catching of the fox. Those Irish foxhunts are like battles or even complete wars, like racing a boat around the world except you come home the same day. She was a talented rider, but as I mentioned, she had many talents. She could paint, and she drew with a near-photographic ability. She was a chef. As for her suggested plan, though, I had to assume she wasn't serious. Spending the rest of our lives camping there on the crippled boat wasn't a viable option.

At the end of a week, there came into port a gigantic containership. This ship must have been half a mile long, and the ship had three elevators. The captain agreed to carry my boat. He took me up to his cabin in one of the elevators. He said it was no problem to help us out, and there'd be no charge, but there were no accommodations for passengers. Gwen and I would meet the ship in Cape Town, and it sailed in twenty-four hours. On the docks everyone jumped into action, and up my "little red monster" went to be nestled into the high-stacked containers on this real monster. My boat was just a speck up there, a toy boat with oblong building blocks to keep it company. Away they went.

In Port Elizabeth I was scheduled for a live six A.M. television interview. Gwen and I went to the studio and survived a difficult interview, for I had to discuss emotional issues with an unseen interviewer, all the while, pretending he was in front of me. I said I didn't know exactly what would happen next, but that so far I'd had tremendous support from the local brandy company and hopefully that would continue. "I had lunch with the branch manager," I said. "Maybe something will come of that." It did.

I ordered a new mast paid for by the brandy company. Gwen and I were trying to patch the broken deck, and we were staying on the boat and having a rough time because plenty of yacht club members were coming by to say, "We told you so." They said they knew we couldn't do it and wondered why we even tried. For a colored South African to attempt something, even to make an effort, was apparently still a threat to them. Things had changed since Slocum's visit. They admitted the earth wasn't flat, but I still had no business trying to circle it.

Fortunately, Gwen and I still had Floyd Romack for company. He wasn't giving up, and neither would we. Race director Mark Schrader lent four hundred dollars from his own pocket. The criticism continued, though. About a week before the new mast was to be stepped, I had to get another passport issued, and Gwen and I were walking down Adley Street, the main street of Cape Town. This is our equivalent of New York's Fifth Avenue. We were walking along, and I heard a horn honking. I didn't look around because the traffic was heavy. The horn honked again. I paid no attention. Then I heard the banging of dustpans. That seemed out of place and at least got my attention. I glanced over my shoulder and saw a big garbage truck. We just kept walking because they were picking up garbage from the curb side, and the banging lids were can lids. Then suddenly, I heard my name called out along with more banging of lids. I looked back, and the calls were coming from the garbage truck which had come to a dead stop in the middle of the road. The crew of six had left the truck unattended and, still banging their lids to get my attention, was coming toward us.

Now other horns were honking, but that was because the truck had been left in the middle of the road, and no one could get around. The garbagemen kept coming, though, for they wanted to meet me and say how much participation in the race meant to them. "Neal, you are our hometown boy!" they were shouting. "You can count on the Cape Flats, you hear!" the lead man shouted as he shook my hand. "You are our hometown boy!" You see, Cape Flats, where I'd grown up, was a neighborhood of few opportunities, one of those places where dreams get crushed by the struggle to survive, and just seeing one of their own actually taking part in an international sporting event was in itself a victory. They wanted my autograph and waited to chat so there we were, chatting and getting autographs. The traffic jammed behind the truck grew and grew, and at the same time the crowd around Gwen and me grew and grew. More and more people crowded in, hundreds finally. People were grabbing scraps of paper from wherever and asking me to sign autographs.

What had started out as a simple hand-in-hand stroll down the street had turned into chaos, which was, of course, exactly what Gwen hated most. She was a private person, not used to crowds, actually, not used to anyone. She had few friends. In fact, she had few acquaintances. Remember, this was the girl who'd grown up on a river barge. She'd often teased her father about being a hermit, but she was a hermit's daughter, and the level of attention we were presently receiving on that sidewalk was for her a true nightmare. Yet having the attention of the public was part of the business of sports, part of getting sponsors who would invest the money necessary to sail the boat. I can't claim that I was bothered. This was exactly the sort of boost I needed, especially because the garbage men, the source of all this commotion, were already dear to my heart, which I tried to explain then and there.

"When I was a little boy," I shouted, "I had some very serious operations on my hip and couldn't move around." And I told them the story of how I would wait for the garbagemen each morning and had promised them that I would pick up the garbage at sea. "I'll take care of the sea," I promised them. "I'll take you all to England with me." Of course, these present-day garbage collectors loved hearing that and started laughing and repeating my earlier promises. "You've taken care of the sea. You've done that, all right!" one added. "Not just England!" another shouted. "You have taken us around the world with you!" Bursting with excitement another shook my hand and stated, "Neal, you've made us proud!" I got more pats on the back and more congratulations, and finally this mob had to disperse; to Gwen's relief we were once more headed off. I felt like I was walking on air. All that rush of good memories brought with it a tremendous sense of renewal. Those garbage collectors were poor. They had the worst-paying job in the city, and most probably had other jobs, maybe even two other jobs to go to. They needed that just to survive. From the age of six on I'd had tremendous respect for those men, and now I was giving them my autograph.

With our morale boosted, the mast was soon set and the sea trials completed successfully. The boat was back in one piece. We set a date to head across the Atlantic. The brandy company gave us a farewell party, and naturally my family and friends were invited. My father had been sober for all the weeks since our talk and was even attending Alcoholic Anonymous meetings, but at the party a waitress passed through the crowd offering drinks. My father accepted one, and I took it from his hand. There was still this tug of war between us, quite literally a tug of war. The branch manager of the company saw the difficulty and came to my rescue. Indeed, the policies of the company and the behavior of its employees made it even more difficult for me to object to their product. The branch manager said he understood my situation but wanted me to know how genuinely pleased they were to be a part of my sailing adventure. Yet, one drink, and my father would have been back to square one. Right then I swore to myself I would never accept another alcoholic beverage sponsor. I would stop racing first.

15

SAILING WITH GWEN

wen and I sailed out of Table Bay. The notorious Cape Doctor saw us on our way. The Doctor is that horrendous southeast wind that blows with enough force at times to knock over double-decker buses. The Tablecloth, the great white cloud that often shrouds Table Mountain, is brought on by the Cape Doctor. The cloud hangs over the flat-topped mountain, making it even more beautiful, and once in place it has a life of its own, flapping like a cloth or billowing down like steam boiling over from a pot. The Tablecloth leaves when it's ready. Gwen and I were more than ready, and with winds of forty to fifty knots, the Cape Doctor was still much in evidence.

Green Point is at the westernmost tip of Table Bay and is composed of huge boulders that were presently wrapped in crashing white water. And thick kelp beds waited to snatch the hulls of the unwary. The few boats following us out were now heeled over by gale force winds, but these winds extended only ten miles from shore. We sailed beyond this "wind line" and for a moment a part of the stern was in a gale and the bow becalmed. We sat there on the far side of this line bobbing and drifting. I still had no engine. We would drift back inside the gale, get up speed and sail out, only to drift back in again. Not a very auspicious start for a transatlantic voyage. Finally we sailed in close to the shore, turned down the offer of a tow from Floyd, and with Job-like patience, poked our way clear of the cape.

Gwen was seasick from the start and never recovered. She hardly came up on deck, couldn't eat, threw up what she did eat, and before my eyes began to lose weight, emaciating quickly toward a skeletonlike appearance. Neither of us should have been surprised, for we'd sailed around Ireland together, and she'd been sick then. Just after she moved in with me, we were sailing back to Galway from a Dublin boat show. This was in a typical Irish winter, meaning gale force winds, strong currents, and big wet seas. Tusker

Rock was just over the horizon, and once passed, I'd have 110 miles of short tacking to do. I went below to catch a nap, and when I woke, the boat was being picked up and thrown. I charged on deck to find Gwen in the cockpit. She was so seasick and cold, she'd finally just put her head down and passed out. We were on the reef, in the white water, and just two hundred yards away the Tusker Light, our beacon of safety, was instead flashing directly over our heads. Fortunately, there was still water beneath the keel. We escaped.

The following summer she sailed from England to Ireland with me, and again she was sick. She persevered, though. She never thought of abandoning ship and took all the discomforts of that lifestyle in stride. When in port, we lived on the boat with no proper amenities—no heat, no toilet or fancy galley. She stayed by my side, lived on the boat, made passages, did public relations, and helped with the maintenance and the fund-raising. Looking back I see she managed this through sheer grit. I suppose I knew that at the time, but I took such determination for granted. She seldom complained, for complaining was not part of what we were about.

Gwen never defined what love was. In all the years we had together, she expressed great and persistent affection and, when necessary, heartbreaking concern, and we both knew this was "love." But she never once came out and said plain and simple that she loved me. I told her countless times. I'd say, "Gwen, I love you." The best I could get in return was "What is love?" Well, what is love? Is it commitment to a dream? Can it be making someone else's dream your own? I wouldn't have the answer until much later.

Halfway across the Atlantic we began to receive word of the race. My old Satcom ID system had been reassigned to Minoru Saito, and I couldn't use the new one without knocking him off the air, which meant that Floyd had to relay the news, and that news was very sad. On March 2 Harry Mitchell's distress beacons had been activated, and since then nothing was heard from him. Race Control had launched a search, and every few hours Floyd gave us the update. The area of Harry's disappearance, fourteen hundred miles from the South American shores, was beyond the range of search planes. The Chilean navy sent a ship, but it met weather so horrific, it'd been forced to turn back. Then Race Control lost contact with Minoru. One minute he was a blip on the radar and the next he was gone. They began a search for him, as well. A week passed. No word from either vessel.

Not even a distress beacon from Minoru. He had vanished. And the weather analysis for that region suggested winds of one hundred knots per hour and eighty-foot-high seas. We feared both men were lost. In our race within a race, these two had been my chief competitors, and I considered both to be friends. Minoru's command of English limited our radio chats, but we'd still looked out for each other. And Harry Mitchell? Well, Harry really was my seagoing father. He was responsible for getting me into the BOC Challenge. He was a seed planter. Harry understood what it meant to dream the seemingly impossible dream.

Under the unhappy cloud of two missing sailors, Gwen and I stepped ashore in Punta del Este, Uruguay. Thirty-eight days at sea, and Gwen was so weak it frightened me. She could barely walk up the street, a street crowded with the celebrants of St. Patrick's Day, the happy descendants of resilient Irish. But once off the ocean Gwen would quickly mend. I should have known that.

That afternoon I met with Mark Schrader. Mark had been a close friend of Harry Mitchell's, a huge supporter of Harry and of me, as well. He welcomed me into the office, but the loss of Harry and of Minoru was obviously preying on him. In addition, most of the boats had been damaged in this last leg. Two had lost their masts and one of these also a rudder. The fleet was patching itself up, licking its wounds, and worrying over the last stretch on to Charleston. Yet, most of the racers still were enjoying limousine rides and fancy restaurants, some very fancy, for this is the "Palm Beach of South America." Gwen and I were enjoying neither.

Of course, I understood that these notions of poverty were all relative.

From Uruguay, a reporter from *Outside Magazine* filed this about my entry: "The red patchwork boat sat, like a soapbox-derby racer in the pits at Indianapolis, at the far end of the dock from Christophe Auguin's swift, sleek world-beater." Still, growing up in South Africa, I'd had two pair of shoes and food on the table. Ours was just a working-class neighborhood of small cottages and dirt lanes, but compared to much of the world, we were certainly well-off.

I understood the relative nature of poverty. That still didn't keep me from seeking out information about sponsorship while we were there in Uruguay. Lunch with someone else's sponsor brought forth the anger of Mark Schrader. In his eyes this was not fact-finding but poaching, and though I could still count on him for help, to this day our relationship has remained strained. I suspect, though, this is somehow related more to Harry's death, perhaps even to the fact that Mark had encouraged "small" boat sailors such as Harry and me to compete. He felt responsible for us all—fleet participation and safety were on his shoulders—in addition to the huge financial and logistical problems of making a race happen. I can't say for certain what caused our falling out, but it was sad to lose not just Harry but Mark as well.

Minora I did not lose. Long after hope was abandoned, he appeared off the Uruguay coast. A severe knockdown had flooded the boat and destroyed all sources of power, and so, unable to send out messages, he had struggled around the Horn. "No radio. Radio no work, steering no work, radar no work," he explained. When the Chilean navy asked if he had panicked, he responded: "Me not panicked. Boat panicked!" He had survived, and four years later we would again race against each other and grow even closer.

One of my favorite memories in this life took place while we were there in Uruguay, and again Gwen's riding was involved—or rather our riding. By then she'd taught me to ride. She'd learned on an English saddle, where you really got the feel of the animal. She looked down on those American Western saddles and called them "arm chairs." Over the years, she'd taught me to be one with the horse, corrected my posture, and showed me how to hold the reins and position my heels down. I'd had other girlfriends who rode, but none like Gwen, who could apparently read her horse's mind and the mind of whatever horse I was riding as well. More than once, my mounts had taken off with me hanging on with no control, and she'd ridden alongside and slowed them with a touch. Payback, I suppose for all those bucking bronco rides she'd taken on the boat, rides where she had to trust I was in control. More or less.

With the very few dollars we could spare, we hired horses and a guide. This was on the famed pampas, open expanses with no fence anywhere and trees only in the far distance. All this was so far removed from the ocean, far removed from any of the world's other cares. Of course, our guide was a gaucho. A real one. If he hadn't been guiding us he'd have been branding cattle with his buddies we'd left behind at the barn. The outfit he wore —high boots, hat, and waistcoat—wasn't for the benefit of tourists. Add to that description an elaborate black mustache and just enough English to understand when we wanted to gallop. He was a perfect guide, the kind that is so much a part of his environment, you forget he's there. That's a rare combination, someone with enough quiet presence to make you feel watched over. Yet at the same time Gwen and I were free to go galloping off on these huge animals through this endless range of ankle-deep grass. Then I was even more reassured by Gwen's closeness. For the first time ever I was on a horse that was completely responsive to my wishes, like a sailboat can sometimes be, and I was free to go galloping off at full speed, for Gwen was galloping right beside me.

In later years there would be times when we'd be sailing in the middle of the ocean, no dry land of any kind in sight, or we'd be driving on a four-lane highway, going or heading somewhere, and Gwen would get this far-away look in her eyes. I don't think she knew where she was, for she'd start mimicking the movement of a horse, as if there were no boat or car, only she and the imaginary horse in graceful motion, galloping, and the sound of the hoofbeats would be formed by her tongue on the roof of her mouth. She'd go on like this for several minutes. Then suddenly she'd realize where she was and that I'd been watching, and she'd say, "Gee, do you think I'm crazy or something?" No. I didn't think that at all. I appreciated her need to escape from whatever we were facing. If anything, I guess I was jealous of that ability to escape, to enter that make-believe place of complete thrill.

Gwen flew out of Punta, and I made an uneventful passage to Charleston, arriving the day before the prize-giving party, a grand party where I was recognized for having taken part. Floyd had made it only as far as the Caribbean and, never one to miss a party, flew the remainder. "Nothing goes to the windward like a 747" was his defense. The next day we had a memorial service for Harry Mitchell down at the city's Waterfront Park and mention was made of Harry's guiding principle: "We call it the present and another word for the present is the gift. Today is a gift to the living." Carpe diem. Oh, yes, seize the day. Be curious. Go! Do it. Don't talk about it. Do it! Those were the lessons imparted by this man who was above all else my hero.

It turned out that even from above old Harry had one last goal that needed to be met. Harry and I and three others had been taking part in that nutrition experiment, the measurement of bone density and fat compositions that was to show how the stress of the race altered our bodies. Harry was gone, but out of curiosity the conducting physician took measurements from Harry's son. This lady doctor and the son hit it off and five days later he proposed marriage. "The old sod didn't get home, but he still managed to play Cupid" was one summation, and all of us laughed and nodded in agreement. Yet for all these lighthearted moments, there was still the inevitable sense of loss, and though I did not realize it at the time, I believe Gwen, too, was greatly affected. She and Harry's wife had been close before and were even closer afterward. She saw what Diane went through, and her own anxiety over my safety while at sea was only increased further. For now, we were making plans to sail together. Whatever the perils, she'd be sharing them.

At loose ends, we'd decided quickly to move on and entered the Bermuda one-two which was single-handed from Newport to Bermuda and then two-handed back. Before leaving Charleston, my mother surprised me by flying over, a secret Mark Schrader helped her to accomplish. Mom took the bus to Newport, and Gwen and I sailed up. "The Racing Capital of the World," Newport was as supportive as ever.

16

CHOOSING CHARLESTON

I had a good race down to Bermuda. Five days out I spotted a boat on the horizon. Here was sailor Peter Chance, an old friend and a designer of weather overlay software that I'd been happily attempting to use. Five hundred miles of racing, and we were neck and neck. Being both friends and competitors, we knew that wouldn't do. Using a blinding rain squall to cover my exit, I slipped away in what I hoped was an improving tack, turned off the radio, and pushed through the night. Where was Peter? Half a mile from the finish line, I notified Race Control of my position. "You're where?" came Peter's voice over the radio. He was three miles behind. I finished second, and he came in a respectable third. Happy with the race, I was soon happier still. With no engine, I was inching my way through the narrow Town Cut, and there, from the rocky western shore, came the call of "Neal! Neal!" Gwen had seen me cross the finish line and now was waving a welcome to our first real tropical island —our first real paradise together—Bermuda!

The boat wasn't broken. I'd sold some books and t-shirts so we had a couple of hundred dollars to spend. One of the local sailors, who the year before had worked through the night to repair my forestay, had been chatting with Gwen via e-mail and now offered us comfortable quarters on his boat. Gwen and I cut loose. We rented scooters and like Hell's Angels went careening down those narrow, twisting lanes. I taught her to snorkel. For the first time ever she saw a parrot fish and all the rest. I carried along a ziplock bag of cooked rice; though we didn't have an endless supply of rice, I couldn't resist the chance to bait the fish up to arms length. Gwen's arms. She would start giggling under water and almost choke because you can't breath and laugh through a snorkel at the same time. Outside of her home, I don't think I'd ever seen her happier, but then I'd never seen her when we weren't under some sort of pressure. We had two hundred dollars in our pockets and a boat that was ready to go.

Of course, in private I'd seen Gwen's little girl side, but now that playfulness was popping out in public. She and Peter hit it off, and with one or two other sailors we'd go off to feast in Bermuda's only cheap restaurant, eating pasta and planning great voyages. On the last night, that twinkle that had come to Gwen's eye took on an added degree of Irish twinkling. She snuck onto Peter's boat, found his coffee, and dividing it into several Baggies, hid them around the boat, hid them well.

The race began, and in an instant thirty-five boats were fending each other off through Town Cut, which could accommodate no more than five. Total chaos, and once away the entire fleet was becalmed, all of us drifting. Gwen couldn't have been happier, though. She called up the coffee-addicted Peter, and he grumbled in reply. "You sound like you haven't had your coffee," she remarked in mock innocence. Then for the remainder of the race she parceled out Peter's coffee to him in exchange for his position and relative sailing information.

Nice winds and very helpful Gulf Stream eddies sped us along, and for the first time Gwen wasn't seasick, not very sick, anyway. She was there on deck to lend a hand and to stand watches, all smoothly done, except for one dramatic exception. A frontal system was coming through, and as we were racing, I wanted the spinnaker up as long as possible. We watched the wind build to around twenty-five knots. Then with me at the helm, she went forward to lower the spinnaker, to douse it by pulling down the sock. The sail wouldn't collapse, and she didn't have the strength to force it. "I'll release this pole line and make it easier for you!" I shouted, emphasizing which line with a yank. She nodded in reply, but she was leaning against the spinnaker pole to which the line was attached. I thought she understood that, but she didn't, and, losing her balance, she screamed out, "Stop!" I couldn't release the line, and she couldn't lower the sail: the next thing I knew the boat was completely on her side.

Spinnaker in the water, mast in the water. Gwen was against the pole, and I was sitting on the hull. She was really screaming, but the wind carried away the sound. Her mouth was moving. I'm certain that every word was an obscenity aimed at me. Every word. Very certain. The boat popped back up. Like a racehorse that's stumbled, she was on her feet, and charging off, still out of control. Over she went again. "Are you trying to kill me?" I heard that. The boat came upright, and this time Gwen abandoned her duty and clambered into the cockpit. She was angry. The winds were up to thirty knots, and the boat still pitching wildly. She took the tiller, and I went forward. Boom! Over we went again. Then we were upright again. Another dip like that, and we were going to lose the sail, maybe even the mast, but now Gwen realized she must release that cursed pole line. The moment she did, I collapsed the spinnaker.

Still, that was only a tiny part of the race, a race that Gwen had fallen into with an amazing competitiveness. I'd never pushed the boat that hard before, at least, never without losing half the mast, but together we not only finished in one piece, we won. We won that leg of the race for our class. Of course, then I had to listen to everybody in Rhode Island say it was because Gwen was sailing the boat, nothing to do with my endless years of struggle and learning. "Gwen's sailing the boat!" I heard no end of that.

It was a happy time of sailing together, but soon after leaving Newport, we took another serious spill. I had a speaking engagement in Florida so we headed down the coast. No engine, of course, and just south of Diamond Shoals we were forced to beat our way slowly into a bit of headwind, which meant the already-damaged sails were beating the seams out of each other. Just this lazy, seam-tearing, go-nowhere situation. Gwen and I were below napping and waiting on a favorable evening breeze when suddenly the boat heeled over. We heard wind, then rain and a squall were upon us.

The boat flew off, but I wasn't worried and took my time going above. Then there was this huge crack, a snap, as if we were inside the world's largest firecracker. I charged on deck and smelled ozone. Then right next to me came another crack, right next to me as in five feet to port. Forks of lightning, lightning all around the boat, and the squall worsened, the wind shifted, and before I could respond, the headsail was back-winded and over went the boat. The mast was submerged, and so were the troublesome sails.

In a way that was an improvement. I thought, well, at least the sails aren't flogging themselves to pieces. The winds increased, though, and the boat was completely pinned over. I was sitting up on the hull, pretty much content. I could release the line to the headsail, and the boat would probably right itself, but then the boat would just be careening about once more and all that canvas would be slapping about and ripping even further. That was my reasoning, and I even remember looking down on the exposed keel and lamenting the fact that I wasn't free to walk over and scrap off the barnacles. Still, all around me were the continuous crack, snap, and boom of lightning and thunder. It dawned on me that I was the highest thing on the hull, so I threw myself down and hugged that red fiberglass until the storm passed, and the boat popped upright. I was up trimming the sails when Gwen came bursting from the cabin in tears. While I'd been perched up there on the side of the hull and confident that we weren't in real danger, she'd been down below imagining that I'd been swept overboard, that the keel had fallen off and we were doomed. As the mattress and all the other contents of the bunk alcove had fallen on top of her, she was trapped below. The whole time she'd been screaming for me, and I couldn't hear her. That was hard on her, and I suppose did much to erase the pleasure of our recent sailing successes, causing her once more to be an anxious sailor.

At the time, though, I was more concerned with what would come next in life. We'd already decided to enter the 1998 BOC Challenge, and we wanted to stay on in America and run our racing campaign from some port on the Eastern Seaboard. Fees from my motivational speeches were now paying the bills, and in addition *No Barriers* and our new line of related merchandise were selling incredibly well. Finally we were getting out of debt. But where to settle? New York? Boston? Miami? Charleston, South Carolina, seemed like the obvious choice. We knew our way around the city, had friends there, and remembered that wonderful southern hospitality extended to all the BOC sailors. We returned to Charleston and discovered the other side of the city. A year before, we'd been heroes. Now we were just castaways. Doors that had been literally thrown open in welcome were shut tight. Our phone calls went unreturned. It seemed we were no longer of the moment, not current and high profile enough. "In another four years," we were assured, "you'll be back in favor. Just wait until the next race." That was an eye-opener.

We were determined, though, to stay in America. We still enjoyed Ireland and flew back there every few months, but Charleston seemed like home, and not all Charlestonians were fickle friends. Some very good people remained supporters and we gained others as we went. I needed an office, a place in the city to set up computers and printers, telephones and fax lines. We had no money. A patron of ours drove me up the main street, King Street, to Sonny Goldberg's Furniture Store. This was on the poorer end of the shopping district, but Sonny had had many years of good business there. He'd promoted himself as "the old King Street singer," and though the radio ads no longer ran, he'd occasionally burst out with "They call me the old King Singer, I sing whenever I'm blue." Not that he was all that blue, but I guess he did have reason to be.

Anyway, I met Sonny and told him we were looking for an office. "How much money you got?" he asked. "None," I said. "How much rent can you pay?" "As little as possible." He scratched his chin and said, "I think I can help you." Sonny carried us back into the store through a maze of armchairs and sofas and whatnots. We came to the bedding department. He pointed at all these mattresses stacked on end and said, "How much space you need?" I motion a width and said, "From about here to here." He started flipping mattresses out of the way, and I helped him to form a mattress-walled cubicle. "Will that do?" "Yes."

That was my first office in Charleston. He had telephones installed for me and set up a couple of rolling chairs and a big desk, all from the front of the store. My office hours were his store hours. He was a wonderful man who really cared about Gwen and me. His days were numbered, though. The discount chains had just about put him out of business, and he went bankrupt seven months later, more or less. While I was there, he'd stop by the "office" and say, "How things going?" I could see he was tired of fighting his fight. It was showing. It was a sad day when Sonny died. The world lost a fine singer.

As far as being comfortable outside of the office, Gwen and I weren't used to much, which was just as well. We still lived on the boat, and, to reach it, we had to cross a couple hundred feet of dock. In the worst of the mosquito season this was like running a gauntlet—slapping wildly and running. On one particular night, we were asleep, and as we had no air conditioning, the washboard was open. We slept in what Gwen called "the coffin box," a cubbyhole bunk beneath the cockpit that gave her (for being smaller she got the narrow side) no more than seven inches clearance. We were lying in our bunk without even a sheet for covers and just melting in the heat, when suddenly we felt these "things" landing on us. We started swatting, rising up and banging our heads and swatting each other as much as the "things." I turned on a light. Termites! A swarm of termites had come aboard. It was like being in the water and attacked by leeches. We were covered. The wings were falling off: flying and crawling bugs and bits of bugs were everywhere. Gwen became hysterical. This was two in the morning. No place to go. No money for a motel. We got into a car, which had been loaned to us, and tried to sleep. But this was a tiny car without reclining seats. We had no choice but to go to the office and lay down on the floor.

We had a new office by then. When the furniture store closed, we'd moved to a "swankier" address, lower on the peninsula and behind a cosmetic shop. We went there. No pillows or bedding of any kind. The roof leaked, and every afternoon thunderstorms rained straight down into the office so the carpet was continually damp and reeked of mold. We wrapped ourselves with newspaper and went to sleep. Gwen stayed with me. I don't mean just that night. I mean she stayed by my side, despite conditions.

Finally, to cope with the insects and those blistering Charleston summers, I installed an air conditioner in the companionway hatch. The winters were actually pleasant, not nearly as harsh as Irish ones. We had bicycles and the loaner car and each other. We had a few close friends nearby. We'd moved the boat to a little low-budget marina to the north of Charleston by the navy yard and stayed on for a couple of years. Ken Bonerigo was living on his boat there, as well, and six or seven others. Doc Joe was a favorite. A radiologist and most unlikely doctor, for he smoked like the nearby paper-mill chimney, he was often our host for dinner, though "dinner" is a bit too grand a description. Two or three times a week Gwen and I and Doc Joe and Ken got together. Ken and I would go out on the dock and cast for shrimp, and sometimes it took hours to get enough. Then Gwen would cook, and Joe would do the dishes. This was on Joe's boat, for his was the most comfortable. After dinner Joe would discuss sea chanteys and Irish literature with Gwen and play music. Ken would listen in, and I'd sit beside them with my laptop, trying to figure out where the next sponsor dollar was coming from.

If Gwen and I had been sitting on a million dollars, I don't think we would have swapped it for a moment of that life. I think I'd finally come to peace with myself, had found a balance between being on the boat and being with a woman that I really, really loved, and I was enjoying being around friends who loved the ocean as much as I loved the ocean. Yet, each of us still had a dream of going off somewhere, sailing away to conquer some ocean and anchor in some distant place. Even Gwen felt this, though she would more likely be exploring on horseback. I kept on telling her that I loved her, and she kept on replying, "What is love?" I asked her to marry me, but she said no. Years later Doc Joe told me he'd questioned her on the subject, part teasing and part in earnest. "Why won't you marry Neal?" She'd gone into a mock rage, swinging her arms about and shouting, "I'm never going to marry anybody."

During this happy time we had what Gwen always referred to as "the weekend from hell." We decided to take a cruising holiday. Doc Joe, Gwen and I, and another couple took our three boats fifty miles down the coast to a semideserted barrier island and spend the weekend. First, though, I needed to get out of our marina, which, because of all the narrow doglegs, could only be done with the aid of the third-hand outboard I had bolted to the stern. The engine wouldn't start. I pulled on the cord and pulled. Gwen started counting: 25 strokes, 30, 31, 32. I was hanging over the stern yanking and yanking. When Gwen reached 135, the outboard sputtered to life. So began our weekend from hell.

We motored out well into the harbor, under the rolling hump of the bridge, and toward Fort Sumter. I got the mainsail set. Joe was single-handing ahead of us. The other couple was behind. We passed through the jetties, and immediately the wind picked up, the boat heeled over, and the outboard was submerged. Didn't matter. We sailed down the coast, Gwen and I arrived well ahead of the others. We waited in the inlet. Getting into the secret anchorage would require Doc Joe's guidance. I tried the engine. Not even a cough. Finally Joe arrived. We already call him "tugboat Joe" because he'd pulled Gwen and me out of the local doldrums so many times. He towed us up this narrow creek, and, with the aid of the inflatable, we got his anchor out. Both boats were to hang on this anchor as in the best cruising tradition. Then in the inflatable we went in search of the other boat. They were hard aground in the inlet. We got them off and also attached them to Joe's anchor. The tide was ripping out now, but the anchor held. We had this incredible view of the dunes and the ocean beyond, and right beside the boat dolphins were chasing mullet, sometimes leaving the water to wrestle with their prey on the muddy bank. We broke out the cocktails and hors d'oeuvres. Someone actually said, "Isn't life wonderful?" That's as bad as asking, "What worse can happen?"

We went to sleep. The next morning I got up at dawn and was doing my thing and looking around at the palmetto tree–crowded islands and the sweep of golden dunes, and I was truly staggered by just how beautiful it all was. Tall marsh grass lined the curving river as it swirled past ancient

Indian mounds. Cormorants perched in a long dead tree. One took off to go fishing. The others stretched to meet the sun. My first impressions of the Carolina lowcountry had been colored by the heat, humidity, and insects, a bug-infected swampland, but that was only for two summer months of the year. For the other ten it could be a paradise, which it was at dawn on that creek.

That's when the anchor suddenly broke loose, and down the creek we went, carried along on this ripping ebb tide, all three boats banging together. Everybody was awake now. I couldn't untie my boat from Joe's, as I had no working engine. They started the engine on the other boat to halt our collective progress, but we still couldn't get Joe's anchor to bite. I tossed out my anchor, but it wouldn't bite either. Joe picked up his anchor in order to motor free, which meant he had to cut me loose. Although my anchor didn't bite, it still made my boat untowable. I was drifting. I hit the first bend and careened into the marsh. Joe pulled me out of the marsh and, in so doing, spun me about. My anchor line was wrapped around my keel. At which point it bit. Bound by its keel, my boat was zigzagging from shore to shore, banging into each bank and tipping violently over. I tossed out the spare anchor, and this fouled with the first.

At this point Gwen offered her opinion. She said, "I'm not doing this anymore. This is crazy. This isn't fun." I don't recall what defense I made, or even if I could have.

Finally Joe got another line on us, and we were pulled free. We decided to wait for the tide to turn, but when it did, the current would sweep us all off in the opposite direction. I decided to dive down and free my two anchors. My hull was covered with barnacles, which ripped into my flesh. Streaked with blood, I returned to deck. I'd freed the anchors, and they were brought on deck. The tide turned. Each of us set his own anchor, and, to my mind, we enjoyed ourselves for the next day and a half. Except we were counting on a diet of fresh-caught shrimp, and we caught none. We caught and ate mullet instead—which the unenlightened consider a trash fish. On Sunday morning we sailed back to Charleston. Gwen was seasick the whole way. She said, "I don't ever want to see the inside of another boat. I'm cold, I'm wet, I'm hungry, and you're covered with bloody welts, and you call this fun."

For ten hours we'd been heading up the coast into a miserable northeast —dark and nasty conditions. Now I had to get through the jetties and across the harbor. We passed the jetties, but the harbor was its usual mass of confusing city and suburban illumination and blinking radio towers, and add to that a bewildering array of red and green lights on the outboards of shrimp casters working well up on the flats. I was watching the depth recorder. It went from thirty-five feet to eight, then seven, six, and then five. We ran hard aground. We had no working engine, and our two companion boats were still out in the ocean. The tide was ebbing.

That's when Gwen officially designated our outing as "the weekend from hell." She said, "If you want to go cruising again, you go by yourself. You know what I want? I want a hot shower and a life back to normal." Actually, our normal life wasn't all that comfortable. The shower she coveted was nothing but a marina stall. I didn't argue the point. A freighter was coming down the shipping channel, and a container ship was exiting under the bridge. I figured a tug must be close by, and sure enough it was. In passing it threw a wake big enough to float us off the bar. Then with just 150 yanks on the cord I got the motor started and we reached the marina thirty minutes ahead of the others. And Gwen stayed with me.

Along about then, we decided to enter the OSTAR, the single-handed race I'd done before. As usual, we had no sponsor, and competition for sponsors was fiercer than ever. Another Charleston boat had been entered in the OSTAR, and that skipper had already gotten the support of Charleston's powers that be, the politicians and the local yachting establishment. Everywhere Gwen and I went he'd been there ahead of us. Who was this skipper? Why was this guy so successful? I asked around and to my surprise discovered that no one had actually seen our competitor sail a boat. No one even knew if he could sail, yet the guy was saying he'd win the OSTAR. A curious state of affairs, but feeling further questions would suggest poor sportsmanship on my part, I halted my inquires. The truth was his boat was just one slip away from us; I saw him often, and he seemed a good enough sort. I answered his questions about the race and preparing for it, and, as a reward for this generosity, the gods who control such matters gave me a sponsor of my own.

Public Broadcasting was airing a documentary of the 1994 BOC Challenge, and, to celebrate the event, we had a big party at a nearby bar, Salty Mike's. We invited everyone we knew, and among those guests was the CEO of an innovative film company. I'd met him only two days before while investigating the possibility of having my own video camera on board.

At the party he took me aside and asked, "What is it you're trying to do?" I explained about the OSTAR and about my background and especially how I would again be taking part in a nutritional study during the race. The CEO was interested in computers, and we needed a specific one to do this study.

The following day, he invited me by his office, but once there, he announced he'd been called away. Would I come with him out to the car? Then walking into the parking lot, he reached into his jacket and said, "By the way, this is something to help you on the way." He handed me a fat envelope, one that contained thousands of dollars in cash. "Seed money," he said. I was to come the next day, and we'd discuss the mounting of 3-D cameras on the boat. My effort in the OSTAR was to be the subject of a three-dimensional documentary.

Of course, I was delighted. His seed money alone was enough to get us to the starting line, and while I suppose all that cash should have made me suspicious, Gwen and I just saw it for what it was—manna from heaven. The next day we deposited our windfall into the bank and set to work preparing the boat. Every day our surprise benefactor would come on board, bringing along computers and figuring out where the camera systems would go. We were to have live 3-D feed from the boat. He introduced me to the scriptwriter. I might become a film star. Then, best of all, he showed up one morning with a state-of-the-art computer onto which we loaded all the nutritional experiment's software. It churned out numbers like I couldn't believe. I could use it for navigation, as well. We'd hit the big time.

Still, no cameras had arrived. He had five people working out the technical aspects of this moviemaking, but no cameras. And then he called me to his office. "The plug got pulled," he announced. The decision was made. Everything already on the boat had to be returned, the computer and all the related electronics. I could keep the cash, though. He told me not to speak of the money, which I didn't until writing this chapter. I never could decide about the money—whether he'd given me cash, knowing an attempt might be made to retrieve it, or whether this was some darker, perhaps illegal aspect of venture capitalism.

No further explanation of the company's withdrawal was made, but the CEO's wife did make the cryptic remark "Be careful of your fellow sailors." What she'd been hinting at wouldn't come out for several months yet. Our resourceful neighbor, the other OSTAR contestant, had camped on the film company's doorstep and, by insisting that he was Charleston's legitimate entry, finally succeeded in having their support redirected to him. What's truly sad about all this, or truly laughable, I suppose, is that this resourceful sailor never even showed up at the starting line. He took money from everyone and slipped away. To this day, I'm not sure he could even sail a boat, much less race one solo.

ANOTHER OSTAR

O n the up side? Gwen and I had the cash on hand to complete preparations, and, for the second time ever, we hadn't been reduced to a state of complete and anxious prerace exhaustion. We sailed over to Bermuda for a quick holiday with my old boatyard friend Ken Bonerigo, and then she and I set off for England by way of the Azores. This was a good crossing, an almost unbroken stream of starry nights and steady breezes. No longer seasick or at least not as sick, Gwen was proving to be a good, dependable sailor—at least on a day-to-day basis. In daylight she was fine, but couldn't bring herself to do a night watch. On the boat or not, she didn't like being in the dark, and unless I was beside her, she insisted on sleeping with a light on. Perhaps she'd been frightened as a child, some event in the night putting this fear in her. Of course, traveling in that boat at night, we did have need to worry, but I can't say that I did, and I'm not sure her fears were based on these legitimate concerns. In any event, the ensuing division of labor worked out wonderfully. We understood what each other's abilities were. She stood her watches in the day and I took those at night, not unlike the nursery rhyme about Jack Sprat and his wife. We handled the cooking in a similar fashion.

Gwen was an incredible cook. Eventually she would study to be a chef. However, at sea she couldn't face the galley, so I cooked then, which in this case meant preparing meals that had been prepackaged and were eaten in accordance with our computerized and much-monitored nutrition program. If nothing else we had at least advanced beyond our days of Mars Bars, and my even more disastrous diet of cold peaches and cold potatoes.

It was smooth sailing as we approach the Azores, with just one mishap to clutter the pages of the log. We woke from a nap to the sight and smell of smoke. But there was no visible fire. Gaining the cockpit, we shut the hatches to deprive the fire of oxygen, and we prepared the life raft to go over the side. That done, I climbed below with a fire extinguisher. Perhaps I'd left something on the stove. Breath held, eyes tearing, I found no sign of a fire in the galley. Back on deck, and I gasped for air, while through the hatch I'd opened, smoke was bellowing up. I gave Gwen the distress beacon and told her, "At the first sign of flames, hit this beacon and launch the raft. I'm going below." Not exactly encouraging words. No use in adding that I was going below only to retrieve our second distress beacon. Smoke as thick as ever, eyes tearing, as I reached for this second beacon I noticed that the charging panel was glowing, and at once I realized this was an electrical fire. I managed to regain the deck and between gasps announced to Gwen that I'd solved the mystery, at least thought I had. I looked over the transom. Of course, we'd continued to sail flat out, and as long as we were moving, our trailing generator was spinning away behind. Nothing more than a waterproof generator with a propeller attached, this devise uses the force of the water to create power, which is forwarded by wires to the batteries. A short in the cabin's switch panel was causing the smoke. I pulled the generator on board. End of fire.

We made a brief stop in the Azores and were soon on our way to Falmouth, England. I allowed twelve days for that passage, but conditions were ideal, and we docked early on the eighth morning. We'd kept pace with a sixty-foot cruising yacht, a feat that surprised my old friend Simon Rabbit, but he and his son still managed a welcome, leading the way to the berth in their bobbing punt. Gwen and I were back among friends, friends who had seen us dejected and on the brink of quitting. This was to be my fifth international sailing event. With a tremendous feeling of success, I began speaking at schools and prepared to compete in the coming race. I celebrated my twenty-ninth birthday, and Gwen flew on to Newport to wait for me.

There was one hitch to the plan, though. I'd been unable to find a liability insurance that I could afford, and I couldn't race without it. Fellow racer George Stricker heard of the problem and offered to pay the bill for me. Four years before he'd given me an additional spinnaker. On our level, at least, this was what solo racing was all about, and even on the million-dollar level such generosity isn't unheard of—just seldom heard of. At the last minute, I managed to find a policy I could afford, but having George's offer as a fallback had removed that all-too-familiar frantic element from the search.

Preparing to sail the
Protect Our Sealife

Besides George, other friends and past competitors were entered: Karl Brinkmann from Germany and Canadian Dave Evans, elderly Phil Rubright on *Shamwari* (his very attractive daughters always drew admiring glances), and Jens Andersen of Denmark, a paraplegic who had designed and built an incredibly fast wooden boat and sailed it by shimming across the deck on his backside and letting his powerful upper body make up the difference. Quite a cast of characters and a tight-knit family as well, all racing away through the English Channel. Harry Mitchell was remembered and sorely missed.

From the start and for several days thereafter I kept crossing paths with a little Belgian boat. We must have been pretty well matched because tacking from Bishop Rock and into the open Atlantic, there she was. It was torment, of course, for each of us wanted to be ahead of the other—not only ahead of, but out of sight, and eventually we did part company. I was hardly alone, though, for the just-mentioned friends and I were in constant radio contact. Plus I was checking in with Race Control and receiving and sending e-mails to Gwen and a group of schoolchildren in Charleston who were witnesses to the nutritional study in which I was the most willing of guinea pigs. Every candy bar or soda from the food bin, every calorie consumed, was entered into the computer. Every pound lost, every inch subtracted from my waistline, had statistical significance. And I was having fun with the e-mails to those kids ashore and also doing my first series of weekly columns for the Charleston paper.

I was connected to the world, and, at least technically, I was leading my class in the race. Two fast boats weren't reporting in, though, and I suspected they were ahead of me. Seven days out, I had my nose into some gale-force winds. My two friends slipped by, but this, I reasoned, was not because of my lack of skill but because of their faster boats. Frustrating. The ninth day the fog was thick as pea soup. No other comparison works. Pea soup. The mast appeared as a vague gray line, and the foredeck beyond was completely lost from sight. The gale continued undiminished with the waves terribly steep. They seemed to have no back to them, and each time you came off of one, you kept hoping water was somehow waiting on the other side. If it wasn't, you'd go sliding down into the trough, dropping twenty feet and then hitting the previously longed-for water, a solid wall of it that exploded against the hull with such force your teeth literally rattled. What am I doing out here? Why do I keep doing this to myself? Is enough not enough? Along with that came the noise of wind screeching in the rigging and the percussion of each slamming drop into the trough. Actually there'd been another noise as well. My radar, which I ran continually, had an alarm system that could be activated to ring when another vessel approached. I'd set it for six miles, but with troughs this deep the alarm never stopped ringing, as it was set off by the actual walls of water, and I'd turned down its sensitivity. The alarm was still set, but its efficiency had been short-circuited. Fog or not, I couldn't see where the continuous ringing of the alarm would do me much good.

I wasn't the only one suffering. George Stricker wasn't too far ahead. He'd lost his generator and, trying to use his main engine to charge his batteries, discovered his fuel was contaminated. He'd have no power for luxuries like autopilots or even frequent radio contact. My boat was canted well over, and I'd braced myself in the companionway hatch so each collapse down a wave front wouldn't sling me across the cabin. Sleep was out of the question. Already my muscles ached from this constant hanging on.

I remember complaining and commenting to Phil Rubright and Dave Evans that while it might be calmer to the southward, I thought I'd stick out the quicker northern route. "I'll stay in the circle," I'd announced with bravado. "If I wanted comfort I'd be down in the Caribbean sailing those tropical waters." Then I added, "Wow! That was a huge wave. The deck felt like it was completely buried." And then I was adding a shouted, "Stand by! Stand by! There's a problem. I'm coming back. Give me a moment! Stay on frequency!"

I charged on deck and stood gape-mouthed, for my tiny boat was scraping down the side of a huge freighter. What I thought was a rogue wave was its bow wave, and now, with me as witness, my boat was being sucked up against this great fog-shrouded wall of fast-moving steel. I was looking straight up, still paralyzed, hearing the wind screeching through the rigging —and now hearing this low thump, thump, thump of the freighter's engines. There was no other sound in that fog-deadened world. Certainly no warning alarm from my radar, but how this had happened wasn't the question I was asking. Should I jump below to protect myself from my collapsing mast? Or address the fact that the boat was about to be sucked under by the propeller wash? The answer: better to die from a falling mast than to be chopped into matchsticks by those propellers. Now, what could I do to save myself and save my boat?

I glanced toward the freighter's stern. Used to hold anchors, two tremendous brackets protruded a good eight feet from the ship's side. If I didn't get clear of that hull in the next few seconds, they'd snatch my rig and drag the boat under. No question then that I'd be sucked into the propellers —and in moments. Yet these few seconds I just described were taking an eternity to occur. It was in slow motion, this seemingly inevitable demise of me and my small craft. I leaped into the cockpit and yanked the tiller hard over toward the freighter. There was enough momentum generated by the dragging to give me steerage, and the bow swung out, and my boat pivoted away. Those deadly "cow catchers" brackets skimmed by the rigging with only inches to spare.

Continuing to pivot, I swung behind the freighter and read her name, a name I was soon shouting into the radio. "This is the sailing vessel *Protect Our Sealife!* You've hit me!" Instantly they responded, shouting in very broken English for me to repeat, which I did. Then I got on the single-side band and called two of the closest skippers, Phil and Dave, and advised them of my situation. It was time to assess the damages. The mast was shift-ing, swaying in a radius of perhaps six inches. Obviously the stays had suf-fered. I took down the mainsail and then the staysail and had a look. The bow was split open like a really overripe tomato, split wide enough for me to see the contents of the forward compartment. There was a second gash on the starboard side. If the boat started moving again I'd be taking on major water. Indeed, the forward compartment was already a third full.

At this point the freighter began honking its horn at the required legal intervals. Laughable, if I could have summoned up a laugh. I went on the radio and insisted they stand by. I told them I did not know if my mast would stay up or even if the boat would keep floating. If I was sinking, I'd need a lift—a lift to eastern Texas, the Russian freighter's next port of call. I couldn't see them. "Can you see me on your radar?" I asked. In the same broken English they told me to hold on, they were warming up their radar. In this fog and in this traffic, they'd been running without their radar on. I returned to my inspection. The chain plate of one forestay had been torn out, well, just about out for it held only out of habit. The gashes in the hull were wide enough to slip my hand into. If I did attempt to sail from here, it would be with a minimum of sail. If? A colossal if.

I went below and used the electric bilge pump to empty the saloon com-partment. It took thirty minutes to pump it dry, but the water was still pour-ing in. I moved this pump into the forward compartment, rewired it, and began to pump again. It had to run forty minutes out of every hour just to keep up. Even if I had the battery power, that little pump wouldn't last. Reduce the water flow? From the outside, I stuffed my sleeping bag into the largest of the cracks and covered the splintered portion of the deck with my storm jib, but I knew that a single big wave might easily undo both patches. I had to chance that. By then the bilge pump had already burned out. I turned to the small manual pump, which quickly brought on muscle cramps and did little good. I broke out a recently acquired "emergency" bilge pump. Built by Edson Pumps, this monster was theoretically portable and could move a gallon of water with each stroke. I placed it in the for-ward compartment, pumped a couple of strokes, and realized it must some-how be fastened down. Just screwing it to the side of the hull took up the rest of the night for a pump eighteen inches wide and with a handle four feet long requires a serious mounting.

That done, I began to pump and pump and pump. Moving that much water made incredible demands on my body. First my arms cramped, then my calves, and then my back. Serious cry-out-in-pain cramps. While I was making progress against the sloshing bilge, the boat was just bobbing among the waves. Once I was underway, the leak could become much worse. I was far from port, and my problems far from over. The Russian vessel wanted an update. "Stand by," I responded. "I'm not releasing you from the scene." I went back to pumping and gradually adopted a rhythm that would serve me well in the days to come. Twenty strokes a minute. I broke into a sweat. I was continually lifting the equivalent of a fifty-pound dumbbell—per arm. My muscles screamed. They can, you know. Forget weightlifting, I was gasping for breath like a marathon runner ill-prepared for a marathon.

By now, I was also in communication with Portishead Radio, Marine Rescue Coordination in New York, and the U.S. Coast Guard, who kept insisting that I abandon ship. I refused to do it. I told the Coast Guard that I was the captain of my vessel and hence I was in charge. I would not leave my vessel until I was 100 percent certain she was going down. The freighter was also requesting that I come aboard her. They wanted to get on to Texas. I was costing them money.

Though she hovered close by, I still couldn't see the freighter. The fog was as thick as ever. Wind gusting to 45 knots. Still those steep seas, with the boat sliding from crest to trough and on and on. I gave some thought to the legality of my situation, but not much. If the freighter had been using its radar, my own radar would have picked up the signal no matter how weak my reception. I would have been warned six miles earlier. Indeed, the moment the other radar was engaged, my own alarm had sounded. We were both responsible for maintaining a constant watch in that fog. Someone may have served as lookout on the freighter's bridge. I was down below. It's allowable to have technology keeping watch, which I was doing and they were not. Obviously, we both had levels of liability, but as a powered vessel, it was required to give way to sail.

I mentioned none of this to the freighter, nor to their credit, did they raise legal questions. Issues of right and wrong would be dealt with once I was ashore. Assuming I got ashore. To that purpose, I now raised the mainsail, raised it with an ambitious second reef. If the mast was to fall over or the leak to overtake the pump, best for those things to happen now. As a concession to the waves, I did set my course for a slightly gentler ride. The mast held, and if I went below every hour and pumped and pumped and pumped, I'd stay afloat. Three hundred strokes each hour, pumping, with brief rests, to move out three hundred gallons of seawater. I thought I could handle that.

I'd have to give up the race, though, or at least detour to Newfoundland to make repairs. One fellow sailor was already headed that way. Eighteen hours after impact I released the freighter, and radar running, they headed on to Houston. The U.S. Coast Guard was angrier than ever and now dispatched a cutter that had been near Canadian waters. The intention was to remove me from my sinking vessel. To calm those officers, I agreed to set a converging course with the cutter. In forty-eight hours our paths would cross, and we'd decide then if the situation required me to abandon my boat. There we were, the cutter steaming at their pace and me at my much slower one. Out of each hour I was pumping twenty minutes, and, in my free time, I fixed a computer-dictated meal, gave my fellow competitors a radio check, and even enjoyed a moment or two of sleep. Then thirty-six hours into this ordeal I would have a curious visitor, one who, if reported, would cinch the Coast Guard's case.

Completely exhausted, I went below and lay down in the saloon berth. I was on my back and looked out the hatchway at the clouds moving by. I closed my eyes. Just a nap, I told myself. The water sloshing up would wake me. Instead I entered a deep sleep, and when I woke and glanced up into the cockpit, there was Harry Mitchell helming the boat. I thought, "Harry's in the cockpit. How fine. I can roll over and finish this nap." And I did. I can't say how much longer I slept, probably no more than a few minutes. Then I sat straight up in the bunk and shouted, "My God, Harry's dead!" I scrambled up into the cockpit just to make certain I was truly alone. That vision was so vivid, Harry sitting there with that big boy's grin of his and those mischievous eyes shining. His expression seemed to say, "Don't worry, youngster. I've got it. Get some rest. You'll need it later." He was right.

Gradually, my body began to adjust to the rigors of this discipline. I learned to position myself to ease the pain and strain. Yet, it seemed inevitable that my strength would eventually fail. If I'd been an Olympic athlete, I would have trained for my event and entered it with muscles already in place. On the other hand, what better training could I have had than this constant regime of pumping? Here I was competing not for a medal but for my life. I'd always insisted there were no barriers. Why shouldn't the pumping itself be the practice for pumping further? Logical or not, that reasoning brought with it an amazing amount of assurance.

I was speaking often with Simon in England and with Gwen in Newport, convincing the latter, particularly, that I was fine. Not to worry. Then came the shocking news that the paraplegic Jens Andersen had hit a submerged container crate, and his beautiful handcrafted yacht has sunk. He was in a life raft, and the U.S. Coast Guard had diverted from me to him. In addition, the *Queen Elizabeth II* was steaming toward him. Who would get there first? The racers were wishing it'd be the *QE II* for the accommodations were so much better. But the answer was neither. The Danish navy was on exercise in the same area, and they weren't about to let the Americans or Brits rescue their Jens. They flew a helicopter from one of their ships and plucked him from the life raft.

At least the Coast Guard was off my back. I could make St. Johns, Newfoundland, on my own. Poor George Stricker was off of Nova Scotia, hand steering and exhausted. I was talking to the other boats and had favorable winds. Five days passed, and I was gaining confidence. I crossed the Grand Banks. The fog was as thick as ever; I weathered another bad storm, and kept pumping. The pump and I had become one. As my body adjusted to the labor, less and less effort seemed to be required.

Three hundred miles off the Newfoundland coast, the winds shifted round. Bucking these, I could still make it into St. Johns in three days' time, and I could be at the finish line in eight. I asked my body, and my body said, "I can pump it." My body was getting quite proud of its new Olympic weightlifter muscles. I turned south.

The U.S. Coast Guard screamed itself to the verge of an institutional hernia, but they had to accept the undeniable—I was still afloat. And my friend Simon smoothed the way by sending word to the Marine Rescue Coordination Center that I was a "crafty" sailor and could make it. I was racing again. Phil and Dave were ahead, but not by much. I added more sails. I decided that the mast wasn't going anywhere. The extra speed meant pumping an extra five minutes every hour. Eat, nap, pump, and then pump five more minutes. I was closing the gap with Dave. I warned him to keep looking over his shoulder for I'd be appearing out of the fog. And after a couple of days I did pass him. I crossed St. George's shoals and discovered that George Stricker had retired from the race. My generous competitor had gotten within one hundred miles of the finish, and then he turned inshore. He said, "I'm exhausted." He was "done with the Challenge." That was a bit of a letdown, but I tried to understand and respect his choice. By then, perhaps he saw just stepping out on any dry land as a major victory. He wouldn't be the first racer to feel that way and was hardly the last.

Coming out the fog, I crossed behind Sable Island and was busy with a sail change. At last I had bright skies and clear, blue water. For some reason I glanced over the side—and again—a classic double take. Straight below me was a right whale. Bigger than the boat, he was swimming upside down and apparently playing, his playmate being my boat. When he finally surfaced right beside me, that exhale of breath had a stench of fish that literally set me back on my heels.

I was laughing. I was back to competing, no-holds-barred competing. Phil was just ahead, but he was pulling away. The seas had dropped. We were facing a headwind. Off the Nantucket Shoals I had to start tacking. Inshore, then off. The fog finally lifted. Sunny skies. I saw a sail on the horizon, and the sail grew and grew. Then the VHF crackled. This other sailboat identified itself. She was calling to the red sailboat. I responded. She was the Belgian boat, the one I'd been sailing beside when we left English waters. Here we were neck and neck to the finish line. Not quite neck and neck, though. He crossed ahead of me by ten boat lengths, and then, with me as a helpless onlooker, he piled up more sail. I said "helpless" because I was already risking more sail than I should.

The Belgian might have a bit more speed, but I reasoned that I knew these Newport waters and he did not. That knowledge could get me to the finish first, but apparently he realized this as well. I kept going offshore. He watched me, then turned and headed offshore. I tacked back inshore. He tacked back inshore. He was mirroring each of my maneuvers. He was already ahead and with each of "our" tacks was pulling away a couple of more boat lengths. I could hardly blame him. This strategy was certain to beat me, and under reversed conditions I'd probably have done the same. We spoke briefly on the VHF radio. Neither of us said anything of substance, nothing to hint of weaknesses or of strengths.

Evening was approaching. I figured we were less than twenty-four hours from the finish line. I studied him with the binoculars. He was sitting in the cockpit. His autopilot was driving. He was comfortable. For no particular reason, I tacked. He was up and shifting sails. He got comfortable again. I tacked again. I had a workable strategy: I was going to wear him out. I tacked, went below and pumped, jumped in the bunk for a quick nap, grabbed the binoculars, saw him comfortable in his cockpit, and tacked again. He's a mile ahead. I started pumping out every twenty minutes. That kept the boat lighter. I pushed toward the shoals and watched the depth finder close. I was into nine feet of water, and I draw six, so there were three feet to spare. I turned offshore. He turned off. He disappeared from the cockpit. I hoped he was trying to catch a nap. I called him on the VHF and got a groggy response.

"Are you going to run night lights?" I asked. "You know, there's a fishing fleet ahead of us, and also I don't want to run over you when I pass by."

In demonstration I put on my own lights.

"Oh, right," he joked. "You will overtake me. I must be prepared."

He turned on his lights.

I continued offshore. He continued offshore. An hour passed. I didn't tack. He called on the radio. *"Protect Our Sealife.* Do you intend to tack?" I didn't reply. I turned the radio off. The night was coming on. I sat very low in the cockpit and watched. Finally, it was too dark to see him—or for him to see me. For company we had each other's mast lights. I continued to pump and sail and pump. Three hours passed. It was 11:00 P.M. I eased the tiller over and put the boat inshore. He didn't follow. Ah, he's asleep. I headed for the shore of Nantucket, and my mast light was soon blending with the lights along the coast. His mast light disappeared on the offshore horizon.

I helmed all night except when I was pumping. I short tacked, catching every bit of the breeze. Early morning, pale dawn, and I turned the radio on. He was calling me. "Where are you?" he asked. "I'm not telling you," I answered. "How far are you off shore?" he asked. "I'm not telling you," I answered. He said, "Well, I'll tell you where I am." I said, "I don't care where you are." I knew I was ahead and in celebration set my spinnaker and headed screaming off toward the finish. With four hours to go, I used e-mail to tell Gwen I'd be with her soon. Then, with three hours to go, his spinnaker appeared on the horizon. All I wanted was one boat length, just to beat him, even if it was by a single boat length.

He called on the radio. He said, "Where were you last night?" "Oh," I replied in complete innocence, "I thought you saw me. I went inshore." He vowed to overtake me, to move heaven and earth and the seas and beat me.

"Not if I can help it," I vowed in return. Race Control called and asked who was where, but they already knew the answer. They'd been monitoring the conversation.

I kept pumping, and shortly after noon on day twenty-four I crossed the finish line forty minutes ahead of the Belgian boat, a boat length plus a bit more. Quite a few spectator boats had come out to greet me, and soon Gwen and several friends were on board. From Gwen I received a hug and the traditional reward of ice cream. I hugged her in return. She felt surprisingly fragile. I was nothing but muscle, a bit like Arnold Schwarzenegger, only smaller and seagoing. She felt a bicep and posed as if she was a beauty queen. Still, that weightlifter's regime was something I was all too happy to abandon, and within minutes I showed my friends the pump handle and made a request. I said, "It's your turn now."

Waiting at the dock was a happy crowd, for I was returning to "the Sailing Capital of the World," a port where I'd already been given the Key to the City and made an honorary member of its famed Working Men's Yacht Club. Now, four years later, I'd raced across the Atlantic, finished third in my class, and in the process recycled the entire Atlantic Ocean through the boat. I had much to be proud of. The first in my class had beaten me by only thirty-six hours. Even before the freighter collision, my boat was far from the fastest in the fleet, and my skills as a sailor and a survivor had made the difference. With a broad smile, renewed determination, and Gwen at my newly muscled side, I came ashore, and the parties started.

18

BACK TO CHARLESTON

After the celebrations ended, Gwen and I sailed back to Charleston. A wonderful passage, but the money problems waiting for us ashore had gone nowhere. The 1998–99 Around Alone would begin in two years, and to compete I would need a major sponsor. I continued to do well on the speaking circuit, and books and merchandise were selling. Gwen and I had food on the galley table and even a new downtown office. The funding doors, though, remained firmly shut, and before they opened, we took a couple of interesting detours.

Besides bicycles Gwen and I had a junk car on loan and were about to drive over to Ken Bonerigo's house for a Friday night of steaks and a video. It had started to drizzle, and, on leaving the marina, we noticed a couple in slickers. We offered them a lift. We opened the rear door from the inside, of course, for there was no working handle on the outside. As a result we soon had new and wealthy friends inviting us to stay with them in California. We accepted, and I did a series of speeches there. After seeing the first of these, a presentation at a Boys and Girls Club, my host (who was state chairman of the clubs) offered his critique. "Use props," he said. "When you tell the children of your dream to be a solo racer, show them your jacket, the one with all the racing patches. When you tell them about stitching up your eyebrow with a clothespin, show them the pin. When you speak of using a sextant, show them the sextant."

In hindsight, something so simple should have been obvious, but as is often the case, the obvious is not obvious at all. With the use of props, I took my talks up ten notches, and I came home from California with a new confidence in my motivational abilities. Soon after, I appeared in Charlotte, North Carolina, in front of a group of the world's best speakers, but I was certain that what worked with children would work here. Visual aids, a properly condensed and exciting story, and interaction with the audience would get my message of following one's dream across. It did. I received a standing ovation, and world-famous speaker Dr. Terry Paulsen christened me "the Hope Merchant of the Speaking World."

I had no intention, though, of abandoning young audiences. I would continue, and have continued, to dedicate the bulk of my efforts toward schoolchildren, often speaking for groups that paid little or nothing. I saw, though, that I could command considerable fees from others and that Gwen and I weren't going to starve after all. In January of 1997, I had just such an engagement in Bermuda, and, to save money, I intended to sail there. Gwen and I'd met Charleston businessman Gene King and his wife, Doris, and Gene wanted to go along on the sail. A big teddy bear of a man, weighing three hundred pounds and six feet, five inches tall, he was, among many other things, a great chef. I've never eaten better. Even in the midst of a raging gale he wedged himself into the galley and served up a three-course dinner. I told him that wasn't a normal routine when the boat was bucking like a horse, and, in fact, this continuing storm was having its effect. That night the winds increased to a good forty-five knots. I reefed down the sails and came below. Overhead Gene could hear the freezing, breaking seas pounding upon the deck. Convinced that he would die, Gene began to video the experience saying, "If I'm going down, you're going down with me. " Perhaps this was his first true inkling that a Gold Card with all the world's cash behind it wasn't always the answer. He had to trust my instincts. As I tried to explain, in businessmen's terms he would understand, the sea was my environment; my real-life horizons were like the metaphorical ones of business, and my instincts and past experiences allowed me to make decisions that would happily affect my future, our future in this case, for the boat and he and I all reached Bermuda unscathed.

As a result I was offered a job as his public-relations director. This paid well. At the beginning Gene had to buy me a suit and a couple of ties, but soon enough I could buy my own. I enjoyed parts of the job. Still, as with most companies, there were all sorts of backstabbing and intrigue going on. I overcame most of that, created team-building exercises, some involving sailing my boat, published a series of articles on motivating employees, using our company as an example, and in general helped to increase profits. Each day when I had to tie my tie, I thought of a sailor's knot. Each day when I went to an office that overlooked the water, I left my boat in the harbor to go there. And each day when I went back to Gwen, I brought this company's problems with me. She was running the sailing campaign by herself. Finally I resigned.

After seven months I was a solo sailor again. Shortly after, the company was sold, in part thanks to my efforts. I had no regrets, not about taking the job and certainly not about leaving. I'd learned a tremendous amount about the business arena. We have choices in life, and business is just a part of life. Negative people can hold you back; positive people can push you forward. Right now Gwen and I needed to find one of those positive people, maybe even two or three.

In the summer of 1997 I approached the South Carolina Ports Authority, a government agency, about sponsorship. In response, I was asked for a formal proposal, which I supplied. Then we waited, but while waiting, I agreed, at the suggestion of friends, to form the No Barriers Education Foundation. My interest in helping children would simply go from an informal to formal format. I was to continue telling children of the power of dreams and to explain that what they learned in the classroom could make those dreams come true. I was to be a living example of what a positive attitude and setting goals could accomplish. My initial goals hadn't changed, and yet this formal organization did lift a huge burden from our shoulders. Finally Gwen and I could separate public time from our private lives. We could stop living on a burned-out, exhausted edge.

In August, the State Ports Authority said yes. The people there felt very strongly about investing in the community they helped to serve, and I was to be a conduit of that investment. I would do public appearances on the agency's behalf, but my main concerns would still be with the public schools in the area. The initial response was disappointing, for no principal reponded to the offer of help. I went out and told them in person what we intended. Six public schools and one private school in the area signed on, and we designed an educational program that would keep them interested in the BOC Challenge, renamed the Around Alone, and educate and motivate at the same time. Enthusiasm from that direction grew and grew and grew, and before I sailed, some of the young people even illustrated a coloring book that dealt with my adventures, and this was published. I had obtained a satellite telephone, so the ability to communicate with these students while at sea was now assured.

Going into the local classrooms, I met a great cross-section of children, black and white, which most often meant "poor and not poor." To the black children raised in the inner city or in rural poverty, it was particularly important (as it had been in South Africa) for them to see a black man who had succeeded in a previously white arena. Many, in fact, had only a limited exposure to the ocean that was at their very doorsteps. A few had none at all. Whether black or white, though, all these children shared one common problem, for all were facing that most troubling and dangerous of oceans, modern adulthood. "We need to have a goal!" I'd shout. "When I go home at night, what do I do?" "Sleep" was the usual answer. Of course, "Watch television!" was another. "No!" I'd shout. "I read. Reading is the beginning of any journey!" Then I would tell them of my struggles as a child and the importance that reading played in the accomplishment of my dreams. More than reading was involved. "Everything you learn in school plays a vital role! Math enables me to estimate the amount of provisions I need, geography teaches me about the climates I'll face, and from history I gain the experience of others." I would explain the power of their dreams to change the reality they faced. "You can make it happen. Those who laugh at your dreams don't understand the power of a dream. Always remember that drugs, alcohol, and cigarettes are killers of dreams." I wanted them to understand that the dreams themselves represented choices they must make, and with the proper choices unbelievable barriers could be overcome. The right choice might even save their lives. At sea that was often the case.

When possible, I brought the children to the boat, for what better visual aid than a big-as-life forty-foot red sailboat? There they were introduced to the nuts and bolts of sailing and, with their own hands, could work the pulleys and winches, raise and lower sails, and even use the radio, each task done in cooperation with others on the boat, exhibiting not only the power of a dream, but the power of the machine coupled with the greatest power of all—cooperative effort. An odd lesson to come from a solo sailor, but prepping the boat for this solo race was exactly that.

In the meantime, other sponsorship opportunities were coming along. My motivational speaking lead to a short and unhappy stint with Coca-Cola and an entirely happy one with Wal-Mart. A member of a local Rotary Club not only helped me to better formulate my own goals and philosophy, but brought along the willing hearts and hands of the entire club. Both financial support and the support crew were growing. In September I was formally announced as a South Carolina race entry. We'd also be flying the Irish and South African flags. The vessel that began life as the *Stella-r* and then was called *Protect Our Sealife* was now renamed *www.no-barriers.com* to signify the foundation's message of hope.

By now I was speaking at schools and corporations all over the state and, of course, continuing with the fund-raising. The boat was in dire need of attention. The State Ports Authority offered to lift the boat with a crane and place her at the old banana freighter pier under the old Cooper River Bridge. Convenient both to city and the waterfront, this was a picturesque spot. To one side was the city's abandoned jail house, nicknamed the Seabreeze Hotel, while above the bridge swooped out across the harbor like a worse-for-wear double-humped camel. Tugboats were docked here, and the port captain's office was just beyond our work area. We were high and dry with plenty of work space, all on the very edge of the busy harbor's comings and goings, and that proved a great advantage. Not only was I getting by without haul-out fees and space rental, but Port Captain Billy Lempesis offered whatever help he could give, a support given freely by many of the port employees—from policemen to crane operators.

Still, there were chores that were beyond even their helping hands. I planned to strip the vessel, break her into her rawest components, and then reassemble her. Hull, deck, keel, rudder, and all the mechanics and electronics would be placed back in, and if not in new, then at least in raceable condition. First of all, I would sandblast the hull, but no company was interested. The job was too small and unprofitable. Then I met Les Phillips. Soft-spoken, gentle, hard-working to the edge of fatigue, Les seems a cautious person from his manner. When you get to know him, you realize here's a risk taker.

He said, "I hope you have deep pockets. What you need could run to tens of thousands of dollars." I was expecting to hear him say a couple of thousand. My jaw dropped. He suggested we help each other. I would promote his company, and he would promote me. He'd take the risk. I had gained a sponsor and, as it turned out, a very close friend. I had a shore crew. Unpaid, Les and many of his workers lent able hands, and, of course, Ken stuck by me. And from the schools where I spoke came teachers and parents to scrape and patch and paint.

By this time Gwen had left Charleston. She had decided to follow her own dream. Cooking was her passion, and she'd enrolled in a cooking school in Ireland. She'd been waitressing, and those savings coupled with my speaking fees gave her enough money to take the four-month course. We knew we'd miss each other, but she'd been supporting me for years and was frustrated that her own interest had been ignored. With e-mail and telephone we stayed close, but now she was the one off on an adventure.

The sandblasting proceeded. Off came layers of paint and patches until we had a naked hull. All the scars were there, every bump from Russian freighter to container crate to iceberg and many more. An odd feeling to be reminded of what I'd faced on the high seas, a bit like a boxer examining his face and body after the match. I'd survived all that, so putting things right shouldn't be that hard, except that I stayed covered with fiberglass dust and was soon getting rashes. Plus we were working in winter on a pier that was totally exposed to those wicked northeast winds. One weekend day in particular the temperature stayed below freezing, and dozens of volunteers were on hand to grind away with the power tools, some standing on scaffolding fifteen feet up. It was a brutal day, but each one of them was putting a bit of him- or herself into that boat, and the boat and I both were being exposed to all those positive people. Perhaps the boat felt then she was meant for greater things. I know I did.

Additional sponsors came on board. Wal-Mart helped to merchandise material, and Prudential Insurance hired me as an inspirational speaker. Busy days were made busier. Since the loss of Harry Mitchell, new safety features were required by the racing organization, among them inboard engines. Ken helped to install this, my first ever. A pinhole was drilled through the propeller shaft and a wire threaded through that and crimped with a special seal. Engaging the propeller would shear the wire, and you would have to explain the nature of such an emergency to the race committee or be disqualified. Rather than waste all this potential power, Ken added a huge alternator to the engine, something to feed the electricity-hungry pumps and satellite telephone. Of course, the weight of the engine and fuel tank meant a shift in the sail plane, and a three-foot bow sprit was added to allow for a broad asymmetrical spinnaker. Prudential Insurance came up with the dollars needed for a new set of Spectra racing sails, made of a special high-tech yarn. A Hollywood producer was interested in doing a film about the adventures Gwen and I had had. His advance went into the kitty. This time round we were doing things right.

In the preceding four years, the BOC Corporation had dropped its support for the race, and those initials were dropped from the title. Sydney was replaced with Auckland, New Zealand, as the second stopover. Probably the most significant differences came from Harry's death, which had brought a change of regulations and training. Race rules now required each boat to have a complete medical kit and the fleet doctor was on hand to teach an extensive first aid course. We were taught to give ourselves injections and staple ourselves back together. For this last lesson, I recall, we used pig's feet, for the flesh has a similar consistency to human sailors. A half-day Coast Guard briefing even included the demonstration of a helicopter basket recovery. I'd had all this training when I was diving in the oil fields: firing flares, flipping from a life raft, and the rest. I found that the prerace courses compared quite well.

Shortly after the boat was launched Gwen returned. She'd finished her chef's course, but somehow the experience had only made her less sure. Rather than focus on what she'd learned, she brooded on what remained to be learned. All her fears and frustrations were now simmering close to the surface. To make matters worse, I was busy with work, speeches, and a team-building program begun for Prudential. Our sailing "family" had mushroomed. Often I'd be taking these new family members out sailing. Gwen would skip those trips. She'd cast the lines off from what was again her floating home and go off to spend the day in the library or at the office.

Growing even more frustrated, she took a cooking job in Italy. She was to work in Tuscany, then come back to Charleston two weeks before the start of the race, and then she would return to her job, which would give her the money to fly to each of the race stopovers. Off she went. We stayed in touch on the phone. She wasn't happy there. She missed the excitement of the project. She loved cooking but still wanted to be in Charleston. Three months earlier than planned, and much to my relief, she flew back.

Gwen and I did have one fight, though. Actually, we'd only had three fights in our whole life together. One occurred when she had wanted to skip that BOC prize-giving ceremony and I insisted that she attend. I said that we were going, and we did. Then when we were living on the boat in Charleston, she got so angry, she threw her good sunglasses overboard, just snatched them off and threw them as far as she could and then laughed at herself. This third fight came just two days before the start of the race. Her father had taught her to drive, and I'd taken her a step further. She'd been a nervous driver, and I'd been a nervous passenger, but gradually she'd gotten a bit more proficient. The stick shift still gave her trouble, and I was still her extra pair of eyes. Neither of us could afford a wreck, for not only did we have no spare money, I had no American driver's license, and Gwen had no license of any kind.

So there we were. Gwen was pulling out of a supermarket parking lot. I knew she was going to bounce over the curb. I said, "Be careful, you're going to bounce over the curve." She bounced over the curb. And then she totally lost it. She threw me out of the car. She drove off and didn't come back, and she was so angry, I didn't go back to the little apartment we'd been lent. I slept that night on the boat. That fight was just from stress, as so much was riding on this race, not just all our struggles of the last eight years but all the money we had as well. Though the sponsors had helped, she and I had doubled that amount. We were spent. Emotionally and financially it seemed we had nothing left to give. More than ever it seemed the race itself was just the iceberg's tip—the exposed one-eighth. After years and years of scrambling after money and making frantic boat repairs, these were now all beneath the surface. The race, it seemed, was not a test at all. It was a reward.

Adding to the excitement was the steady stream of sightseers and well-wishers who came. They'd mill along the docks, mix with the working crews, and compare the boats, complimenting and questioning. Over the weeks an elderly gentleman kept coming by mine. Unlike most others, he asked personal questions such as how do you feel about facing death? All I learned in return at that time was that his name was Gamel and that he was Egyptian.

The opposition? Seven entries in the superboat Class I division, among these the well-known Frenchwoman Isabelle Autissier and, also from France, the controversially quiet Marc Thiercelin, both veterans of the brutal Vendée Globe; an Italian, Giovanni Soldini (who would win); two Englishmen, Josh Hall and Mike Golding; a Russian, Fedor Konyukhov; and a Canadian, Sebastian Reidl. Some of their boats had evolved considerably in the last four years. Using hydraulic rams, keels could be swung from side to side, along with dagger boards, increasing directional stability and speed and decreasing the need for weighty water ballast. To obtain better sail shape, the mast could rotate. To make this work, ten-foot outriggers extended from each side, thus increasing the hypothetical beam, and the average speed had increased proportionately. These rooster tail–throwing boats could approach thirty knots.

In my class, the smaller forty-to-fifty foot boats, some state-of-the-art racing machines were again entered, and some were sailed by egos that matched. (All of us racers had healthy egos. They're just not always loud-voiced, high-maintenance egos.) Robin Davie, George Stricker, and Brad Van Liew of the United States; Neil Hunter of Australia; J. P. Mouligne of France (who would win Class II); Viktor Yazykov of Russia, Michael Garside of England; and my old friend from Japan, Minoru Saito, made up this Class II division. Again I had the smallest boat, and, besides being home-built, it was also one of the oldest and again probably the least given over to comfort.

19

LEG ONE

The gun fired. As was often the case, I was first across the line. The others would catch up soon enough. Immediately, in fact. The first leg of the race was completely uneventful, no coming apart, no sinking, no drama at all. The first week's summary: A single flying fish came aboard, but it was not large enough for a breakfast, so I let it go. A spider built a web in a corner of the stern. Light winds, steady progress. For the first time in my life I had the time and money to get things right, and what a difference that made.

Gwen had precooked the meals and canned the curries, stews, and soups. For the first time ever I wasn't losing weight, and, instead of pumping or sewing canvas, I could tend to other projects. Among these were an ongoing e-mail dialogue with the children in the No Barriers program and writing the column for the *Post and Courier,* the Charleston newspaper. Instead of a nutrition experiment, I'd be measuring for sleep deprivation. I'd be filming with a video camera and would continue to work on a new book, a sequel to *No Barriers.* In between all this, of course, I'd still be sailing the boat, and as it turned out, there'd even be time left over for boredom —and time for missing Gwen.

Modern technology had put an end to the isolation of solo sailing. No longer was I truly alone, and, with no desperate drama to survive, the highlight of every day became my five- to ten-minute telephone chat with Gwen. What was happening in Ireland? How had she spent her day? Had she gone to Dublin? Had she worked in the garden or baked a cake? Such things seemed of monumental consequence now that we were apart. Of course, she didn't see such mundane activities in the same light.

My other source of comfort lay ahead in Cape Town. Since the last BOC Challenge, my sister had married and had a baby. On board was a teddy bear I hoped to deliver for a first birthday. And I would meet my new

Twenty-seven thousand miles to go. Photograph courtesy of Chuck Hooker.

brother-in-law, Graham, who was already handling my South African publicity, and handling it well.

Fifteen days out, I caught sight of Minoru Saito. I had just enjoyed a squall-produced shower, the kind where I rushed to soap myself and then didn't get rinsed in time. I was searching the horizon for another squall so I could finish my bath. I thought I saw a sail, and yet it wasn't there. I looked out of the corner of my eye—an old trick—and, yes, I was convinced I saw a sail.

I had no idea whose it was. Checking the latest report, I noticed Minoru and I were an equal distance from Cape Town. I took out the binoculars. I still had the bar of soap in my hand. Someone was there, and after an hour I could see clearly that it was Minoru. We were both drifting toward the same squall. His boat did better in the light airs for it has more sail area and a bit more waterline length, so without a lucky break he was going to sail away from me. The squall hit. I was soaping up again. A big wind shift came, and it occurred to me that Minoru might not take advantage of this. I dropped the soap. And in the darkness of the rain I tacked. We'd been talking some on the VHF radio, but I didn't tell him I was tacking. The rain lifted, and I was gone. He called and asked, "What you do?" I said, "I ran away."

News came that Sebastian Reidl had dropped out to the race. He was an environmentally conscious skipper, sailing *Project Amazon,* a high-tech boat, and I was disappointed for him, as I am each time a boat withdraws from a race. My competitive spirit didn't run in that direction. It ran in the direction of beating Minoru to the finish line, but apparently now he was hiding from me.

Five days later, butterflies were keeping me company. Orange with black spots, they flittered around the boat but would not land. Minoru called on the radio, and we attempted more conversations. Beyond his boat's name, the word "geisha," and the names of a few food dishes, Japanese was beyond me, and his version of English was also beyond me. He did see the humor in this, though, and in much else. "My position . . . my position . . . I think longitude . . . longitude . . . I think . . . , *No Barriers,* how you today?" Sometimes I didn't even know what language he was speaking. Anyway, I got the impression he was fine but frustrated. So was I. Again I saw him on the horizon. Again a rain squall descended, and for several hours I helmed. The rain stopped, and again I was alone. Eventually, by continuing to leap along from squall to squall—connecting the dots—I broke through the Doldrums ahead of him.

Goodbye to the Doldrums and the vivid dreams they induced, ones in which I had conversations with friends, normal conversations, enthusiastic or confidential or simply everyday talks. It was as if I'd been sitting in their homes. Gwen called. Here was my link with sanity. She was having lamb for dinner, while I was having leftover tuna pasta, a slice of ham, and an orange.

The next day I discovered that both incoming and outgoing phone calls would be charged to me. Without knowing it, I'd run up several thousand dollars in bills, money I didn't have. So, no more phone. I couldn't give up my call to Gwen, though. She began to tell me how she and her father discovered thieves removing belongings from her father's home. The intruders escaped, then returned and were discovered by Gwen and her father —at which point in our conversation a squall hit, and over the boat went. Some hours passed before I could sort out the damage, return to the phone, and learn that justice had triumphed. Her brush with danger seemed so much more important than my own, and in fact it was.

Twenty-five days out: my naps had increased in length. I was timing these for the sleep-deprivation study. I was giving them less and less to study. I was about to run out of books. I had only one left for the entire other side of the equator. Plenty of music was blasting away, though.

Twenty-seven days out: I crossed the equator at dawn but waited to make my sacrifices to King Neptune. I needed proper light for the video. At midday I filmed myself wrapped in a towel and wearing my sponsor-decorated t-shirt. I'd built a crown from sailing gloves and a sail tie. "I ask you to protect me in your ocean and to accept this gift from me." Overboard went the leg bone from a piece of smoked pork.

A week or so later, the Brazilian coast, or at least the Brazilian island of Fernando de Noronha, was on the horizon. The next landfall was Cape Town.

A week after that the winds were gusting to thirty-five knots. With new sails my old boat took off, literally leaping out of the water as she crested each wave. I was airborne and counting from one to as high as five before splashing down with a deafening thud that vibrated both hull and rigging and frightened and vibrated me as well. But "can she take this?" is a game my boat has always played with me. I turned up the CD player to drown out the banging, and I let her pound her way on to Table Bay.

So it went. I increased my lead over Minoru to two hundred miles, overate, and got seasick. Just swallowing my fortifying green algae pills was enough to bring that on. A second boundary was passed, one solo sailors speak less about than the equator, but one just as significant, the sailing-naked boundary. I put on some clothes, for it was too cool to sail naked, which I and many others often do. Who cares what we look like or smell like for that matter? Still, a bit of personal hygiene, a bucket bath and a toothbrushing are good morale builders. I did both, and instead of watching a lonely albatross circling in a drizzling rain, I pretended I was about to take Gwen to the movies.

The next day I trimmed my mustache, using the video camera in place of a mirror. Ah, technology. As if in revenge, I was losing telephone contact with Gwen. I'd be with her soon, though, and the radio reception to Cape Town was now strong. Three weeks out of port, I began to do daily spots on Cape Town radio shows. What was happening on the boat? Was I nervous about the next leg of the race? The talk show was fun and led to a national TV coverage of my arrival. With a southern approach, I was passing by the landmarks of my childhood—Slang Kop, which translates to Snake Head; the Twelve Apostles; Lion's Head; and from there a glimpse of Table Mountain. Then after Signal Hill I'd be home—except that the television crew hadn't arrived yet. I was sailing along beneath that grand Table Mountain, anxious to get my ice cream and to hug my mother. Fifty-four days at sea (fourteen days better than my first passage), and the message "Slow down!" came, so I reefed the sails.

Most of the boats had finished long before, but in my class I was still well placed, for Minoru Saito, Neil Hunter, and Robin Davie were all several days behind. I wasn't in danger of being overtaken, but the frustration of that moment is still a vivid memory. Then came word that the cameras were ready. I have a second vivid memory, of my parents and sister waving from the towboat (my sister telling my nephew, "There's your crazy uncle"). In an inflatable my brother-in-law, Graham, and Race Director Mark Schrader approached with the film crew. Gwen wouldn't arrive for another four days. By then I would be settled. For now I celebrated my homecoming. An incredibly joyous moment, yet this arrival was still far different from the one four years before. In the harbor no tugs were spraying welcoming arches with fire hoses, and waiting on the dock were a dozen people instead of a thousand. Something had changed.

I had sailed into one of South Africa's most prestigious harbors expecting, as a South African, to be honored.

The twelve days in port were certainly hectic enough. Graham had done an excellent job with the press, with radio and television, all that. Actually there were more demands than I could possibly fill. And Gwen had arrived. We'd made plans to ride horseback through some garden wilderness, taste wine in vineyard arbors, and lounge on an isolated beach. My Charleston sponsor, Les Phillips, had flown in to lead my shore team—to be my shore team. That meant a lot.

Quickly, I did dozens of media spots. One television magazine with a tremendous Sunday night audience filmed me speaking to children and interviewed both my parents and me in the backyard in front of the "dream tree" I'd "sailed" as a child. I had plenty of publicity, but, oddly enough, no one was stopping me on the street to chat or ask for an autograph. The one constant was the response of the schoolchildren. I continued my lectures to those groups and especially enjoyed returning again to my old high school, Livingstone.

Then an old friend from my yacht-club days, Rob Kamhoort, set up a meeting with Netcare, a large health-care group, and suddenly I had a broad audience. I began at once to speak to hospital staffs, to address adult South Africans who were struggling to adapt to the changes in their country. Yes, they now enjoyed political freedom, but in the workplace morale was down. More responsibilities, but less resources, plus affirmative action created all types of insecurities. It was an odd situation, this feeling of uncertainty, of being cut off from a social standard, which, though hopelessly flawed, had kept the economy functioning. They had dreamed. They still dreamed. How do you make a dream a reality? That question was a familiar one.

Under Netcare's direction, I was also flown to several orphanages it sponsored. One village, in particular, made an impression. This was a village created within the city of Port Elizabeth, a community of children within a compound with dormitories, a dining hall, a music room, an arts and crafts area, and all surrounding a small play park. Four hundred children from toddlers to teenagers were there, kids taken off the streets, kids who were so full of love and so full of life, kids like I'd never seen anywhere before. I tried to concentrate on the older boys, for they'd spent years on their own and hence endured the most. I said, "Yes, you have dealt with hardships in your life, but if you give up hope, you give up your life." I can't say they were happy, but these children had big, open, always-smiling faces. They didn't know how bad off they were, especially by international standards. They just knew that they had to survive and that being in the orphanage was their best chance. They were respectful and hungry to learn. I was scheduled to spend an hour with them and stayed for five and a half. When I flew off from that village, I left a piece of myself behind. I plan to return.

I had a full twelve days. Hectic! I was meeting people at the airport, going to family events and public events, working on the boat, and speaking, with not much sleep in between. And it turned out that my hospital sponsor was quite literally a lifesaver. A friend of my sister's was working on my engine and slipped, opening a seven-inch gash in his thigh. Then Minoru Saito came into port. He'd lost all feeling in his fingers. The Netcare physicians diagnosed this as the early signs of heart fibrillations and treated him for free. A second life was saved. Minoru took the medicine and got ready for the next leg. Even after I left port, Netcare would treat my father for free. I could not have asked for a better sponsor, yet even this relationship was about to take a hard knock.

The hospital logo had been put on the sails, and I took the boat out into the harbor for publicity photos, shots taken from a helicopter of the sails with the city and the mountain in the background. I had my father and two Charleston friends on board. I was due that evening for a reception at the Royal Cape Yacht Club and knew I'd be a few minutes late. We tied up the boat, and Gwen and I were off. I walked in the door of the yacht club and immediately saw a couple of old friends, both paraplegics in wheelchairs. As a teenager I'd sailed with them, and I went over to chat. Then this guy, David Bonges, comes up behind me and in Afrikaans said, "I see the hotnot is back." "Hotnot" is the equivalent of the word "nigger."

I'd been in the yacht club three minutes, a club I'd once been a member of, and I was greeted with a racial slur. On the faces of my two friends was this look of shocked amazement, and even I was surprised. I suppose I'd been lulled in a false sense of somehow belonging, of thinking, yes, I belong here. With anger beginning to boil up, I excused myself from our conversation, turned on the new arrival, and said, "You have no right to speak to me like that!" He said, "But you are back." He put his arm around me. He was drunk. I pushed him away and went over to Mark Schrader. I told him I was leaving and why. Gwen and I walked out.

Of course, the taunt of this single drunk might not seem to be my worst encounter with racism, yet in some ways it was. It brought back so many negative memories, memories of hearing similar things as a child, and sailing was supposed to have been my way out, a path toward freedom. As a teenager, I'd been a member of this yacht club and had only stopped being a member when I sailed off to Ireland. Then four years before, the former commodore of this same club had stood up in front of everyone and announced that I did not deserve to have my dream realized. I was back in the same room where that comment had been made and hearing, "The nigger is back." I went home and thought about it. Some members of this club were still claiming that my boat was "a floating coffin," that "Petersen's boat will never survive the Southern Ocean," and, no doubt, some still felt that yachting should forever belong to the privileged class, and, no doubt, a few were still asking in private the ridiculous question "What does a black man know about sailing?" But some in this club had been kind and encouraging. They'd treated me without prejudice and had taken me on their boats. In place now was a youth-oriented sailing program, and thus the skills I'd struggled to obtain were opening to many others. Progress was being made, but how much of this was just the "veneer" of progress? The question of whether I sailed a floating coffin would be settled soon enough by the Southern Ocean. The question of how I was to be treated as a man must be settled now. I decided to fight back, to take nothing less than a public apology.

The reporter from the Charleston paper, Tony Barthelme, called and I told him of the incident. He asked if he could do it as a story, and I said do what you like with it. Then I called Eben Human, the sports editor of the Afrikaans paper, and discussed it with him. He said I had two choices: ignore the slur and keep quiet, in which case it would be heard again and again, if not by me, by somebody else, or I could let him run it as a front-page story—go after David Bonges with national publicity. I said, "Do it." Eben called the present yacht-club commodore, Paul Mare, and asked him for a comment. I had sailed with Paul as a child and respected him. He called and asked if there was any way to stop the story. He would investigate the incident. By then, though, the ball was rolling. I started looking forward to the resumption of the race, to escaping South Africa once and for all.

The next day I went into the yacht club and made a statement regarding the incident, and David Bonges went in and made a statement. He said he was drunk, didn't know what he was saying, and apologized. He was expelled from the organization, but I can't say that satisfied me. I decided to finish the race, to take the South African flag off the boat, and from then on to make my home in America. That just left the problem of my new sponsor, Netcare. They'd asked me to drop the story, because having my name on the front page of every newspaper in this manner was exactly what they didn't need. Attention was fine, just not negative attention. I told them no. If they couldn't stand beside me, we needed to rescind the contract, and I'd give them their money back. In the last four years South Africa might have become a democracy, but racial prejudice was very much in evidence, and I was going to demand nothing less than a dignified reception in my old homeland. They stayed on board.

The night before my departure, a big party was given in my honor, and Netcare was doing things right. They'd even bottled a wine with my name and picture on the label. Five hundred people, including the region's doctors and politicians and all the local dignitaries, were in attendance. I spoke to them of my career and what it meant to have their support. I didn't say what I was thinking at the time: that this would be my last public appearance in South Africa, that I'd had enough. I just thanked them.

And while I was thanking them, my father kept shouting, "That's my boy! That's my boy!" Disconcerting. He was sober now. He attended Alcoholic Anonymous, a particular comfort since the special "Neal Petersen Wine" was readily available. Still, my father was an unruly emotional bundle, and in the four years I'd been gone, he'd suddenly grown old. When he walked now, he shuffled. He tried without success to make his way forward, and he kept shouting. Of course, all this was in complete contrast to my proud, reserved mother and my sister, who with one hand was cradling my nephew and with the other pointing out to him his famous uncle.

I thanked all in attendance, came down from the podium, and, with my infant nephew in my arms, began to mix with the crowd. I couldn't find Gwen, though, and hadn't spotted her while I'd been speaking. It turned out she hadn't been there at all, and I asked Les Phillips to hunt for her. He did, but without success. I left the party and with a dozen others started looking. I personally searched the car and the boat, not finding her then. We continued to look for hours and finally found her on the boat, asleep in the bunk.

"I want to be out of here" is what she said when we were alone. "I can't take any more of this." I understood what she meant. I was having a hard enough time, but Gwen had had all the attention she could handle and much more. We hadn't seen a horse or a beach or a vineyard. Except for a brief trip up Table Mountain, we had failed miserably at relaxation. I felt a shift in her attitude toward me, but once the race was finished, we'd straighten everything out. Anyway, there were two of us who could hardly wait for the starting gun.

My mother fired that gun the next morning, and mine was the last boat across the line. Every sailing decision I made that morning seemed to backfire. It was as if Cape Town had a hold on me. The rest of the fleet was sailing out of sight, while I still struggled to get offshore. Once again, I was far more exhausted leaving South Africa than when I'd arrived, and, once again, I was headed off into some of the worse conditions of the voyage. Just ahead was the Southern Ocean and the site of my dismasting four years before. At least I was free of the land, and when the cape shore finally disappeared from sight, I felt a sense of physical relief. It was as if an actual weight had been lifted from my shoulders, as if the cape's hold had lifted. Let the ocean do its worse. Nothing could top what I'd just been through.

Of course, that's the sort of reasoning that brings on trouble.

20

LEG TWO

Two days out, two days without Gwen. Winds were blowing from thirty to forty knots and great, green swells breaking over the stern. I was already surfing at fourteen knots and began to drag a length of chain behind, a strategy that I hoped would compensate for the narrowness of the extended stern. Instead, the chain wrapped around the paddle of the self-steering system and bent it. My other innovation did work. I'd added a second foresail to the roller furler, and now the two sails extended out before me like butterflies' wings. Quite a sight, especially the next morning when the winds were gusting even higher and the waves were the height of two-story houses. I felt it was safer to be below. And that's where I was when a knockdown—caused by a big wave forcing the boat over onto its side—flung me out of the bunk for a distance of ten feet and tore the bunk from its mounting. Besides which, in clutching for a handhold, I tore the radar screen off of its mounting. My feet smashed into the electrical panel, breaking switches and the ammeter casing. My head lay across an unlit burner of the stove. No serious harm done. The content of lockers and my cargo of fresh fruit were scattered about the cabin. An hour of tidying restored all.

I had decided on a conservative strategy. I would stay out of the southernmost waters and keep the sails to a minimum during the worst of the weather. I'd try and stay competitive, but I'd also try and stay alive. I'd get to Auckland, New Zealand, with as few dramas as possible. Yet, even in this cautious mode, I had taken that first knockdown, one I had half-expected would remove the mast. Having survived, I began gradually to add more and more sail, testing myself and the boat, looking for that edge, the one that goes along the border of total catastrophe. It was the cold that I miscalculated—and the loneliness.

Four days out, my heater died. The cold was incredible. I put on all my clothing. By the time I passed the site of my previous dismasting, I could see my breath even when I was below deck. Four days without Gwen. I ate one of her canned curries and called her twice just to hear the sound of her voice. She had returned to the green hills of Ireland.

Five days without Gwen, and the prospect of the approaching Roaring Forties filled me with dread. This section of the world's oceans had taken two of my good friends, and both were exceptional sailors. Yet I couldn't turn back. Again I called Gwen. After 178 seconds on the telephone, I found that my courage had returned. I told her that I loved her and knew that she was there for me.

I went from gales to not even a breeze. I sat on deck, watching the Southern Cross, a great speckling of stars low on the horizon and sometimes misted over by clouds. The moonrise was almost beyond words. Moon and all the stars in the sky, moon reflected in the sea, stars reflected in the sea, and mixed among the waves was the phosphorescence of a billion tiny sea organisms. Water sloshing over the stern entered the cockpit bright blue. The hull and sails were only dark shapes in this starlit and moonlit world that had no top or bottom. At last I had a breeze.

Fog greeted me on the following day, and I dropped to the south in search of stronger winds. There were e-mail comments and questions arriving from some of the No Barrier's schoolchildren. Many expressed hopes that I would not sink. Some hoped that I would win the race, as did I. And a few asked about my family: what was it like to see them again after a four-year absence?

Twelve days out, the barometer was falling, and my hip was beginning to ache. I was having trouble with my electrical system. I had passed Minoru Saito, but now he was catching up. "A boat and a star to steer her by." That day had passed. I needed more than stars or a compass. I needed electrical power to tell me where I was and where the weather was and to keep the boat on course.

Fourteen days and a sunset so spectacularly red, the sea, boat, circling birds, and even I, the skipper, were all tinted by its fiery glow. An ocean on fire. Better yet to say, "Red skies at night, sailor's delight." I filmed this sight with the video and the still cameras. I missed Gwen, who had gone off to Dublin, I presumed, to shop for Christmas. At one Netcare hospital I had met a seventeen-year-old waiting for a heart and lung transplant. I thought, *let that be his Christmas present.* I knew this and I knew that Gwen knew it, too, but, out here, the fact really comes home: there are some things in life that are worth having and then there is just stuff. Out here in the ocean there is very little stuff. Cherish the day. Seize the day, Harry Mitchell would have said. That was my final thought as the red, red sun extinguished itself in the blackening sea. Cherish the night as well.

Sixteen days out. It was my mother's birthday. She had witnessed three-quarters of that turbulent century. She had given my sister and me the gift of life. She continued to give to us—not only to us, but to thousands of other children. For forty-three years she taught biology and encouragement to the young of South Africa, and now in retirement she was a volunteer in the educational center at Kirstenbosch Botanical Gardens. Gwen and I had spoken of someday opening No Barrier schools in South Africa. The mighty oak would be our symbol, for oaks from little acorns grow. We would let Mom plant the first of these. I had sailed beyond the reach of telephone communications with either Gwen or her. By e-mail I sent a "Happy Birthday, Mom."

I had entered a no-man's-land of voiceless ocean, where I could hear only my own and the singers on the CDs. A bold blue sky gave way to a hairline moon that in the twilight three albatrosses appeared to circle. "The gulls way, and the winds way." A plastic bottle encased in barnacles floated by, plastic enduring forever.

Another boat had dropped from the race, that of my old OSTAR competitor George Stricker. I felt his disappointment. A day passed and another. I managed to make one nautical mile in four hours. That divides out to a fourth of a knot an hour. Is that better than being adrift? Thick fog collapsed on the boat, but before that curtain I'd seen the dorsal fin of a whale in the distance and a pair of seals. I began to read *The China Voyage,* by Tim Severin. I'd met Tim and one of his crew members, men who, in these pages, were drifting across the Pacific on a bamboo raft. While they drifted between the covers of the book, I drifted—and longed for the arrival of a predicted gale. I longed to hear Gwen's voice. One phone call and I'd have been happy. I wanted to call Tim Severin as well and tell him that at that moment I shared the frustration he once felt, except that, compared to his raft experience, I was relatively dry, well fed, and usually moving about four times faster than he had on that raft. I was cold and frustrated and a chatty e-mail from Gwen brightened my mood only a bit.

Twenty days out, I'd entered a true no-man's-land, a section of the race's path so remote, I was beyond the reach of search and rescue sent out from either South Africa or Australia. For help I could count only on Minoru, who, with a stronger boat and an attitude that at times now seemed irrational and dangerous, had stayed far to the south, and on Neil Hunter, who fortunately was just behind me. Twenty days out, I had my gale. Twenty nights out, a sudden gibe crashed the boat out of control. I had broken a control line on the wind vane, and what followed was a ghastly struggle with sails and screwdriver-enforced adjustments. Returning to the cabin, I tried turning the heater, which I had rebuilt, to a maximum discharge, but it was already there, and now with a black billowing of smoke, it halted altogether. Enough. Enough, for the next day is Christmas. Ho-ho-ho.

The wind had been gusting as high as 50 knots, and the waves were now raised to three-story apartment buildings. I reduced sails to a minimum, only enough to maintain steerage, and still I had roared down one wave at a record, for me, of 19.8 knots. I was scared, willing to make a deal with God or the devil to get me out of that mess. I faced my fear, though, for there are no deals. Then the winds shifted, and, wedged tight into my bunk, I took three knockdowns. Christmas dinner was a bar of chocolate, supplemented by Christmas gift treats from schoolchildren and other well-wishers. I recorded all this with the video. This was the first Christmas Gwen and I had spent apart in six years. I repaired the heater again. Water had somehow gotten into the exhaust.

A bad night followed with more knockdowns and a boiling sea. The boat tossed, agitated as if in a washing machine, an angry washing machine. One surf lasted over thirty seconds, the longest I'd encountered. Surely it was some mountainous sea—some Himalayan peak of a sea—and if I had broached, the boat would have certainly rolled over. As I returned from changing a sail, a wave broke into the boat, soaking my bedding and clothing. I was thankful the heater was working.

Four days of this followed, and finally the sea eased to a lumpy gray, a rain-pricked and drab hillscape, a wilderness. I managed to boil two eggs and fixed a cup of hot chocolate. I passed the time reading *Madiba,* an excellent biography of Nelson Mandela, written for the young. I worked on my own manuscript, completing the story of my own journey up to my arrival in Ireland. For this leg of the race I'd reached the halfway point, with South Africa and New Zealand at equal distance. I had to move eastward, for to the east was the satellite's path and hence phone contact with Gwen and my family. I had begun to write of Ireland.

Gwen and I were entering our eighth year together. On board I celebrated the New Year by disassembling and reassembling the troublesome heater. No champagne. The heater once again was broken.

Days passed. My feet stayed wet and had begun to tingle, as if stuck by many pins and needles, especially the left one, as there was a hole in that boot. I kept the boot on. I had been ignoring this wet-boot problem and, having no choice, continued to ignore it. I stayed below deck whenever I could, reading and listening to music on tape. Over and over again I listened to Flatley's "Lord of the Dance" because it reminded me of Ireland and of Gwen. I listened over and over to Michael Jackson's "I'm Bad" because it offered pure escapism, and escaping from the present was also very important. I sailed back inside the satellite phone-coverage area and began speaking to Gwen again.

My left foot began to hurt even more, and the pins and needles were being replaced with numbness. I still hadn't taken off my boots. I hadn't changed my clothes either. I knew I stunk, but there was nobody to offend but myself. Finally I entered waters at least a degree or two warmer and decided to give myself a proper washing. I took off the boot, and I'd never smelled anything so rotten. I took off my left sock and the toenail came with it. I remember saying, "Oh, crap." The flesh was peeling from that toe. I e-mailed a digital photograph of the foot to the fleet doctor in Boston. My high school classmates had given me dozens of books on tape. I happened to be listening to *Into Thin Air,* by Jon Krakauer, which dealt with the 1996 Mount Everest expedition. That fit perfectly. The doctor rang back with the news that I had trench foot, a mild form of frostbite. Since I had no heater, again, his advice was to sail north at once, for I needed to get warm, but that would have put me a thousand miles or more behind and I'd never reach New Zealand in time for the next start. "All right, then," he told me, "drink lots of hot fluids and foods and stay off the deck." I got in the bunk and waited for the pins and needle feeling to return. I'd be getting better when the foot started once again to "hurt like hell."

Word came that Minoru's distress beacon had been activated, and as I was closest to him, I plotted a new course—south, not north. Twenty hours should put me there. False alarm, though. His beacon had loosened in its mount and then gotten wet and activated.

Over the phone, I spoke with my breakfasting Rotary Club in Charleston, while the boat steered herself among fickle winds. To stay warm, I remained below in complete boredom and listened to the rest of the *Into Thin Air* tape.

Compared to the Everest climbers, I actually had it pretty good. Then I got an e-mail from one of the Netcare patients I'd visited. The son of a hospital matron, he was waiting for a heart transplant. His condition had improved. I also received an e-mail from a hospital worker. Her husband had stomach cancer, and she was asking for my prayers. I responded to him, urging that he have faith and make the most of his remaining life. Whatever my condition, I still had control of my destiny, a freedom not given to those in hospital beds, especially those with terminal illnesses. Actually, I felt guilty in a way. The distresses I was suffering were self-inflicted.

Still, I was suffering. The frostbitten foot was healing, and the pins and needles were back in full force. I returned to the deck to soak in the sun. Once more, Minoru and I had drawn within sight, for one brief glimpse. I was determined to pass him. Once more this was our own "race within a race."

We were entering the Tasman Sea. Only weeks before, sailors in the annual Sydney-to-Hobart race had been caught by extreme weather here, and six sailors had died—professional racers from all over the world. No such storm greeted us, only much needed strong winds, and I helmed both day and night. Surfing at times to speeds greater than eighteen knots, the boat threw up not only rooster tails at the stern, but great wings of spray from beneath her belly. Plus the sun was out. Warmth, blessed warmth, for the first time in six weeks; I could strip completely. Like five-foot platters, sunfish floated on the surface. They flopped about searching for jellyfish meals. In contrast to the purposefully graceful dolphins, they seemed comically clumsy, each an odd, flattened disc with a waving dorsal fin. The sunfish flopped, the dolphins leaped, and hundreds of birds circled above. I closed on Minoru. I was racing again.

We were entering the great "Tasmanian Parking Lot" when the hull struck something, perhaps a plank. There was no apparent damage and on the day following absolutely no wind. Eight hundred miles from the finish line, I was drifting and practically next to me was Minoru Saito. We talked on the radio and mutually cursed. Where were the fierce winds? The answer: this stretch of sea is notorious. It's either fluky winds or else you're having your nuts kicked out. We had the fluky winds. Birds were landing on the water and swimming around our boats. They swam past and seemed to be taunting us. Actually, I could swim faster than I was moving. I'd dropped from one hundred miles a day to twenty. I was frustrated and helpless. Then I got angry, as there was still no wind and nothing I could do about it. I would rather have a storm than that. I shouted, "What am I doing out here? Am I nuts. Please let this end!" A puff of wind and I set the spinnaker. I overtook Minoru and then stopped. Then he got a puff and overtook me and stopped. We stared at each other. I decided I should have stayed south. I stomped around the deck. I now had two good feet under me, and I could stomp. Minoru reported that he couldn't get his engine started, and, with no way to charge his batteries, his refrigerator wouldn't work.

Like me, Minoru had a minimum of sponsors and to help him out, Les Phillips gave him provisions as well. On our level of the race, there was still that sort of camaraderie. I told him to drift over toward me and I'd take some of Les's frozen meat off his hands. "No. No! Cannot do that!" There were limits to camaraderie. We sat there. Finally the weather broke.

Of course, it broke with a vengeance, going from calm to a tropical cyclone. We had winds in our faces that started at fifty-five knots and moved up. Huge seas were coming off the deep water and onto the continental shelf. Then the winds turned 180 degrees. Again we were surfing. I lashed myself into the cockpit with two harnesses and set off with the boat bucking like a wild horse, a runaway wild horse. The autopilot couldn't handle this. I had to drive. I had eaten the last of Gwen's curries and was forced to eat "manufactured ones." And Minoru was now ahead of me. Both were intolerable situations. I was three hundred miles from the finish and determined to arrive there ahead of him. I plowed through waves, rollers that come over the deck and buried the mast, buried the boom and hit me full in the face. I leaned into each wave, stretched against the harnesses. If I didn't, my back would be broken. I gagged continually from the water forced into my nose. These were the seas that had recently claimed so many lives.

Enough. I made a short tack in toward the New Zealand coast. I'd pop in behind the island and then head for this leg's finish line, the same strategy that had just sent the leading boat onto the shore and out of the race. I didn't plan to sleep and would see that sort of trouble coming. I hoped that, and hoped correctly. When the next positioning report came out from race control, I was thirty-one miles ahead of Minoru. He couldn't believe it. How had I jumped ahead of him? He was sputtering over the radio. A broken English sputter. I didn't bother to tell him that I was well up in a bay that I now had to tack out of. The race coordinates are taken as the crow flies—or gull in this case—and I couldn't jump a headland. He beat me to the finish line, but he beat me only by one hour.

21

LEG THREE

hough we'd raced seventy-nine hundred miles, Minoru hadn't thrown the rotten meat overboard. I was told that the spectators could smell him coming. Those helping him from the boat had become sick. The smell had come on slowly as he sailed. Somehow, he'd managed to ignore it.

Though second to my friend, at least my entry into the harbor was a bit more heroic. I crossed the finish line wearing my favorite green socks, very lucky lime-green socks. Crisp white shorts and lime-green socks and a beautiful young woman, an Irish lass with ice cream, were waiting for me. She shouted, "What took you so long?" Which translated as "You're alive. You made it this far." Maybe she was thinking, "What am I doing here?"

I had two weeks of rest in Auckland. It's called "the City of Sails" and with good reason. The masts along the docks resembled a bamboo grove, and it had been that way even before New Zealand won the America's Cup in 1995. Now the port was concerned with retaining that honor. We could see these tremendous sheds holding the entries. Serious business. One boat syndicate apparently had sixty million dollars in funding. All of this money and organization was going into boats that race for two or three weeks in relatively calm water. In comparison Mark Schrader referred to us as "the warm-up," though I doubt he meant that.

I did get a good boost when I tried to renew my American visa. The embassy called and said I'd have to apply in person and to ask for the deputy ambassador. I thought there must be a problem but couldn't imagine what. I entered the embassy after hours, was shown into a room, and waited. Then the deputy ambassador entered with my passport in her hand. She said, "I follow your racing, and I just had to meet you."

I got a knock, as well. At one of the parties, I was told that Brad Van Liew had bet another of our competitors that I would never make it to New

Zealand. Brad was a hard-partying Californian and by my standards well-off financially. We were, in fact, from completely different worlds though trying to sail around the same one. Neither Brad nor this other gambler (even better financed) thought I had any business in the race and apparently weren't shy about saying so.

Gwen and I were patching up our relationship and going to parties almost every night, with none of that stress we'd endured at Cape Town. Our hosts, Ann and Trevor Hackett, were the best imaginable. Trevor's company, KZ Marine, became a sponsor, and Trevor took over the supervision of many of the repairs. A couple of gashes in the hull got patched over, the keel bolts were tightened, and new bearings went into the rudder. Shrouds were replaced. Nothing was left to chance. I even visited a dentist. I had many distractions: I recall an Asian market with cheap and exotic, colorful and delicious, foods; and Malcolm had shown up from Iceland. He planned to stay three days but met a New Zealand woman and entered into a great romantic adventure that lasted a month or better.

What really stood out, though, were the disturbing conversations I had with Minoru at some of the gatherings. Over the years we'd grown closer and closer, and now he approached me in this buzz of happy partyers and said, "Neal, Harry calling me." Of course, I was already guessing what he meant, for back on my hard-pumping Atlantic crossing I'd heard from Harry Mitchell myself. Still, I asked, "What do you mean?" He said, "Harry calling me. I go to him." Minoru intended to sail to Harry Mitchell's last-known coordinates. This was way down at fifty-six degrees south and not even midway across to the Horn. I said, "That's suicidal. You're crazy." He said, "If die, I die."

On several occasions we continued this discussion, and for the first time he revealed that he'd had a Japanese girlfriend, a young woman whom he loved. Just before he'd sailed off on his second BOC Challenge, she'd given him a hand-stitched pouch that hung around his neck. He always wore this beneath his shirt. It held his heart pills—and you could say his heart, as well. She, too, was a racer, and while he was gone, she had crewed in the Whitbread Round the World competition. She'd been washed overboard and lost. He was getting old, and he'd lost both Harry Mitchell and his lover. Now Harry was calling. "I go!" he said.

Maori warriors gave us to a traditional send off. On the downside, these warriors and their women are at the bottom of the social structure and face challenges similar to those of the blacks in South Africa or the Gypsies in Ireland. They, too, are a proud people and have a particularly rich heritage. For the ceremony they were dressed in native costume, the huge guys covered in tattoos, and they would put their faces right against ours, and you didn't know if you were going to be bitten or licked. This is to scare off the evil spirits and welcome in the good. Finally you rub noses. One stunning girl rubbed my nose and instead of leaving, I wanted to stay. But for a send-off, Gwen had already treated me even better.

A grim beginning, for an hour after the start, a small plane crashed into the ocean. Ahead of me I saw a helicopter flying a search pattern and several powerboats arriving. There was fuel on the water. I offered to search, but by then the two bodies had been recovered, and the search was over. Only in Punta would I learn that these were journalist friends of Giovanni Soldini.

I settled down. New Zealand was sorry to see me go. So sorry it took an entire day to sink the coastline. Night came, and a perfect moon rose in a perfectly cloudless and windless night.

Four days out, the current carried me across the International Date Line, then carried me back over it. I gained a day and lost a day. Just like life. It doesn't always go the way we want, but in the end we find it works out. I crossed the line again and stayed across.

Five nights out, I dreamed that an associate of the No Barriers Education Foundation was giving me advice. We were in Cape Town, and as he was speaking, a scriptwriter was trying to incorporate the discussion into a motion picture. The dream was so vivid, I awoke wondering where they'd all gone and how I'd gotten into my present situation.

Valentine's Day: Gwen was traveling the North Island of New Zealand with her cousin Malcolm. The valentines of my younger days were mostly married now. I had a lot of making up to do with Gwen. Cold nights had returned.

On February 15 word came that Isabelle Autissier's distress beacon had activated. Though days away, even I began to calculate my position in reference to her own. Was she alive or dead? Practically everyone racing was emotionally connected to this spirited woman. Another sun rose before we heard that Giovanni had rescued her from her flipped boat.

One of the two sailors who bet I wouldn't make it to New Zealand had already lost his mast—not Brad, but the one with the most ego and financial backing. Of course, it was tempting to say, "What goes around, comes around." It really was. Still, I don't want to believe some sort of God is keeping score. And I'm not one to risk bad karma. Negative thoughts have never been my thing. Racing mishaps simply aren't arranged so. Out of the sixteen boats starting the race, only nine remained. Isabelle Autissier, who was one of the most considerate sailors I knew, a woman who never spoke a bad word about anybody, had flipped over in this particularly tricky approach to the cape. (Her rescue was accomplished by another considerate sailor—and a true gentleman.) If you don't push, you don't win. There was such a thing as just plain luck, and when you're slipping along at thirty knots, you need a healthy dose of it.

With thirty-five hundred miles to go to the Horn, I heard from Gwen that she was going camping alone in the New Zealand countryside. I was doing live radio programs, stitching sails, and once more disassembling the heater. Another day passed, and I discovered a stowaway, a Carolina palmetto bug, otherwise called a cockroach. So far it was live and let live. Once more I'd traveled beyond the reach of telephone service. With infinite patience and by following e-mailed instructions, I got the heater blasting out hot air and smoke once more, certain proof that in life there are no barriers, only solutions.

Two weeks at sea: I reached a decision. As captain, I was judge, jury, and jailer of this craft, and in that capacity I decided to let my stowaway cockroach (named "Cockie") stay aboard. More good karma. Anyway, he was too hard to catch. Actually he was too well hidden. There were conditions, though. He was not to interfere with the running of the vessel or attempt mutiny—or produce companions.

Twenty days out, I dreamed of steak and a hot bath and, of course, Gwen at my side. It was a waking dream about to be answered in an excellent fashion. I was in the cockpit. With three reefs in the mainsail and the headsail poled out, the boat was barreling along, riding those giant Southern Ocean swells. There was a low mist. There's always a low mist, but at least on this day I had a good half mile of visibility, and, looking straight up the mast, I could even see a vague blueness, a suggestion of the sky. For the Southern Ocean this was a very nice day. Then I looked astern and saw something on a wave cap. Something? I looked back and glimpsed it again. Then nothing. I kept looking and yes, something faint and white was definitely dancing along the tops of the waves. It was a fairy. An Irish fairy. Was I losing my mind? Or was this merely a hallucination? I kept watching the fairy. She came off a wave cap and danced upward, fell back almost to the water and then jumped back into the sky. Closer and closer. A feather! Finally, I realized my fairy was only a feather. Albatrosses and other birds had often been circling the boat. Here was a snow-white bird feather dancing like a ballerina from wave cap to wave cap. It passed me. It overtook the boat and went dancing off toward South America.

That was a highlight of my Southern Ocean travels. An Irish fairy had blessed me and departed. Everything was right in my life. I was aligned once more. I'd been blessed by a feather.

Meanwhile Minoru was, as he promised, keeping well to the south. Neil and I had been watching a horrendous weather system approaching him and tried to communicate. We could hear him, sometimes only every tenth word or so, but we knew he was alive, and he was receiving our calls. Then we heard nothing for a couple of days. By then Neil was well to the north. He'd been ahead of me for the first nine hundred miles but now had decided on a conservative race. Plus I suspected he had a few bottles of wine on board. Like Mike Richie, my old and honored friend from Newport days, Neil had opted for a comfortable crossing. Not so with Minoru. He was a fierce competitor, and, in a sense, it was Minoru that I was racing around the world. I suppose I felt him to be my responsibility. I set my own course further to the southward. If Minoru needed rescuing, I would be the one to do it.

Minoru survived. He'd gone through hundred-mile-an-hour winds and horrendous waves. "Bloody weather! . . . Crazy winds!" Though the message was garbled, I knew he'd survived. Gradually, his signal grew stronger, and when we were finally able to have a conversation, he confided that he had seen Harry Mitchell. "Harry not want me," he said. "Harry tell me not come." Of course, having met Harry under similar conditions, I understood what that meant. Still, I was worried that Minoru might just walk off the stern at this point. Not that he was emotionally unstable. He was as sane as any of the rest of us, and I don't mean that as a joke. Minoru had a deep spiritual connection to the world, one that the rest of us envied. That didn't mean suicide wasn't an option, but the Japanese warrior sailed on. I set my course back toward the calmer northern waters, and for a few days, at least, I got plenty of sleep and enjoyed the cruise.

Gwen was returning now to Ireland. By e-mail she briefly mentioned exploring Jakarta, Indonesia, and Singapore on her own. I could tell she was pleased by her success as an independent traveler. I was happy for her. Still, the South Pacific hadn't been all the travel brochures suggested. Right then it seemed a bit cold, wet, and unfriendly. As they say in those tropical isles, "The wind was blowing dogs off their chains." By e-mail my No Barriers students were debating the fate of Cockie. Does he come along or swim for shore? Actually, I'm not sure I could catch him, unless the open-hatch drenching I occasionally took floated him to the cabin's sloshing surface— which it didn't.

The time had come to turn the corner and head south. To approach close to the coast of Chile meant risking the frequent southwesterly winds that in rough weather could push me up onto the rocks. The trick would be somehow to slip around the Horn with the least amount of risk, and I can't claim that I managed it all that well.

On March 6 I wished Gwen a happy twenty-sixth birthday. Four years before we had celebrated her birthday, or failed to celebrate it, while fighting a gale together in the approach to Punta. Eleven days later, I had bought her dinner with ice cream for dessert. Gwen was my best and most loyal friend. To see her smile—but it was impossible to wish myself ashore.

Another day in what the old sailors called Godless country, a setting so bleak not even God himself dwelled there. From the roaring forties I passed into the screaming fifties. There was a rip in the genoa, the electric bilge pump failed, was rebuilt and still failed. I pumped out by hand. Then fixed it. The heater also failed. I stripped it and found unburnt gummed up fuel. I hated to use the word but only "hopeless" described the heater. I had to fall back on the hot-water bottles and thermal gloves the No Barriers children had thoughtfully placed aboard. I was closing on the Horn, a landmark that my entire adult life had been spent getting to. My favorite cap had gone overboard. My ears were freezing. My fingers were already frozen, numb from the cold.

It was March 11, and I downloaded the weather map. A system was headed my way. It didn't appear too bad, and, anyway, I was already pointed south. Still, intuition told me otherwise. Sure enough, the next report had the storm increasing in intensity and heading south as well. Gusts of fifty-five knots were forecast, which down there could be ugly. I kept going. The barometer kept falling, quickly reaching what had been predicted for the next day. I should have been feeling winds and was not. A bad sign. After lunch the forecast winds began, and I shortened sail, taking the mainsail down to three reefs and shortening up on the headsail. My hip started hurting, a particularly biting pain. I was certain then that trouble was coming. Minoru was already around the Horn, but Neil Hunter was behind me and a bit to the north. We both agreed that the forecast was wrong, but he thought me overly concerned.

In less than two hours the barometer fell another ten millibars. I lashed the mainsail down and shortened the headsail even more. Thirty-five knot winds. I was scared. What was I doing here? If I got out of this storm, I promised I wouldn't tempt fate anymore. I returned to my chart table. I was three hundred miles from the Horn and two hundred miles off the coast of Chile. I set the GPS navigation guard zone on the closest rocks.

Did I have enough room to get by? Assuming seventy knot winds were behind me, even running under bare pole, I'd be making six knots, which would clear me around the Horn. At sunset the bottom fell out of the barometer, thirty millibars lower than predicted. I sent an e-mail message to Gwen. I said, "We have a problem here." At dark came sixty-knot winds. I was running under bare pole with the wind vane steering. I put on a double harness. The winds gusted to seventy knots, and I started taking knockdowns. I sensed a huge sea building, a shift of motion in the boat. I was helming and began to override the wind vane. Still we took knockdowns. Pitch-black dark, but that wasn't a surprise. I hadn't seen the sun all day. By midnight the winds were gusting to eighty-four knots, the worst I'd ever seen. The boat was totally out of control. She was surfing on monster waves, waves unseen and unheard. The wind shrieked through the rigging, squealed and howled like an angry alley cat. The tips of the waves were blown horizontally into my face, assuming there was a horizontal.

I've heard others say, "thank goodness, it was pitch-black dark." If I had been able to see my actual circumstances, I'd have lost heart. I didn't want to see. On the other hand, in such visual isolation, there were no reference points, no horizontal, no vertical, just what was perceived. Under these conditions the imagination could be as dangerous as the sea. I began to come off those waves at what must be a forty-five-degree angle. Pitch poling seemed likely. The boat would go end over end. I couldn't leave the tiller. The wind vane couldn't do this alone. Under bare poles the boat was surfing at twelve to fourteen knots—faster speeds than I'd ever sailed her. I was headed due east toward the rocks of the South American coast. That means that if the storm lasted another twenty-four hours, I was finished.

I'd been over the charts. There are channels among those islands, but I'd never find them under those conditions. I was trying to push the boat southward, or at least suggesting to her that we push that way.

In this black night, I came up close to the South American coast, and the Horn was another forty-five minutes of latitude below me. It's best to round the Horn, not to bounce off it. Still, if I turned directly to the south, the seas would be broadside, and the boat would roll—roll over, and over, and over. The path was narrow and my control limited.

I felt each wave pick up the boat and then pass under her. We were of no more concern to that ocean than a paper airplane sent out into the stratosphere. An incredible feeling. I was going as fast as I'd ever gone in a race. On the one hand I was frightened, and on the other I was feeling this passionate joy; and on the third hand I was feeling totally at peace with myself. A rush of pure adrenalin in my bloodstream like I'd never experienced had coupled with the calm of someone who thought they were perched on the top of the world. Then there was the anticipation of seeing Cape Horn.

Well, not quite the top. Every so often a wave came along, and I felt the boat rising but not rising as it had on the previous wave. I knew then that I was inside a tunnel of water, and in a moment I would feel the wave break. It was breaking behind me and in front of me and then straight on top of me. Totally submerged in the cockpit, I held my breath. Overhead were five or ten feet of water.

On and on this went. The boat was nothing more than a surfboard, and the waves were like those pipelines the Hawaiian surfers ride through. I was inside the tube. I was gagging and gasping for breath half the time. I had on a double harness but no life jacket. A life jacket would only have tried to pop me up to the top of these waves. And in the midst of all that I was suddenly going fifteen to sixteen knots, then seventeen, eighteen, and the boat was over on her side—a total knockdown, a 180-degree inversion. I was half underneath the boat and clinging to a web of rope that was twisting around like spaghetti. The mast was in the water, the keel in the air.

That's the closest I have ever come to being dead, to getting death's grim wink, and yet it was also the closest I've ever felt to being absolutely alive, being so alive that death had somehow become incidental. Not that I planned on dying. That sudden burst of speed had been caused by the lashing of the mainsail giving way. Up the mast went the sail. Only seven or eight feet had been able to rise, and over I'd gone.

As the boat righted herself, I realized I had to go forward on the deck. I unclipped from the cockpit and for the briefest second had only one harness to trust. Then both lines were on the jack line that ran from bow to stern. This could be done, as long as I didn't flip over as it was being done. A knockdown now and my life really was over. I crawled forward, was blown forward actually, and I remember having the odd notion that I was like a rag doll I'd once seen tethered in the back of a speeding pickup truck. I could see myself fluttering that way. Then I had the mast in my arms, and with the wind holding me vertical against it, I started pulling the sail back down. Lashings held the remainder, but that loose canvas was enough to destroy the boat. I pulled on it hand over hand, the force of the wind pulling in opposition. I was using such force that my fingers began to bleed and the sail began to rip. I had a torn mainsail. My headsail was already shredding. Big challenges were coming up.

A couple of days before, I'd considered slipping behind an island and changing that headsail, but a lull in the weather had allowed me to switch mid-ocean. I had put my big number-one racing headsail on the rolling furling system. A brand new and very heavy sail, and now it was shredding. What was in the locker? I went on mentally switching around sails, all the while clawing the mainsail the rest of the way down and lashing it in place. Then I headed back to the cockpit. I might as well have been climbing Mount Everest, for the wind was against me now, not only holding me back but blowing into the hood of the foul-weather gear. When I raised my head, the hood snapped like a hangman's noose, and the spray struck my face like sandblasting—sleet blasting. On my knees and hand over hand, I hauled myself back into the cockpit, a fifteen-foot journey that felt like fifteen miles, and as soon as I was there, over the boat went. Up she popped again.

I was safe. I'd made it to the mast and back, and it was only then I realized how cold I'd gotten. That foul-weather slicker of mine wasn't designed for total immersion. I was soaked and beginning to shiver, to shake, which was how I knew that I was cold. What I was actually feeling was the same incredible adrenalin rush that'd kept me alive in the last few minutes, that and nothing else.

That high stayed with me. Hour after hour, I sat in the cockpit, clinging to the tiller, and guiding the boat from wave to wave. After thirty-five knockdowns I stopped counting. Thirty-five knockdowns, and then what's the point? And for those 35 I'd drastically altered my definition of a knock-down. Until reaching Cape Horn a knockdown might have the mast barely touch the water. Now, a knockdown was having the mast and boom totally under and the keel in the sky. Anything else didn't count. Of course, I was expecting any one of those hits to bring on a 360-degree roll. With a boat like mine I'd have little chance of keeping my mast. Oddly enough, I'd stopped worrying about pitch poling. Going end over end would definitely dismast me, but I'd decided that if I hadn't pitch poled by now, I wasn't going to. I'm not sure that was a completely logical view of my situation, but then hypothermia was coming on, and, with it, my ability to make judgments and act on them was lessening.

I realized, finally, that I had to go below. If I stayed topside the cold would have me. I'd be too numb to think or act. I had to get warm, or at least warmer. Engaging the Monitor wind vane, I sat there, and, free from my correction, the boat went on wave after wave. As I watched the instrument panel, the glowing dials showing the boat speed and the wind strength were just numbers now, ones difficult to associate with my surroundings. As I held on and watched, the boat suffered knockdown after knockdown, yet each time she managed to right herself. By letting her go like that, I was gaining some suggestion of peace of mind. I was going down below to sleep, and the boat would have to sail herself. Would she look after me? After eight or nine more knockdowns, I decided she would, and, at that point, in middle of all the excitement and fear, the suspension between those two extremes, I remembered what the media in South Africa and the yachtsmen in South Africa, what all those critics in South Africa had said about my boat—she was "a floating coffin." That night would be the telling. Out loud, I said, "Tonight they're either going to be right or wrong." I went below.

That meant opening the washboards—and finding a foot of water over the cabin floor. The force of the seas had been continually squirting water around the edge of the washboard, and gallon by gallon I was in the process of sinking. Once through the hatch, I slammed the boards back in place and immediately was thrown to the lee side. A knockdown, and naturally I was thrown leeward. Several hours before, I'd lashed the boom to the starboard. With the boat biased in that direction, she'd at least fall to the right, which was south, and I had to go south if I was ever to round the Horn.

Plus there was less of a surprise, a better opportunity to brace, if I knew in which direction I was flipping.

Fortunately, I'd learned a valuable lesson in 1996, when I'd pumped by hand across half the Atlantic Ocean. After that I'd rigged out with a large electric pump, the same one I'd just repaired. I flipped the switch, and within four or five minutes I had the water out. Of course, more was coming in with each monster wave, gallons and gallons squirting around the edge of the washboards, but the pump could handle that, which left me free to boil some water. I really didn't have much choice, for the only way to warm myself was the hot-water bottle. Still suited up in my foul-weather gear, I scooped up a kettle full of salt water from the bilge, braced it on the gas stove, and braced myself in the galley beside it. There seemed to be some rhythm to the knockdowns. I'd timed a few, and they appeared to be coming about ten minutes apart. I knew I'd need longer than that to boil water and the last thing I needed was to have almost-boiling water flying around the cabin. I lit the stove, and that alone began to warm the cabin, but I'd still need the hot-water bottle. I held the kettle in place for five or six minutes and then took it off and cut off the stove. One hand clinched on the grab rail and the other holding the kettle, I waited. Over went the boat, then up again. I lit the stove and put the water on again. I did that twice. Two knockdowns, and I had boiling water and filled up the bottle.

My Neoprene gloves and the hot-water bottle had been gifts from the children and teachers of Springfield Elementary School back in South Carolina. The hot-water bottle had even been signed by the teachers. To this day, I don't think they know how special those gifts were. At that point I was hypothermic: that hot-water bottle saved my life.

I stripped off all my clothing, and, wedging my backside against the hull, I pulled my sopping-wet sleeping bag over me, placed the hot-water bottle against my chest, and went to sleep. But only for a minute or so, for soon the boat was on her side and I was thrown from the hole I'd burrowed into my wet mattress. My face was pressed against the hull, and I was pelted by the bilge and the objects floating in it. The chart table and the computer were still bolted down. Everything else seemed to have come loose and was floating and flying free. Still, I did manage to sleep. For six hours I lay braced in that bunk. I didn't know how strong the wind was blowing. I didn't care. I didn't know how big the seas got. I didn't care. Hey,

I was alive. That was the level I was operating on. I've drawn another breath. Imagine that.

At dawn up went the barometer. As fast as it had fallen, up it came. The winds dropped. My mast measured 63 feet. The seas passing by were far taller than that. I remember looking up and saying out loud, "Yep, that wave is taller than my mast." And that was just the seas, the white water. The swells themselves were easily 150 feet. And as I'd suspected, there were tunnels of water. I could see them. I sat in the cockpit and guided with the tiller. Every so often, I looked along the side of a wave, and I saw up into its middle. In the dark I'd been surfing those pipelines. I should have died. I went below and sent Gwen an e-mail. It began, "Dear Gwen, I am alive."

That was March 12, and I've come to think of it as my second birthday. I knew from that day on I would never wake up and not be able to smile— no matter what. They call it "the present" because that's exactly what it is, a present, a gift that we so often take for granted. What else I knew was that I built from scratch a boat that could carry me just about anywhere and I had a great deal to be proud of. She wasn't a floating coffin. Far from it.

On the second night following the storm, I saw the blink of the Cape Horn light. Blips. Bright heartthrobs on the horizon. With dawn approaching, that light grew bigger and bigger. Up above me in the rest of the world were six billion people. I'm down here alone at the bottom of the world. At daylight I saw steep, treeless peaks, a rugged salt-blighted, wind-bitten piece of eroding mountain, a sight that had fascinated and plagued sailors for at least four centuries. Less than three hundred people had sailed by the Horn alone, and I was one. Except I was becalmed, more drifting by than sailing by, and totally in awe. The dreams were now my reality.

Thirty-five days out of Auckland and at last it was the Horn and me. Me and all those hundreds—no thousands of other people—who had made this moment possible: Joshua Slocum and a dozen more like him who showed the way; Richard Broadhead, who told a fourteen-year-old Cape Town boy he could circle the world; Harry Mitchell, who attempted the Horn twice and died on the third try. In memory of Harry I tossed a single earring into the sea. Gwen, my parents, Mama who raised me, all of them, along with eighteen years of risk, strategy, and planning involving so many people, had made this possible. "Thank you," I said out loud. And let me say it again now. "Thank you."

Before piling on more sail, a passing ship altered course for a closer look at me. It was outbound from Argentina, headed for South Korea. The officer asked how large my crew was. I told him, and he responded with a whistle and said, "So far south, such big seas, and alone?" Yes—except for all those just mentioned.

I was back in the warm Atlantic Ocean, and, of course, feeling more and more confident—and filled with joy. Minoru was just ahead, and since he had torn practically every sail, I was sure to overtake him. I chatted with Gwen for five or ten minutes every evening. She was in Ireland and preparing to fly to Punta del Este, Uruguay. It looked like I'd reach there a day ahead of her. I heard from the Hollywood film producer Gerry Li. He'd had an interesting and productive time with my parents, but the bulk of the film was still to be shot in Ireland.

I passed by the Falkland Islands. No sign of the stowaway roach. Did he round the cape? Perhaps a palmetto bug isn't the indestructible pet I was promised. Just at dusk I came upon a strange sight. A wall of fishing trawlers was working their way toward me—hundreds of boats, towing in a line two and three deep, miles and miles, outrigger to outrigger. I couldn't imagine a fish could find its way through all that webbing or that I could find my way through all those outriggers and then tack around what by then looked like a city of lights. Cape Town was somehow transported across the sea. For miles I sailed parallel to the fleet so that I could eventually get by it.

Two days from the finish line, I struck a sunning sunfish. I'd been below deck and heard a thud, the kind made by hull-busting flotsam, but, rushing on deck, I saw only the poor sunfish wallowing in my wake. Diamond-like scales glittered in the water, but it seemed uninjured, which was certainly my hope. The next morning the breeze freshened, and I felt secure enough to set the spinnaker. Still, I was on guard for more trawlers and any suggestion of bad weather, and, looking over the stern, I noticed some white water at one spot and then white water at another. Odd, but I was not taking chances. White water meant wind, and I pulled down the spinnaker and pulled up the headsail. That was not enough canvas to pass Minoru. I was determined to beat him but too concerned with freak storms to take a chance.

By now the white water was all over the place, and I realized it was approaching fast. But these weren't waves. I'd been looking at the leaping bodies of dolphins, thousands and thousands of dolphins, far more than I'd ever seen before. They covered the entire horizon at my stern and behind the front line were more and more. Finally, they caught up with me. They came by doing backflips, frontflips, rolls, every sort of jump possible. Perfection. This was a complement to my journey around the Horn and in some ways was just as memorable. I had something else fine to share with Gwen.

I could smell the land. Not a "clean" smell, but against the musty smell of my cabin, it was still a "good" smell. Actually, since my diving days, my sense of smell had diminished, but with a good breeze I could still smell the land. Four huge ships had passed within two miles of me. I took my electric razor apart, scratched away at the rusty innards. No "on-off" switch. Just slip in place the previously misplaced battery, and within minutes I'd made myself presentable for Gwen.

22

LEG FOUR

I reached Uruguay ten days ahead of Minoru and one day ahead of Gwen. The second time ever she hadn't been waiting for me. I popped the bottle of champagne but, without her there, found little joy in being a circumnavigator of the world. By now, though, she was on the bus coming from Buenos Aires, and in a couple of days we'd be riding with the gauchos on the plains. I sat in the yacht club, staring out the window in the direction of the bus station, and finally she was there, walking toward me, carrying her backpack. All that chestnut hair blowing in the South American wind.

This layover in Uruguay was nothing like the last. For one thing we now had money. Not much, but enough to eat in restaurants and to shop for a new CD player. Mine had quit. I had ten CDs I listened to continually, and I was having music withdrawal. They were Gwen's choices. Before I met her, I'd had different taste in music. She threw my collection out. We compromised and listened to what she liked.

Les Phillips and his son flew in from Charleston with spare parts. Les and Gwen were a team by now, and they went to work helping me repair the boat, but we played as well. Teddy Turner and his wife, Leslie, had arrived—they came on a private jet with his father, Ted Turner, and Jane Fonda—and we took time out to have four-hour lunches with Teddy and Leslie. I've got to admit it's hard to say no to "vulgar" living, to self-indulgent living when you've got good company sharing incredible meals that take hours to serve and consume. Especially if the boat's not back at the dock sinking or threatening to sink. The worse was behind us. I'd rounded the Horn, and this last leg could never knock me around like that. The boat was ready; I was ready.

Gwen and I met a Brazilian fashion designer. He rode his bicycle down to the dock and said, "Hey, how can I help?" Gwen followed the doings of the New York fashion houses and recognized his name. A delightful, down-to-earth guy, he carried us off to a small hotel restaurant set high on a hill-top, a place with only half a dozen tables and a view that stretched all the way to Brazil. That lunch lasted five hours and like the other Punta cele-brations was an extreme switch for me. On the boat I had Gwen's gourmet cooking but not in these portions. In Punta's restaurants, if I wanted another lamb chop all I had to do was ask. Four years before, we'd almost starved while in this port. We'd envied those who lived this way—but we'd had the simple pleasure of riding on the pampas. Now we couldn't find the time to ride. Instead of sleeping on the boat, we were at the yacht club.

Still, we did have some work to do on the boat, and Les tried to keep us focused on the job. Of course, Gwen worked, but she'd begun to ask how much longer this prepping would take. And just as often I was asking her to marry me. "When we get back to the states will you marry me?" She would say, "We'll talk about it later." She was preparing my meals for the last leg. At night we'd discuss the future. I wanted to enter the Vendée Globe in one of the high-tech craft and do it in a boat that had a chance of plac-ing first. She wanted that to happen. I wanted to continue my career as a motivational speaker, to work my way up to the five-thousand-dollar range. She told me I was worth more than that for I had experiences that few oth-ers could match. I said, "Marry me?" She said, "We'll talk about it later."

The approach of the final leg brought an excitement to the docks, a lit-eral "buzz." We took the boat out for a quick trial sail, stowed the gear, and topped off the water tanks. I was having trouble with the generator. The engine hadn't been serviced since Cape Town, and Les and I had to fine-tune it, or I'd have dead batteries and no electric pump or communications. That completed, I was filling jerry jugs with water, and Gwen asked, "Well, do you think you're ready to go to sea?" I said, "The boat's done."

She went up to the yacht club to use the restroom. That was at eleven in the morning. Minoru was tied up beside me, and we were kidding each other. Gwen was gone an hour. I found her in the yacht club living room, sitting with several others. I sat down beside her, and she said, "Let's take a walk." She went out ahead of me and leaned up against a palm. She said, "I'm leaving you." "You mean tomorrow," I said. After the race started, she'd be taking the bus out. She said, "No. I mean I'm leaving you. I don't want any part of this. Not anymore. I'm out of here." "What are you talking about?" Shocked almost voiceless, I was whispering frantically. "You can't just walk away from eight years together. Not like this." I was dumbfounded. "I want out," she said. "I brought your computers with me from Ireland. I brought your logbooks, your trophies, all the things you had in Ireland. I've put them in a travel bag and stashed that in the stern. I'm gone." She retrieved her backpack from the club living room. I went along, trying to reason with her. "Why?" I kept asking. She said, "I don't think you care about me anymore. I don't think this relationship is what you want anymore." I'd been asking her to marry me. Over the last eight years and especially over the last week, I'd been asking.

She walked off toward the bus station. The pack was under her arm; her beautiful hair was swinging across her shoulders. I realized then she'd been planning this for months. Even when we'd been making love, she'd been planning this. I took a step in her direction. She hadn't looked back. Not once.

Then I went back to the boat. I lay in the bunk. If she wanted a house with a white picket fence, I could manage that. If I had to choose between her and my racing career, then I'd choose her. She had an uncle in Argentina. She was probably headed there. If I followed her, though, took the next bus, and found her at her uncle's, then I'd miss the last leg of the race, a race I'd been working toward for eighteen years. And what if she couldn't be persuaded? Then I'd lose both the girl and the dream of the race.

After a couple of hours I found Les Phillips, who I trusted completely, and told him all that had happened. I kept saying, "I love her." He said, "If you want to go after her, I'll buy the tickets. If you think you can put this back together, I'll do anything you ask." I went off and found the race director, Mark Schrader. My relationship with him had become tense; he was under a lot of pressure. We went for a walk, and I told him Gwen had left, and I might go after her. I might not be at the starting line the next morning. As I'd done with Les, I went over all the options with him, tried to understand things from her point of view—and from my own. And in the end it came down to this: Do I abandon an eighteen-year dream by trying to salvage an eight-year relationship? I wouldn't have gotten this far without Gwen. I didn't doubt that. All the other contributions put together didn't match hers. If I followed her to Argentina, would she change her mind? I really didn't know.

I had less than twelve hours to decide.

I chose the race. The next morning Les and his son came on board. They'd be seeing me off. For the first time since the 1992 OSTAR, Gwen was missing. At every start she'd been the last one off the boat. I'd give her a big hug and a long kiss, then help her down into the inflatable that took off the shore crew. I'd hold her hand to the very last second. When I'd reach the next port, that hand was the first thing I'd touch.

I let Les and his son off the boat an hour and half early. Les said, "The best thing you can do now is cross that starting line first." I agreed. I needed to focus on that line and ignore the bottomless pit that represented the entire rest of my life. I concentrated and put myself in that solo state of mine. I focused on the tip of the bow and its relationship to the starting pins and aligned myself with a range on shore. To be first, I'd have to cross within ten seconds of the gun. The ten-minute gun fired. I approached the line, turned back for the five-minute gun, and was at the line for the one-minute countdown, the longest minute of my life, for I was facing the notion of being alone not only on the boat, but simply and plainly alone. I crossed the line five seconds or so behind the gun.

First away, I stayed with the fleet until we rounded the first mark and headed out into the Atlantic. We turned north, and depression hit me. It was as if every good and positive emotion had drained away. I was fearful at the very thought of Gwen. Suddenly, I just wanted to sleep. I stopped caring about the race. I stopped caring about the boat. All I could think about was the two of us apart and what I could have done to keep this from happening. Two days before I'd assumed we'd be together forever.

That night the barometer took a radical fall. A storm came out of the northwest and it was horrendous. Caught off guard, I tore sails, and a crashing tack took out the radio antenna. Both mishaps could have easily been avoided. Even worse, I didn't care. Still, I'd been lucky to escape more damage. In the same storm Brad Van Liew had lost his mast and was headed back to Punta. Though Brad had been belittling my own efforts, news of his misfortune only increased my depression.

I could head inshore and short tack up the Brazilian coast, but to pick my way past the points and fishing boats, I'd have to stay on deck. Or I could set the wind vane and head offshore, which I did. Instead of coming on deck when the wind shifted to the south, I just said, to hell with it and stayed in the bunk.

I lay in the bunk asking myself over and over again, "Why? Why? Why?" What had I done? What had she done? How could we drift so far apart? All that night, all the next day, I lay in the bunk. By then the boat was pointing southeast, heading toward South Africa and straight away from the finish line. For two days I sailed out of the race. Ten minutes on deck and I'd have been back on course. I didn't care. For the first time in my life I was totally down. I didn't care if I lived or died. A freighter could hit me. A rogue wave would be a relief. From the bunk I could see the light on the e-mail flashing. I knew that would be Race Control asking, "Where are you going?" I ignored them.

Donald Crowhurst had sailed alone in the 1968 Golden Globe race. Instead of circling the earth, he stayed in the Atlantic and radioed in fabricated positions. To win, all he had to do was sail back to England, but he couldn't face what he'd done. He walked off the stern of his boat. They found the boat later. With that in mind, I finally went on deck, and it wasn't to change course. I sat in the cockpit and thought about taking my own life. I could walk off the stern of my boat. That was an option I seriously considered.

I'd spent years speaking to schoolchildren and to adults about the importance of a positive attitude. In all those talks I'd been using myself as a model. That thought alone was enough to put suicide from my mind, but, in addition, I had family and friends that were a vital part of my life. What right did I have to bring such an unnecessary tragedy into their lives? I turned the boat around.

Of course, by then the winds had completely died out.

Raising all the sail possible, I tacked to the north. I hadn't done a log entry or contacted Race Control in two days, so I e-mailed them, reported my position, and said I was okay. I didn't access my e-mail or turn on the telephone. I still wasn't ready for that kind of contact. Instead, I tended to the boat. The wind vane was damaged, and the radio antenna had snapped off. This last would keep me from contacting my two nearest competitors, Minoru and Neil Hunter, who would be worried at the silence. Yet, what could I say to them? I didn't want my plight to be made public. I kept silent, and after another twenty-four hours I logged into my e-mail. I was hoping for a message from Gwen, one that said, "I didn't mean what I said." I was hoping that she'd say, "I'm sorry. I'm wrong." There was no message from her.

My parents would have to be told. I waited until the middle of the night to call. My mother was distraught. She and Gwen had started out on the wrong foot, but over the years they'd grown close. She asked me to phone every day, but I said I'd just have to call when I could. I was still worried about the media getting hold of the story and generating exactly the kind of attention that Gwen had always hated. I reached Tony Barthelme, both a reporter for the Charleston paper and a friend, explained the situation, and asked him to print nothing and if necessary ask the other reporters to do the same. As a courtesy such "love interest" stories were usually played down, and he agreed that both Gwen and I had earned a privacy pass on this one.

I fixed a meal, my first in days. Of course, this meal had been prepared by Gwen. Realizing these were the last meals of hers I'd ever taste brought on a flood of conflicting emotions. Had she ever loved me? She'd cared enough to fix the meals in Uruguay. Once that was done, she'd begun to ask, "Is the boat ready to go to sea?" I should have known then. She was telling me that her job was finished. She'd done her part. All I had to do was get to Charleston. If she really hadn't cared, she could have just stayed in Ireland and telephoned her goodbye. I couldn't get angry at her, not then or ever. It took courage for her to show up and face me. With that in mind, I felt a little better and pushed the boat a little harder. Some of my friends did know, but they didn't pry. Once more, I began doing live interviews over the telephone. I was racing again.

I tacked in and passed close to the shipping lanes and to a coastal area thick with oil fields. To avoid that tangle, I kept going toward the shore which proved to be a good move. Neil Hunter did the opposite and ended up becalmed. By closing in on the beach, I managed to pick up some shore breezes and favorable currents, as well. Without those, I'd have been stuck, for the ocean was now flat, calm. Not a wave or ripple. I reached Victoria, Brazil, and on the beach I could see people, bathers. I could see the color of their hair, the color of their suits—the cut of bikinis. Only ten feet of water was beneath the keel.

On the radio I joked that I was going inshore to order a delivery pizza, for in the sailing chat rooms, I was being accused of unseamanlike behavior, of taking unwarranted risks. It's hard to imagine what Joshua Slocum or Francis Chichester would make of that, of having their solo sailing second-guessed by strangers watching from an electronic "chat room." Those critics were partly right, though. Coming close to shore does involve the risk of going to sleep and running aground or being hit by some coastal vessel. Still, I felt I was safer inshore. I didn't bother to explain that. And I could hardly give my second reason—I needed to see other human beings, to know that I was not alone on the planet. I sailed along like that for several days. In the afternoon, I tacked offshore, then around midnight tacked back in. I had to stay awake. The sun rose, and before long I'd be looking once more at couples walking hand in hand along the beach. They waved to me.

The holding-hand days were over for Gwen and me.

Cockie, my palmetto bug pet, reappeared. Briefly. Very briefly. He'd survived the Horn. He hadn't jumped ship in Punta.

I developed a sore throat and an accompanying dizziness, which was successfully treated long-distance by the fleet physician, Dr. Carlin.

Then came a night of amazement. With the full moon setting in the midst of a light rain squall, I saw a moon-bow. Imagine a rainbow, but instead of colors imagine only white, a great arch of crystal-like white light, and I was sailing directly toward it. Only the second time I'd seen one. The next morning, at sunrise, there was Minoru on the *Shuten Dohji II*. He was pushing himself again. He thought he'd lost his centerboard and, passing me, sailed close so I could have a look. He heeled over, and it did appear to be missing. Then he headed toward the horizon. He'd get bored soon, though, with looking over the stern for me, and I'd have a chance to slip by him before the finish line. In order to be ready for that push, I began to stitch up a fifteen-foot rip in my headsail, a chore that left me with bloody fingertips and in a state of mind both hopeless and contrary. I decided to phone Gwen.

I dialed Ireland, and we had a conversation—a painful one. She said that when she left the yacht club and got on the bus, she half-expected and half-wanted me to follow her—to plead with her. Yet, she was still standing by her decision. She was going back to Italy to work in a restaurant. She had a few things in Charleston she wanted me to send. We had some financial matters to untangle. We'd speak a couple of more times. I hoped to salvage a friendship with her—but she wasn't going to reconnect, even to that extent.

A great night at sea. Photograph courtesy of Chuck Hooker.

Another day, and I passed Minoru, then dropped behind again.

The next day, with following winds and helming through the night, I set a new record for my boat, 201 miles in a single day. To celebrate my record I had one of Gwen's stews. Then like a wall came the Doldrums.

I finished the food in my fourteen-day bin and the first of my seven-day bins. I discovered that water had gotten into the packages and much of my remaining food supply had been destroyed. Chocolates, rice, pasta, all were waterlogged and moldy. Only Gwen's airtight meals and a bit of chocolate remained, enough supplies for just a couple of weeks, unless I rationed it.

One night in Punta, I'd come home from one of those mammoth meals, and, looking out of the bedroom window, I saw a man rummaging through a garbage bin for food. That was such a sad experience, a glimpse of the world's state, but a sight that spoke to me of choices. A few bad choices and that could have been me. Choices. I was sailing into a new life and yet dreading the end of this race, this race I was struggling to finish quickly. I considered, then, the actions of Bernard Moitessier. In the 1968 Golden Globe, he'd rounded the Horn and was headed for England with a first-place finish all his. He veered off for the Cape of Good Hope again, circled the world again as far as Tahiti, and settled there. That would suit me fine. I'd cross the finish line at Charleston and turn off shore for Tahiti. Except what would I eat? I'd been fishing without success for every strike broke the line.

Drinking more liquids quelled the hunger, but that strategy wouldn't get me to the South Pacific.

The Doldrums. By now, I knew that piece of the ocean well. I set the spinnaker. And since I was crossing the equator (for the sixth time), I paid tribute to King Neptune. Cockie, my palmetto bug pet was disobeying my injunction. He'd been told to bring no women on board, but now I was overrun with his young. I called them "Cockie's bandits." I was in no mood to share my meager rations with these other stowaways. Cockie could stay, but, as a sacrifice to King Neptune, overboard went his family. This seemed to work. The breeze picked up. I entered the northeast trades.

With two thousand miles left to Charleston, I sailed under full sail with a full genoa, but Minoru still pulled away, and Brad Van Liew was catching up. Then with lighter winds, I was able to overtake Minoru, but in turn Brad Van Liew passed me. Then with twelve hundred miles to Charleston, perhaps ten days to the end, I continued to helm and tweak the sails. Brad didn't pull away, and on one day I even overtook him for a time. We were skirting the islands; ships passed. A lightning storm came on with strikes just beside the boat, the smell of ozone, and the sound of sizzling water heard even above the deafening roar of thunder. I was squeaky clean after that one. Brad Van Liew was now over the horizon.

Coming home. Photograph courtesy of Chuck Hooker.

I had three hundred miles left to make Charleston, and there was wind, then no wind, then wind switching directions. I had one soft drink left, one meal, and some barely drinkable water and the last bite of chocolate. For over a month, I'd been rationing a single chocolate bar. And for almost that long I'd been suggesting to Race Control that they put off the homecoming party until Neil, Minoru, and I had all entered port. They'd been refusing. Brad Van Liew was also behind schedule, which meant only four of the eight finishing boats would be on hand. The party was put off two days.

I was about to cross the finish line. An eighteen-year-long dream had finally been realized. A radio journalist was welcoming me live on the air as I crossed the finish line, and the telephone kept ringing with congratulations from friends and sponsors. Though the conditions were fairly rough a fleet of small boats had come out. Then my mom and some friends, including Tony Barthelme, were scrambling from the inflatable boat. Mom came aboard limping. The pounding of the waves on the inflatable raft had knocked her down, and she'd twisted her ankle. She ignored that and urged a great barrage of hugs and ice cream on me.

23

FINISHED

Over all, I finished the race seventh out of eight, but also seventh out of the sixteen who began the race, which made it a respectable placing. The crowds waiting on the dock must have thought so. The group looked a bit strange, and I realized finally that so many hundreds had showed up to greet me, the floating dock was sinking under their weight. Over four hundred people were on hand, more, possibly, than for any other racer, and over half of them were schoolchildren. Some of these were shouting "Welcome home!" and others were chanting "Neal Rocks!" Mayor Riley of Charleston was there to give me a hug. He'd showed up only for me. "This is the impossible dream come true," he said. "You have our everlasting congratulations!"

"My mother was my greatest teacher!" I said, and I toasted her with the champagne bottle. And she took an uncharacteristic swallow herself. The champagne was flowing, and the television cameras were broadcasting live. I was a celebrity.

I had only one last bit of torment to endure. Normally, when a boat crossed the finish line, as the race director, Mark Schrader would go below immediately and check the seal on the gear to make sure the engine hadn't been engaged. When I crossed this time, he said he'd do it later, that it didn't matter. Then the next day while the two of us were alone in a car, he questioned me about my performance during the last leg of the race. How had I done so well? I told him I'd helmed a lot and conditions were ideal. He asked, "What's your waterline length?" An odd question, but I answered it. Brad Van Liew had a fifty-foot boat. How had I managed to stay up with him? I answered that I helmed and had my spinnaker set and that I had no idea what Brad was doing, and then I asked, "What's going on here?"

It turned out Brad had accused me of using my engine. By then I was in a rage. This is the same man who'd bet another sailor I'd never reach New Zealand. Instead, I'd completed the race, and on the last leg I'd almost beaten him and his superior boat to the finish line. I said, "Mark, let's go down to the boat and look at the seal." We did. We drove straight there. Not only was the seal in place, but the cable that engaged it was rusted tight. Even if I'd been in danger I couldn't have engaged the propeller. Ridiculous. After Punta, Brad had been sailing with a heavier mast. The whole business was crazy, and to this day I don't understand why Mark hadn't just checked the seal when I crossed the finish line, instead of entering into that bizarre cross-examination. Still, in the great scheme of things that insult was more irritation than a profound injury. I could think of it as "just business as usual" for someone like Brad.

For me and others, that race was not just about who crossed the line first. Among the crowd that waited on the dock was the Egyptian, Gamel, who had asked so many questions nine months earlier, odd questions such as "Are you afraid to die?" This time he only had one. "Will you come to

A proud mother. Photograph courtesy of Chuck Hooker.

dinner?" A month later, when we dined, his wife would tell me the reason for all his questions. He had terminal cancer. Facing his own mortality, he equated my struggle to get to the starting line with his own efforts to rediscover himself, his inner strengths, and the accompanying peace. Each day as I sailed around the world, he journeyed to the doctors for chemotherapy. For three more years he continued to fight. Finally the cancer beat him, but by then we were incredibly close friends.

Also pitted against any negative distractions was my mother's fierce pride. On coming ashore, she had announced to the first journalist she saw, "This is a great day for South Africans. This is a great day for the oppressed peoples of South Africa." She didn't say, "This is a great day for my son, Neal." That went without saying. Obviously, she felt responsible for raising my sister and me, but her obligation didn't end there. It began there. Her responsibility was to inspire all children, to get them all to reach their highest potential. She prepared the field and planted the seeds, but she expected those plants to mature and in turn seed the adjoining fields. In that sense, my success was an extension of her own efforts, her efforts to get all children to dream of a better future. Her son was living his dream and that would inspire other South African children, indeed children everywhere, to aspire to something more, and they in turn would inspire others. Yet, I must confess, even knowing all that, it wasn't enough to lift my spirits.

The following night was the closing event in celebration of the race. Thousands of people attended, and, walking up to the podium, I was greeted with a thunder of applause. That should have been the greatest night of my life, but I think back on it as one of my worst. I know this pain was in part related to the sense of letdown that I seemed to feel after every race, only in this case multiplied by a hundred. My entire life had been leading up to this moment. So many said it could not be done. My entire adult life had been a struggle to reach this spot at the podium. It was done. The answer to Charles Dickens's question "Will I be the hero of my own life?" was evident. What would I do now? I'd run out of challenges. At the bottom of this sadness was the unanswerable question: where was Gwen? The one person who'd made all this possible wasn't here to see me welcomed as a hero. She was my soul mate, and then gone. Just gone. In her honor I accepted the trophy in silence and the next day flew off with my mom to begin a series of speaking engagements, and another life.

24

A NEW START

That first set of speeches behind me, I decided that I needed a home, a place to put my life back together, and I wanted it to be near Charleston. I intended by hook or crook to enter the ultimate solo race, the Vendée Globe, in 2004. In the meantime, I had a book and the script for the television documentary to finish. During the race, I'd taken hundreds of hours of video tape and had hundreds more from the other networks, all to be reviewed and edited.

In the last couple of years I'd made business decisions that would eventually pay off and had recently signed a contract to speak at innovative charter schools in Michigan, the National Heritage Academies, but for the moment I was, as usual, without sufficient funds. I didn't have the finances to get a decent place to live, especially not on the water, so when a friend from the Rotary Club arranged for me to have free use of a cottage on nearby Bohicket Creek, I jumped. A hell of a deal, I figured, until I saw the cottage. Like David Livingstone pioneering in Africa, I had to bush axe my way into the house and then spend weeks making it habitable.

My new home had been abandoned for years, vandals had broken in, the ceiling was collapsing, and cockroaches and snakes had to be evicted. I loved the place, though, and soon had it livable and safe enough for the electric power to be turned on. I had an outbuilding for an office, a commute of ten feet, and my computers, manuscripts, and all my paperwork— including a lifetime of logs and diaries and the documentary script—were there at my fingertips.

On August 2, a Monday morning, I lit a large pile of oak limbs, dead limbs I'd cut off trees. I spent the day keeping this going, and that afternoon hosed down the site. A friend came by, and I asked him to keep an eye on the pile while I went for groceries. I had a date coming over. When I returned, he was hosing the pile down again. He wasn't happy with the way it was still smoking. He left, and my date arrived. We had dinner and watched a video, and she left. I checked the pile. No smoke. The next morning I checked the pile. No smoke. I went off to Charleston to meet with Mayor Riley. Then I had an early date in Charleston. Since returning I'd been seeing a number of women, none of whom expected a serious relationship out of me. They understood what I was feeling. I would always love Gwen but was getting over the rebound. This young woman and I had dinner, and I headed back to Bohicket Creek.

When I approached the cottage, I noticed the light that usually burned in the pump house was out. The breaker must have flipped. I had the car's high beams on to watch for deer on this dirt track. Circling out on the bluff, I parked facing the cottage. Nothing seemed out of the ordinary. I got my bearings for the front door, cut off the car lights, walked up the steps, opened the front door, and reached my hand inside to flip the interior light switch. No light came on. The main breaker must have thrown. I stepped inside, and there was a crunchy sound beneath my feet, which I looked at. My eyes still hadn't adjusted to the night. I set my briefcase down and eased toward the kitchen. The crunching sound beneath my feet continued. I looked toward the kitchen, and instead of a wall I could see the river and the lights on the far shore. Finally, I understood. Except for the front facade, my entire house had burned down, and out in the yard where there'd been a huge oak, there was no oak tree now; where I'd had an office, there was no office now.

Apparently the fire from the burning pile had gone underground into leaf mold and roots and, though there had been no smoke in evidence, had simmered on. Then I'd gone off and the dry summer grass of the lawn had caught; fanned by strong winds, the fire spread toward the house. Ordinarily, that wouldn't have mattered, because the cottage was on a high concrete-block foundation and the flames were only a few inches high. The week before I'd had a 150-gallon propane gas tank placed in the yard. The tank ignited and acted as a flamethrower, sending a roaring burst of fire across the side of my office to the oak tree and onto the house. The fire department was called. It took them forty-five minutes just to find the isolated house. It took them another hour to get the propane-tank fire extinguished and to save the front of the house. Nobody knew how to contact me. They coiled up the hoses and went home.

My friend Gene King came by. We sat beside the ruins, and he said, "Petersen, something good is going to come out of this."

All I could think was "What is happening? Is this a test?" I'd lost the love of my life, Gwen, and now I'd lost all the mementos, photographs, and letters, not to mention the written records I'd kept of my life. There were no backups. I was reduced to zero. No, not quite. A planter had fallen over on my copy of Joshua Slocum's *Sailing Alone around the World,* and, though badly scorched, it had been saved by the dirt. And my sextant, the one I'd had since leaving South Africa, was badly warped, but still recognizable as a sextant. It could be used as a visual aid when I gave speeches. Not a complete zero.

I started house-sitting for various friends. I did have plenty of good friends. The Rotary Club was going to help me rebuild the cottage. I wasn't going to be defeated. Then I was driving down the highway, and my car began to slow down and finally came to a complete halt. The transmission was gone. I was homeless. And I was now without transportation.

I stood on the edge of that narrow highway in that August heat. Summer in the lowcountry was never my favorite time. I had sailed all the way around the world single-handed and here I was stranded—up against what seemed an insurmountable problem. But at least I wasn't in danger of drowning or even dying of thirst or being run down by a freighter. There was no apartheid regime threatening to take away not only my dignity, but my very life. I just needed a way to get around. But as luck would have it I ended up with so much more.

When I lecture to schoolchildren, I start by telling them to be the best they can dare to be. "Nothing is impossible," I say, "when you have knowledge and dedication and determination. Everything that you learn in this classroom, every subject you take, you will apply in your life. Knowledge is all around us, from the people we encounter to the books we read, but it's up to you to seek it out. What you don't know is the greatest risk you will take." Some just sit and stare, passing time, but many sit up, absorbing and hungry. "We are creatures of habit. Those who succeed are not lucky ones. They succeed most of the time. When you don't, its not failure if you keep trying, keep working hard with faith. That's a setback. We all have them. Winners never quit. We don't recognize failure as an option. It's our choice, and we each have the choice to succeed. One success is built upon another.

It is built with respect and dignity, and having the right attitude and outlook on life. Success is up to each one of us."

The day after the car gave out, a dealer called to say that he had the wheels I was looking for—something within my budget limitations, something that rolled. But I needed to get to his lot immediately. In search of a lift I made call after call in vain. Then my cell phone rang. A stranger was on the line. The *Post and Courier*'s story on the fire included the bank account number if anyone wanted to donate funds to help rebuild the house. This stranger, Darlene Kristi, had deposited $118 in that account. I called to try to thank her but didn't get through and left a message instead. Now, she called back offering help. She had some tools, time, energy, and some money. I asked for a lift to the car dealer. We arranged to meet at a gas station on the way. My first sight of her was a beautiful strawberry-blond woman in a black skirt, pumping gas. Our eyes met. We both smiled. Not realizing who it was, I went to the back of the station where we were to meet—at which point she called out, "I'll be with you in a minute."

The initial car deal fell through, so Darlene and I went to a movie, then dinner. We chatted till one A.M. We felt comfortable with each other and spoke openly about many things. For instance, I learned she hadn't dated in six years. A long tumultuous relationship had depleted her. She said, "I wanted to have a relationship with myself before sharing in someone else's life. How else could I come into a relationship as an equal?" Then she added, "And if a man is not in my future, I will still be happy and fulfilled."

She drove me back, and before getting out, I leaned over and gave her a soft kiss. I expected her to turn and give me a cheek. Instead, I leaned in again and gave her another kiss on the lips, this one filling my soul with the possibilities of romance. With a pounding, risk-taking heart, I asked her when I could see her again. "Tomorrow," she responded. "How about dinner? I'll cook."

Dinner: I had no flowers. I took a walk on the sand dunes and found wild daisies growing beside the path. I picked a bunch and took it to Darlene, not knowing it was more special to her than a dozen roses, rising another notch in her esteem. Two days later we had a second meal, a spontaneous picnic on the beach that lasted till four A.M. with the two of us talking, just talking for hours, oblivious of time. We spent a lot of time together getting to know each other, and the hours passed more like seconds. Quickly

Me and Darlene on our first wedding anniversary in Ireland

I knew how similar our views of, and attitudes toward, life were. In November I had sailing plans in the Caribbean and shared them with Darlene. Would she like to spend two weeks island hopping? We were never apart and did not feel the need for space away from each other on a cramped vessel. I learned just how well Darlene could cook, and it was an even bigger bonus that she did not get seasick. The most important discovery was that I could spend my life with her and feel complete. Together our foundations were stronger than they would have been individually. Darlene is the rock that one builds a lighthouse on: ever guiding, always lit, a beacon of hope and capable of weathering any storm. One can spend a lifetime looking for the right person. I had found my shipmate and guiding light, and I was her ship sailing into port. On New Year's Eve of the much-celebrated millennium, in a small chapel in Annapolis, Maryland, Darlene and I exchanged wedding bands and vows that included "through health and seasickness." I also gained an incredible stepson, Rick, thirteen months my junior.

Seven months later we found our dream home in McClellanville, South Carolina, an hour's drive north of Charleston. We have three acres surrounded by forests. The house is lovely, rustic, and cozy with a fire continually burning all winter long. We have vegetable gardens and fruit trees to fuss over, plus sixty thousand honeybees, a pond filled with fish and turtles, and nine roving chickens and a proud rooster. The neighbor's black Labrador, Cuba, comes over for breakfast, lunch, and dinner. Darlene and I run our companies from our home offices, mine being a treehouse, the "branch office," complete with communications, creaking wood, and dreams. Cuba just hangs out. Oh, we do travel—often on both business and pleasure. This is the ideal day I've been describing. When the evening star rises I pause and think of my mother and South Africa and just how far I've journeyed. And how far I have to go.

So here I am this morning, sippining coffee with my wife on the porch swing. For now I am contented. Saint Regis is the saint of impossible dreams. We must be friends, for I made it. My old boat made it. We rounded the Horn. My boat, the vessel of so many dreams, rests on chocks at the far end of our property, a very large, red fiberglass garden ornament. Pine cones and needles flow across her deck. Oh, she needs my attention, but I'm burned out on maintenance, and I know she's patient. She'll wait for me. Someday soon I'll rake the deck and brush the cobwebs from her interior, give her a new interior and go off to the Caribbean. And, of course, I'm dreaming of a new boat, something capable of winning the Vendée Globe, some supersonic wedge of technology-loaded plastic. I'm dreaming of business deals that I'm involved in and more deals after those are completed and speeches that I've already booked to make and the ones I'll make after those. And, with Christmas coming, I'm dreaming of a trip home. We should never stop dreaming, and when a dream comes true, we should recognize it and be thankful. I've learned the power of a dream.

I've raced a sailboat solo around the world and in the process found what perhaps I was searching for all along—a woman as deep, as mysterious, as changeless and changing as the ocean, someone to love, to build dreams with, who tells me every day, "I love you."